The Complete Book of
CHRYSANTHEMUMS

The Complete Book of
CHRYSANTHEMUMS

by
Cornelius Ackerson

Illustrated in full color,

half tones, and line drawings.

THE AMERICAN GARDEN GUILD, INC.
and
DOUBLEDAY & COMPANY, INC.

Library of Congress Catalog Card Number 57-11 406

Printed in the United States of America

CONTENTS

	FOREWORD	ix
1	CHRYSANTHEMUMS AS A HOBBY	1
2	THE MODERN CHRYSANTHEMUM	4
3	FUNDAMENTALS FOR A SUCCESSFUL HOBBY	21
4	SOURCES OF PLANTS	24
5	SOILS, FERTILIZERS, AND SOIL CONDITIONERS	29
6	PROPAGATION OF PLANTS	36
7	INSECTS, DISEASES, AND OTHER TROUBLES	47
8	PLANTING AND SUMMER CARE	66
9	AUTUMN ACTIVITIES	78
10	WINTER PROTECTION	84
11	BIG MUMS IN THE GARDEN	89
12	FROST-PROTECTION COVERS	100
13	CHRYSANTHEMUMS UNDER GLASS	108
14	HYBRIDIZING AND GROWING FROM SEED	122

15 OUT-OF-SEASON MUMS 130

16 LANDSCAPE AND DISPLAY PLANTING 144

17 ARRANGEMENTS 154

18 CHRYSANTHEMUM SHOWS 172

19 MAKING A PROFIT FROM MUMS 179

20 HISTORICAL BACKGROUND AND MODERN DEVELOPMENT 187

21 CLASSIFICATION OF BLOOM TYPES AND SPECIES OF CHRYSANTHEMUMS 199

22 VARIETIES FOR EVERY PURPOSE 217

23 CALENDAR FOR A CHRYSANTHEMUM HOBBY 233

Appendix A — CODE LIST OF CHRYSANTHEMUM SUPPLIERS 239

Appendix B — EQUIPMENT 241

Appendix C — GLOSSARY 245

ACKNOWLEDGMENTS 249

INDEX 251

ILLUSTRATIONS

COLOR

A cascade specimen display
Cascade chrysanthemums in a basket
Chrysanthemums in a landscape picture
A greenhouse display of chrysanthemums
Between pages 142–143

An asymmetric triangular arrangement
A Myra J. Brooks oriental composition
An arrangement of large-bloom chrysanthemums
A driftwood composition by Myra J. Brooks
Between pages 158–159

Bloom Types in Color

Class 1 Single—JOAN HELEN | 199
Class 2 Semidouble—RONALD | 201
Class 3 Regular anemone—CRIMSON GLOW | 201
Class 4 Irregular anemone—QUEEN ELIZABETH | 202
Class 5 Pompon—MASQUERADE | 203
Class 6 Incurve—INDIANAPOLIS WHITE | 204
Class 7 Irregular incurve—WHITE TURNER | 205
Class 8 Decorative pompon—CARNIVAL | 206
Class 9 Aster-flowered pompon—APACHE | 207
Class 10 Regular reflex—GARNET KING | 208
Class 11 Irregular reflex—MUTO'S CRIMSON | 209
Class 12 Single spoon—CHARM SPOON | 210
Class 13 Quill—MISS GENA HARWOOD | 211
Class 15 Spider—CHERIE | 212

HALF TONES

Undisbudded large-bloom chrysanthemum, 18

Disbudded large-bloom chrysanthemum, 19

Chrysanthemum cuttings, 25

A mist propagating system, 43

Chrysanthemum cuttings in a cold frame, 45

A mulch for chrysanthemums, 68

The results of a pinch, 70

A typical garden sprayer, 73

Mum spacing and supporting, 77

Winter storage of stock plants, 87

A method of winter storage, 88

A mum support system, 91

Large-bloom disbudding, 93

Plunge-pit mums outdoors, 97

Plunge-pit mums in bloom, 98

Mums in bloom under a frost cover, 102

Frost cover erection, 104

Frost cover in place, 106

Frost cover in mild weather, 106

Bench-lighted mums, 137

Mums in a perennial border, 148

Mums in a landscape setting, 149

A shady retreat among chrysanthemums, 151

A Chinese composition by Myra J. Brooks, 157

A line mass arrangement, 161

A line composition by Myra J. Brooks, 167

A driftwood arrangement by Myra J. Brooks, 170

DRAWINGS

Chrysanthemum types

Class 1 Single, 6

Class 2 Semidouble, 6

Class 3 Regular anemone, 7

Class 4 Irregular anemone, 7

Class 5 Pompon, 7

Class 6 Regular or Chinese incurve, 8

Class 7 Irregular or Japanese incurve, 8

Class 8 Reflexed or decorative, 8

Class 9 Decorative or aster-flowered reflex, 9

Class 10 Regular or Chinese Reflex, 9

Class 11 Irrregular of Japanese Reflex, 9

Class 12 Single spoon, 10

Class 12a Semidouble spoon, 10

Class 13 Quill, 10

Class 14 Thread, 11

Class 15 Spider, 11

Bush-type growth habit, 13

Large-bloom-type-growth habit, 15

Chrysanthemum enemies, 55

Chrysanthemum diseases, 61

Bench support system, 112

A specimen chrysanthemum, 113

A typical sunpit, 118

A bloom ready for pollination, 126

Shading system for chrysanthemums, 133

A mass arrangement, 164

A line arrangement, 165

A tall vase arrangement, 166

Foreword

As a small boy I followed Grandpa around the garden, holding the brown paper bags he placed around each bunch of ripening grapes. These were not ordinary grapes to be casually treated; they were Grandpa's pride and joy, destined for exhibition at the Trenton State Fair. This was my first horticultural experience and one which taught me the appreciation of nature's beauty and the care of which it is worthy. When I was old enough to ride my bicycle out to our farm in the country, I unconsciously furthered my knowledge of nature's growing cycle while doing the things which come naturally to any boy on a farm. I watched the yellow and orange blossoms of the squash and melons turn into fruit; cut spears of asparagus by plunging the knife into the right spot on the side of the hilled-up row; and followed behind the plow in hope of finding Indian arrowheads. Such experiences gave me a familiarity with growing plants that made gardening a natural hobby for me.

When I began adult life I fortunately built my home on the site of Grandfather's garden. The fertile ground was ideal for many types of flowers and I made the maximum use of it. Daffodils and early spring bulbs started my gardening year and, of course, chrysanthemums were a natural choice to close the gardening season. In these early years no particular flower seemed more important than any other. At least, my gardening efforts were more or less equally divided, until I succumbed to chrysanthemania.

By chance I went to see a display of chrysanthemums grown in pots, with one large bloom atop a five- or six-foot stem. The plants were staged according to height, and there were several thousand plants of many varieties. Here was a challenge that has influenced my gardening ever since. Such ethereal beauty as I had witnessed seemed out of the question for an ordinary gardener who had no greenhouse. As time went by I found that not only could such beautiful flowers be grown in the open ground, but also that anyone who had been bitten by the chrysanthemania bug could produce prize winners.

Having proved to my own satisfaction that the chrysanthemum is not at all a difficult or temperamental flower, I have avidly explored every avenue of chrysanthemum culture. I have seen the same starry-eyed look on the faces of visitors to my own chrysanthemum garden that I must have had when I first found the one flower which could have such a profound effect on my gardening activities. The desire to reach out and project that feeling beyond the confines of my immediate acquaintanceship has prompted me to write this book.

I have tried to cover the answers which I discovered to my own questions, as well as the answers to the questions I am most frequently asked. In growing chrysanthemums, as well as in any phase of horticulture, there is a practical explanation for each problem that does not need to be couched in technical terms to be correct. I have tried to make this a practical, down-to-earth type of book. One that will be helpful to those who wish to grow chrysanthemums with a minimum of labor for the sheer beauty of their long-lasting flowers, as well as for those who wish to grow either exhibition-quality blooms or profitable cut flowers. It seemed logical, therefore, to separate the cultural chapters into basic and advanced sections. Also, it is often difficult for the neophyte grower to find the varieties of chrysanthemums he desires. One complete chapter is devoted to a selection of varieties suited for each type of culture, with a list of dealers cross-referenced in the Appendix. Sources of equipment and materials useful in the culture of chrysanthemums are also listed in the Appendix. If the contents of this book help increase the satisfaction gained in the cultivation of such rewarding plants, my own reward will be exceedingly great.

CHAPTER 1

Chrysanthemums as a Hobby

GARDENING has become a pleasurable method of relaxation in this fast-changing modern world in which we live. Within the overall hobby of gardening there are many phases of horticulture to tempt the person who likes to watch things grow, but for diversity of bloom types the chrysanthemum has much to recommend it as a specialized hobby. Mums are not a new flower, yet the oriental growers of twenty-five centuries ago would have difficulty in recognizing the offspring which have been developed from their original plants. The cultivation and development of chrysanthemums over so long a period have resulted in a wide range of sizes, shapes, and colors, although the most intensive part of this work has been done in the past fifty years. This period has seen the emergence of the chrysanthemum as the bread-and-butter crop of the commercial florist; so it is not surprising that agricultural experiment stations, colleges, and commercial propagators have probed its innermost secrets. The results of their experiments have not only given the florist a dependable year-round flower, but they have opened up a broad field for the amateur grower.

By far the greatest number of chrysanthemums raised by amateur growers are grown outdoors. Proper selection of varieties will provide bloom from late summer until mid-November. Of course, some means of frost protection will be required for the late-blooming varieties in many localities. It is surprising how much ingenuity is displayed by chrysanthemum hobbyists in devising types of protective coverings, but, as in the case of most worth-while endeavors in life, where there's a will there's a way.

The hobbyist who grows chrysanthemums outdoors has several paths along which his hobby may develop. He may wish to grow chrysanthemums that are particularly pleasing in landscapes. In this case, there are low varieties, medium tall, and tall varieties in many shape and color combinations to make border, wall, and foundation plantings. Where greater interest lies in the arrangement and decorative uses of chrysanthemums, they may be grown in special cutting beds. Here a much wider selection of varieties may be grown to provide the sizes, shapes, and colors suitable for many styles of arrangements. There are many people who find their greatest satisfaction in a hobby which develops competition through comparative exhibitions. The great number of classes it is possible to provide for all of the bloom types of chrysanthemums make it possible to stage, even in a local chrysanthemum show, a very diversified exhibit.

The gardener who owns a greenhouse or sunpit has a distinct horticultural advantage, for his hobby is freed from the limitations imposed by nature. By using the new techniques developed for commercial growers, the chrysanthemum hobbyist may have his pets in bloom at any season of the year. The chrysanthemum was called the queen of autumn flowers by the early Japanese growers, and its right to this title has never been challenged; so it is perhaps a mistake to force it to compete with spring and summer favorites. However, there is little floral competition during the winter months, so there is no reason to limit the blooming season to the autumn months. There are greenhouse varieties of chrysanthemums which bloom normally in December without special equipment. In addition, the favorite varieties of November can be made to bloom during the winter months by means of the growing technique described in Chapter 15.

It is also possible, without any great outlay of money or time, to turn a chrysanthemum hobby into a profitable part-time business. Chrysanthemums are so prolific that it is possible to realize $500 to $1000 from a 50-by-100-foot chrysanthemum garden. There are many ways to supplement income from a chrysanthemum hobby in addition to the sale of flowers. This phase of the hobby is covered in Chapter 19.

Friendships can easily be made in any gardening hobby, for it is characteristic of gardeners to form a society for the promotion of their favorite flower. The chrysanthemum, rose, African violet, dahlia, lily, orchid, and many more flowers have their devoted followers who exchange garden visits, trade surplus plants, and vie with each other for blue ribbons at flower shows.

The chrysanthemum is ably represented by the National Chrysanthemum Society, which was founded in 1946 to provide the friendly atmosphere that would draw together those gardeners whose special interest lies in the cultivation of chrysanthemums. The quarterly publication of the society contains much of interest to the neophyte as well as to the advanced grower. The regional chapters located throughout the country provide a much closer local interest among growers by means of monthly meetings and regional shows. The national show each year, however, is the most important event for the chrysanthemum hobbyist who grows exhibition mums. Much of the enjoyment of a chrysanthemum hobby comes from the experience of sharing it with others.

CHAPTER 2

The Modern Chrysanthemum

THE chrysanthemum and the wild daisy of the fields have a great deal in common, for they are both members of the same flower family. In fact, their relationship in the Compositae family was much more apparent many years ago than it is today. By the taxonomists, whose task it has been to trace the development of our modern mums from their earliest beginnings, the original species is pictured as a small yellow daisy. The same type of ray petals surrounded the central disk of smaller tubular petals to produce the composite bloom which is the distinguishing characteristic of the family. It may have been an enterprising oriental gardener who started the chrysanthemum along the road to its present highly developed state, or perhaps one of the unpredictable quirks of nature produced a deviation that carried on to future generations of mums. At any rate, the chrysanthemum became the symbol of royalty in the Orient, while the daisy has remained a neglected roadside relative.

In order to facilitate plant identification, taxonomists have subdivided plant families into genera that include the further division into species. The plants within any species are very close and easily recognized, since they differ only in such things as size, color of flowers, or markings of leaves. The word Chrysanthemum is the generic name for a group of species including pyrethrums, ox-eye daisies, and the feverfews that graced Grandmother's perennial border. However, the species *morifolium,* because of its development to our familiar mum, has usurped the generic name for all except those who have a botanical background. The countless generations of hybridizers, who have been responsible for the chrysanthemums we grow today, accomplished the wide diversity of bloom types by selective crossing of only a few species in this one genus. This is rather remarkable, for the diversity in bloom types almost equals that within the orchid family, where intergeneric crossing has produced many new hybrids. For example, species in the orchid genus of Cattleya have been crossed with Laelia species to produce a large-lipped flower having well-formed sepals. The genus Brassavola added a frilled lip to the existing hybrids. Then the genus Sophronitis brought a pleasing red color into the hybrid progeny. These changes in the orchid are quite apparent when the hybrids are compared with the parent species. In the case of the chrysanthemum, however, the large-sized blooms seen in florists' windows were obtained without benefit of hybridizing with the dahlia or other generic branches of the Compositae family. Perhaps the long history of the chrysanthemum, as compared to the century-long period of intensive orchid hybridization, accounts for the results that have been achieved.

BLOOM CLASSIFICATION

Some form of classification is required to separate the hundreds of modern varieties into a recognizable pattern of types for comparative purposes. The florist has a 3-part grouping which serves very well when chrysanthemums are sold for decorative purposes. The standards or disbuds include all of the large varieties which have only one bloom to each stem. The word "disbud" indicates the process required to obtain only one bloom, for the chrysanthemum is naturally a multiflowered plant. A further distinction within this group is obtained by division of standards into commercial and exhibition varieties. The florist rarely grows or sells exhibition blooms. He uses the term "commercial" to indicate the stiff-petaled type of bloom which will stand the rigors of shipment. All of the multiflowered mums grown by florists as sprays, which normally bloom from November through January, are called pompons. These varieties are usually grown in greenhouses, although they may be flowered outdoors if protection is given. All of the other spray types are classified by commercial growers as hardy garden varieties, although the emphasis of the word "hardy" is an injustice to the many other varieties that may be equally hardy with respect to winter survival.

The National Chrysanthemum Society has made a very complete descriptive classification of chrysanthemum types based upon bloom structure, but it is much too detailed to include in this early chapter. A summary of this classification, however, is necessary for ready reference, so it will appear here, with further explanation in Chapter 21. It often is not apparent, but every chrysanthemum has both disk petals and ray petals. In some varieties the ray petals are greatly elongated and curl inwardly to hide the smaller disk center, while other varieties exhibit a greatly enlarged disk. With but very few exceptions, all of the varieties of modern chrysanthemums will fit into one of the following N.C.S. classes:

DIVISION A

SECTION 1 — Disk conspicuous.

Class 1 — Single. All of the distinctly daisy-type mums belong here.

Class 2 — Semidouble. As the name implies, all of these varieties have many rows of ray petals with the disk apparent in fully opened blooms.

Class 3 — Regular Anemone. These varieties are similar to those in Class 1, with a greatly enlarged central disk and regularly arranged ray petals.

Class 4 — Irregular Anemone. Like Class 3 except for the irregularity of the ray petals.

SECTION 2 — Ray petals incurved, with disk apparent or concealed.

Class 5 — Pompon. These are the small globular blooms grown in sprays by florists.

Class 6 — Regular or Chinese Incurve. Most of the large blooms worn as corsage flowers at football games are included in this category.

Class 7 — Irregular or Japanese Incurve. These are the largest varieties, with ray petals interlaced and twisted into an over-all globular shape.

SECTION 3 — Ray petals reflexed.

Class 8 — Reflexed or Decorative. All the characteristics of the pompons in Class 5 except that the ray petals are reflexed.

Class 9 — Decorative or Aster-Flowered Reflexes. These varieties are similar to those in Class 8 except that the ray petals are longer and narrower in proportion to their length.

Class 10 — Regular or Chinese Reflex. All the characteristics of the regular incurves of Class 6 except that the ray petals are reflexed.

Class 11 — Irregular or Japanese Reflex. This class has all the characteristics of the irregular incurves of Class 7 except for reflexed ray petals.

DIVISION B

TUBULAR FLOWERED

Class 12 — Spoon — single. The varieties in this classification have much in common with those in Class 1, except that the ray florets are tubular with a flattened spoonlike tip.

Class 12 A — Semidouble and Double Spoon. This class differs from Class 12 in the same degree that Class 2 differs from Class 1.

Class 13 — Quill. The ray petals are long and tubular with the tips often spoonlike, but they may be closed to the tip and slightly curved.

Class 14 — Thread. These varieties are similar to the closed tip quills, but they differ in the greatly reduced number of tubular ray petals.

Class 15 — Spider. Here the long tubular ray petals are similar to those of the quill varieties, but they are definitely coiled or hooked.

Representative varieties of all of the above classes of mums may be grown by the amateur grower, either in the open garden or in a protective structure. While the changes in bloom form have been many, the natural growth cycle of the modern chrysanthemum remains the same as that of the original species. Man has learned how to change the blooming characteristics of mums and has even wrested from nature her unique method of timing the blooming date, but the chrysanthemum grower must still co-operate with nature.

HOW A CHRYSANTHEMUM GROWS

Fortunately there are only two basic growth patterns which produce the 15 types of bloom. Those blooms which normally appear as sprays are produced on growth which is distinctly shrublike in form, hence such varieties may be called bush types. The chrysanthemums which are normally grown to produce but a single bloom per stem are the standards or disbuds of the florist's classification. Of course, in the centuries of chrysanthemum hybridizing there have been developed some varieties which may be grown either way. The grower should decide at planting time whether he wishes to grow these varieties as bush types or large-bloom types. In general, these dual-purpose varieties will be found in rather limited numbers. Chapter 22 will contain a table of the aforementioned varieties.

The two types of growth are not at all difficult to understand, although nature has endowed the chrysanthemum with several growth processes which make it differ from annuals and most perennials. The first difference is a bud which does not bloom, but it does force the production of side branches from a point immediately below this nonblooming bud. Later on in the course of chrysanthemum growth, similar buds which are larger and more like the eventual blooming buds may be formed. The first bud formed after the nonblooming bud is technically known as the "first crown" bud. A second or even third crown bud may be formed on plants which have been started early in the season. These buds also force side growth, but each successive bud becomes closer in size to the blooming bud. The second trick of nature occurs much later in the season and it concerns the actual blooming of the plant, as discussed later in this chapter.

Perhaps this would be the logical place to combine a pictorial description with the written explanation of the chrysanthemum growth cycle.

The bush-type chrysanthemum plant starts the season as a rooted cutting which may be planted as early as May 15 in the 40- to 45-degree latitude. In *Fig. 1* the left-hand series of panels illustrate the natural growth as it would occur if the grower made no attempt

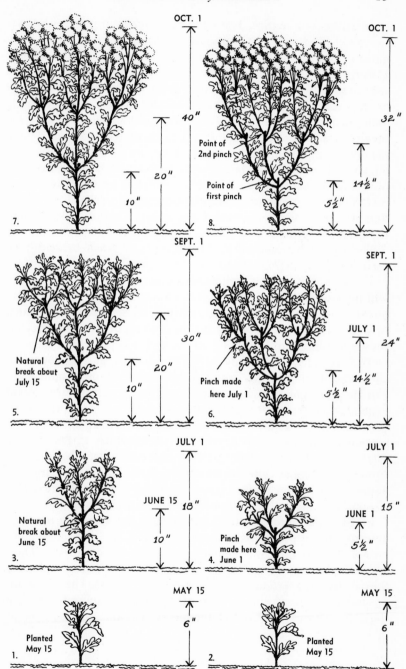

OCT. 1

40"

20"

10"

7.

OCT. 1

32"

Point of
2nd pinch

Point of
first pinch

14½"

5½"

8.

SEPT. 1

30"

20"

10"

Natural
break about
July 15

5.

SEPT. 1

JULY 1

24"

14½"

5½"

Pinch made
here July 1

6.

JULY 1

JUNE 15

18"

10"

Natural
break about
June 15

3.

JULY 1

JUNE 1

15"

5½"

Pinch
made here
June 1

4.

MAY 15

6"

Planted
May 15

1.

MAY 15

6"

Planted
May 15

2.

Fig. 1 — Bush type

to interfere with nature. The right-hand series of panels illustrate the effect produced by the process of pinching. The plant grown naturally will produce a very small nonblooming bud about June 15 (*Fig. 1, panel 3*). Since this bud stops terminal growth and forces side breaks it is called the "break" bud. Later in the season the process is repeated so that the number of branches is considerably multiplied (*Fig. 1, panel 5*). This time the bud which caused the breaks is a little larger, but it still does not bloom. This process may be repeated once or even twice more on plants that are set out early. Eventually the bud which caused the last side breaks will bloom at the same time that the flower buds on the branch ends bloom. The reason for this odd plant behavior is related to the second of nature's tricks, and it will be explained in this chapter under the heading, "How A Chrysanthemum Blooms."

The right-hand side of *Fig. 1* indicates a pinch made by the grower on June 1 (*Fig. 1, panel 4*). This process of pinching means removal of the top half inch of terminal growth, and the method will be covered in Chapter 8. This pinch produced the same result as the break bud, but it occurred earlier and delayed the formation of side branches longer. Thus, the pinched plant is shorter than the unpinched plant on July 1.

The second pinch on July 1 (*Fig. 1, panel 6*) again produces the same result as the buds formed about July 15 on the naturally grown plant. The shorter height and better proportion of the pinched plant show the advantages which can be obtained by growth control of bush-type chrysanthemums. Long stems of well-proportioned bloom will develop from this pinch as illustrated in *Fig. 1, panel 8.* The cushion mums which produce 12- to 18-inch mounds of bloom differ naturally from the taller-growing bush types. They do not require pinching, since they will branch sufficiently without it. The large-bloom types of chrysanthemums are naturally taller growing than the bush types, although the same bud-formation procedure occurs.

Fig. 2 shows the same relative sequence which occurred in *Fig. 1*, but in this case the grower also controls growth by removal of unwanted stems produced by the pinching process. The cuttings of large-bloom chrysanthemums look the same as those of the bush type at planting time, so it is unnecessary to illustrate them in *Fig.*

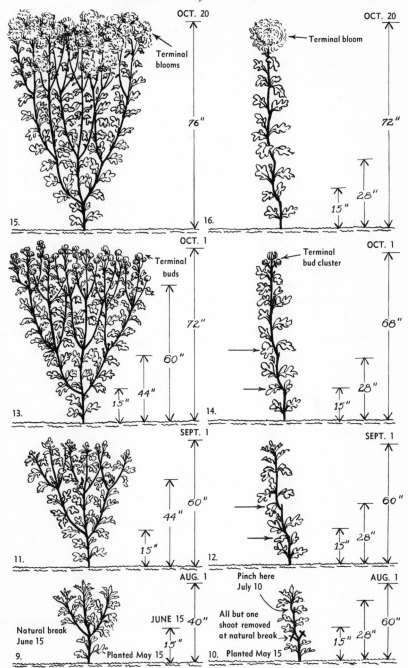

Fig. 2 — Large bloom

2. However, since most varieties of large-bloom chrysanthemums grow much taller than bush types, it is customary to delay planting until June 1 to June 15 in the 40- to 45-degree latitude belt. To compare the sequence of bud formation, the planting date of May 15 has been used for illustration in *Fig. 2.*

The pinch indicated in *Fig. 2, panel 10* was made July 10, in accordance with a schedule which will be discussed in Chapter 11. It is possible that the plant may have produced a break bud before that date, as illustrated in *Fig. 2, panel 9.* Undoubtedly such a bud would have formed if the plant had been set out before June 1. This still does not alter the time of the pinch. However, if a break bud did form, the grower would have to determine how many stems he would permit to develop. Then he would pinch those stems on the scheduled pinching date. In the case illustrated in *Fig. 2, panel 12,* only one stem is permitted to develop to produce the maximum-sized flower. Note that the pinch of July 10 eliminated formation of the buds which developed about September 1 on the unpinched plant. These buds on the unpinched plant are called "second crown" buds. It would be possible for the grower to develop this unpinched plant from its condition on September 1 to produce blooms equal to those of the pinched plant. Many growers do exactly this and avoid the necessity of pinching on a prescribed date. The grower could select the strongest break which developed around the second crown bud. All other breaks around the crown bud, and the crown bud itself, should then be removed. The plant would develop a "terminal" bud cluster similar to that of the pinched plant shown in *Fig. 2, panel 14;* however, there would be a definite offset in the stem where the first and second crown buds had formed. Thus, a timed pinch, by elimination of the first crown bud, produces a straight stem from the point of the pinch to the terminal bud cluster (*Fig. 2, panel 14*). When the side buds around the central bud of the terminal bud cluster are removed, one large bloom will develop as indicated in *Fig. 2, panel 16.* Without this bud removal the blooms are small and crowded as shown in *Fig. 2, panel 15.*

One other difference between the bush type and the large-bloom type varieties becomes noticeable about the time the first crown bud cluster is formed. From the axil of each leaf of the large-bloom varieties a shoot will begin to grow. These shoots begin near the base of the plant and progressively develop from each leaf axil up the stem. If they are allowed to remain on the plant they will eventually develop into terminal bud clusters which would bloom as shown in *Fig. 2, panel 15*. The grower who is interested in the production of one large terminal bloom on each stem will remove these shoots as they are formed. It is better to remove these side shoots systematically as they are formed, in order to keep the remaining stub as inconspicuous as possible. They may be pinched out with the fingernails when small, but if allowed to develop to a diameter of ¼ inch, it will be necessary to cut them with a knife.

The terminal bud clusters shown on both plants on October 1 differ from the previously formed crown buds. Unlike the side buds surrounding the crown bud, the side buds in the terminal bud cluster will not grow out as new shoots. They are true flower buds. The use of the word terminal in this case means the last bud to be formed by the plant, in addition to its normal horticultural meaning of the bud formed at the top of a branch.

All of the buds in each of the terminal bud clusters on the plant will bloom at the same time, on a date which rarely varies more than a few days from year to year. However, if all of the buds were allowed to bloom, there would be insufficient room for all of the buds to develop properly. By disbudding or removing the buds surrounding the central terminal bud, the grower may obtain one large perfectly formed bloom for each stem he has permitted to develop on the plant.

HOW A CHRYSANTHEMUM BLOOMS

How the chrysanthemum could bloom with such precision remained as much of a mystery as its unique growth cycle, until the influence of day length was discovered. Technically, the chrysanthemum is called a short-day plant. It naturally blooms when the short days of autumn provide the trigger action that diverts plant energy from vegetative growth into bloom production. Since the length of day is the same in each locality from year to year, it is easy to see how nature can time the blooming date of each variety in any given latitude.

The large-bloom variety, Detroit News, allowed to grow naturally with no disbudding or side shoot removal. (*Photography by Roche — courtesy* Flower Grower Magazine)

The large-bloom variety, Detroit News, disbudded to produce one large bloom. (*Photography by Roche — courtesy* Flower Grower Magazine)

The sequence pictured above may seem confusing, since it is possible for some unpinched plants to produce second or third crown buds and terminal bud clusters at the same time. The central bud of any crown bud cluster is actually a true flower bud, for if all of the side buds are removed, it will bloom on the normal blooming date for the variety. In fact, most English growers prefer a crown bud bloom, but they are careful to select one which develops late in the season. One that is formed in early August would become hard and leathery in appearance. Also, there would be a 12- to 18-inch stem having a few small leaf bracts in place of the true leaves which develop on the stem of a terminal bloom.

The crown bud thus acts as a test of blooming conditions, for if length of day and temperature conditions are not right the side buds will continue the upward growth of the plant. The crown bud will then be isolated from the direct-line flow of plant food between the roots and leaves. As a result it becomes starved. Once the right conditions have been reached, all of the buds on the plant bloom to fulfill nature's goal of perpetuating the species. This is a difficult task because blooming occurs late in the season when pollinating insects are few. Thus, nature relies upon the early bud formation to force plant growth into as many branches as the plant can support; then the maximum number of buds are available for flowering at a period of year which is least propitious for seed production.

Man is not interested in seed production, for he can perpetuate a given variety by asexual reproduction. His goal, for a bush-type variety, is a well-developed plant having many well-spaced flowers. In the case of a standard variety, he desires the largest bloom it is possible to obtain on each stem permitted to develop. Man may achieve his goal by a process of pinching and bud removal without upsetting the normal flowering instinct of the plant.

CHAPTER 3

Fundamentals for a Successful Hobby

THE name "chrysanthemum" is a composite Greek word made up from the word *chrysos* (meaning golden) and *anthemon* (meaning flower). While the name aptly described an early chrysanthemum species which resembled our modern sunflower, it also emphasizes the chrysanthemum's need for a place in the sun. There are no special requirements to make a chrysanthemum garden differ from the type of garden used to grow vegetables or most types of flowers; however, to have success in any kind of gardening requires a knowledge of the likes and dislikes of the plant material to be grown. All types of mums will get a good start if the basic requirements for a sunny, well-drained location are met. Everything else required in the culture of mums becomes a refinement that can be learned as the plants develop.

LOCATION

Any location which receives sun for a major portion of the day has possibilities as a mum garden, for chrysanthemums refuse to do well in locations where they receive natural shade, such as that from buildings and trees, for more than 4 hours a day. The actual fertility of the soil and its composition, while important, can always be corrected; so in choosing a location, make sunlight the deciding factor. The only other must for chrysanthemums is a well-drained location.

DRAINAGE

Chrysanthemums are relatively shallow-rooted plants, but there are many tiny roots which radiate out into the top 6-inch layer of soil. Such a root system is designed to absorb its needed water requirements in the layer of soil which is alternately watered and dried by the normal action of rain and sun. The plants that have long taproots are designed to draw water from the subsoil that is usually very wet. Obviously a chrysanthemum dislikes constantly wet feet. The proposed chrysanthemum site should be checked at intervals after spring rains to see how quickly it dries. Unless the site drains well it is best to pick another, or else make provision for positive removal of excess water. Improvement of a poorly drained site can be handled in two ways. A drain tile system that can be pitched toward a lower point will work satisfactorily if it is placed 2 feet under the garden.

Where it is not feasible to construct a positive drainage system, the ground level may be raised. This is done by placing a course of cinder blocks around the bed on top of the poorly drained soil. The enclosed area is then filled with good friable garden soil. Such a bed will be in good condition at planting time, but in periods of drought it will require considerable water.

TEMPERATURE

Of course, temperature may be considered as a basic requirement in successful mum culture, for obviously, in a latitude that becomes consistently cold early in autumn, it will be possible to grow only those varieties that are early blooming. Experiments at several of our agricultural experiment stations have demonstrated that a 60-degree temperature for several weeks is required during the bud initiation stage in the majority of varieties tested. A few will initiate buds satisfactorily at 50 degrees. Once past this critical period in a chrysanthemum's development the temperature can drop to slightly below freezing without damage to the flowers, providing frost does not fall on the petals. The period when outdoor-grown chrysanthemums stop vegetative growth and start blooming bud production occurs about 1 to 2 months before blooming. In any areas that are subject to early cold spells, followed by periods of warmer weather, varieties should be chosen that will either bloom early or develop their buds in lower temperatures. In the beginning phase of the chrysanthemum season, temperatures are not so important, except that new growth cannot stand the same low temperatures that have no effect on mature plants. If plants are set out early, it might be advisable to be prepared with some type of protection in case frost or below-freezing weather threatens.

EQUIPMENT

There is no special equipment required to insure success in raising mums. The standard spade and trowel owned by every good gardener will do very well for a start. Of course, wire, stakes, plant labels, favorite insect sprays, and well-advertised fertilizers will be accumulated along the way. The potentiality for expansion in the hobby of growing chrysanthemums is tremendous. Their normal blooming season extends from August through December, and can be made year round by special cultural techniques; they range in flower size from ½ inch to over 8 inches; and their shapes and color combinations are almost endless. It is difficult for a gardener to get the feel of growing chrysanthemums without wanting to go on and on. This leads to cold frames, frost covers, and eventually to a greenhouse.

WORKING VOCABULARY

The working vocabulary of the chrysanthemum grower increases in proportion to his interest and skill in raising flowers. It matters not whether his efforts are directed toward beautification of his home and grounds, or whether his efforts are stimulated by thoughts of blue ribbons. The lore and language of the chrysanthemum hobbyist are made up of a mixture of technical horticultural definitions and time-honored cultural terms. To avoid needless reference and explanation as these words appear in the text, there is a glossary of the terms used by growers and exhibitors of chrysanthemums in Appendix C.

CHAPTER 4

Sources of Plants

MOST gardeners start growing chrysanthemums because they have been given plants by a fellow gardener. Chrysanthemums have brought so much pleasure to the seasoned grower that he is always looking for an opportunity to indoctrinate the friends he meets with the joys of his hobby. Gift plants are the best invitation to join the mum fraternity.

The neophyte chrysanthemum grower soon finds that his hobby demands a wider selection of plants than he can obtain from neighboring growers; so his next step is the purchase of plants from a commercial grower. Each mum plant that starts growth in early spring is capable of producing up to 15 or 20 new plants. The ease with which these plants can be propagated, plus their vigorous growth, makes them easier to handle and transport than most perennials. This should make them both cheap and readily obtainable. To a large extent this is true, but, just as with any plants, bulbs, or seeds, there are bargains of good quality and there are bargains that turn out to be no bargain at flowering time. As far as price is concerned, it is only natural that the price of one plant of a variety will be higher than will be the individual plant price on an order of 50 of a variety. Also, a new variety will cost more than one which has been popular over the years. The retail price of plants ranges between 25 and 75 cents a plant for older varieties and may go as high as $2.00 or $3.00 for a new introduction. Price alone should not be the determining factor in the purchase of plants, for a reliable chrysanthemum specialist uses the newer scientific methods of producing disease-free plants; his plants will be correctly named varieties, disseminated by recognized hybridizers; and he will adequately pack the shipment to assure safe arrival.

PLANTS FROM THE CHRYSANTHEMUM SPECIALIST

The catalogues of the chrysanthemum specialists begin to arrive in January when most northern gardeners are more concerned with shoveling snow than in digging up a garden. However, unless plants are ordered early there are liable to be disappointments at blooming time. It is an advantage to both the seller and the purchaser of chrysanthemum plants to have orders placed early. Perhaps an insight into the problems faced by the dealers will serve to emphasize this need. The chrysanthemum grower, who has to keep track of as many as 500 different varieties, reserves as stock plants enough of each variety to meet his anticipated demand. Based upon the orders he receives, the grower schedules his production to provide plants at the right stage of development for shipment. All commercial growers ship rooted cuttings that are produced from the new shoots growing up around the stalk of the previous year's plant. Some of the exhibition varieties produce only 2 or 3 available cuttings, while the majority of hardy varieties are more prolific. The top 3 to 4 inches of these shoots are cut off and inserted in the moist sand of a greenhouse cutting bench, and, after 2 to 3 weeks, roots will have formed at the base of the cuttings. These are plants which will

Typical cuttings as supplied by a commercial chrysanthemum specialist. *(Geo. J. Ball, Inc.)*

bloom the same year and they are shipped to all parts of the country. Suppliers of retail plants place the rooted cuttings between strips of moist glass wool or sphagnum moss and roll them in waterproof paper; or else transplant them to 2¼-inch paper pots several weeks prior to the shipping date. The wholesale growers ship their bare root cuttings in special cardboard containers divided into sections, each of which holds 25 cuttings. Since the cuttings are rooted in sterile sand, they must be shipped as soon as they are well rooted, for if they remain too long without nourishment they will become so starved they will never recover. The stock plants require 3 weeks to a month after removal of the first cuttings before another batch of cuttings is available. This creates a problem in timing that can only be handled by having orders available far enough in advance to plan efficient use of valuable bench space. Orders that are received too late are often subject to substitution or cancellation.

TIPS ON BUYING PLANTS

To assist in purchasing plants, a list of varieties for various uses is contained in a later section of this book, and it has been made as complete as possible. There is a code reference to the list of growers for each variety in Appendix A. It may be possible to get all the varieties desired from one, or perhaps two, dealers, thus keeping the transportation cost at a minimum. Always read the conditions of sale in each catalogue thoroughly before ordering plants. These contain the terms under which the grower is willing to make a contract with the buyer. A signed order makes these conditions binding whether they have been understood or not. It is always good insurance to order a few extra plants above those called for in the chrysanthemum plans for the year. These plants can be grown separately for use as replacements, if necessary. More and more concerns are using post cards to acknowledge orders. A new customer should request acknowledgment to be sure the order was received. Since some dealers ship potted plants, while others ship bare root cuttings, there is a difference in the cost of the plants, the length of time the plants can remain packed, and the cost of delivery. If bare root cuttings are to be shipped a long distance, the use of air parcel post or express, while more expensive, may be safer. Closely packed bare root cuttings may dry out if there is too little water at the roots, and too much water, in the presence of heat, may cause rotting or mildew.

In order to take advantage of quantity discounts, it will be better for a beginner to order fewer varieties and gradually build up a wider collection as the years go by, or else order and exchange with other growers. Some dealers sell plants both wholesale and retail, while others are strictly in one category. Where it is possible to do so, it may be advisable to join with other chrysanthemum growers, or garden club members, to order plants on a wholesale basis.

ADVANTAGES OF EARLY DELIVERY TO THE GROWER

Early delivery of plants has so many advantages that it should be specified by every serious chrysanthemum grower. If cold frame space and a supply of 3- or 4-inch pots are available, the cuttings can be scheduled for delivery the latter part of April in the latitude of New York City. Plants delivered early have a longer period of cool growing weather in which to become established before the heat of summer. When finally set out, these early plants will be more resistant to the depredations of cutworms and other early spring enemies of tender young plants. It is also possible to have a 100 per cent dividend from early plants, for, if facilities are available for rooting cuttings, it is possible to take cuttings of the newly arrived plants as soon as they are making active growth. This will result in two plants for the price of one, and they will both develop into good specimens by blooming time.

CARE OF PLANTS DELIVERED EARLY

When the plants arrive they should be potted in 3- or 4-inch pots in good, but not overly rich, garden soil, and placed in a cold frame. If standard clay pots are used, it is advisable to bury them up to the rim in moist sand in the cold frame to prevent them from drying out quickly. Plants in 3-inch pots can remain as long as 2 weeks in the cold frame without becoming pot-bound, while those in 4-inch pots can remain several weeks longer. Another method which is very satisfactory is to use wood veneer plant bands in place of pots. These are usually obtainable through garden centers and they come in a variety of sizes. The 2-inch size is adequate if the plants are to remain in them for only 2 or 3 weeks. They are open at the bottom when ready for use, but are shipped in a flat, folded condition. They should be soaked in water before using and are easily snapped open without breaking when damp. In using them, the soil is firmed around the cuttings with the hands, using the fingers on the open bottom of the plant band and the thumbs on top. There are also paper pots and organic pots, through which the roots penetrate, that are suitable for temporary potting of plants. One advantage of the plant bands is that they will fit closer together and the plants will dry out less than in other types. The plants should remain in the cold frame until all danger of frost is over and the ground in their permanent location has been prepared.

CHAPTER 5

Soils, Fertilizers, and Soil Conditioners

THERE is no one soil that can be recommended as best for growing chrysanthemums. Pure sand, if it could be alternately wet with a nutrient solution and allowed to dry out to permit entrance of air, would make an ideal growing medium; but this of course is impossible, except in a greenhouse. In an outdoor garden, sand would dry out too fast. The opposite extreme would be a clay which never dries without baking. Between these two extremes there is a wide variety of mixtures of sand and clay which, together with organic matter, make excellent growing media for chrysanthemums. If the soil in the proposed site has been used for growing garden plants, or if it is reasonably good topsoil, it will provide a good start toward a mum garden. The best soil-conditioning method would begin in the fall with a 2-inch layer of barnyard manure turned under. Superphosphate at the rate of 3 to 4 pounds per 100 square feet should then be spread over the surface. An added refinement that is worth the effort is the planting of a cover crop, such as rye or clover, that can be turned under after it has made a good green growth in the spring. This will supply additional organic matter which will build up the soil. This step is particularly advisable wherever the soil is very sandy.

If the soil contains a high percentage of clay, the use of manure often intensifies the poor aeration quality of this type of soil. What is needed here is a material which will loosen the clay to produce particles that promote good drainage. Then oxygen can enter the soil to sustain the aerobic, or oxygen consuming, bacteria so essential to the decomposition of organic matter. Sand will accomplish this, except where the clay content is so high that the sand required is excessive. Cinders also will help this type of soil, but, in extreme cases, where readily obtainable materials do not produce the desired soil texture, it is advisable to use a chemical soil conditioner.

NATURAL SOIL STRUCTURE

The soil to which we entrust our plants is so complex that it is well worth the time required to study its composition and effect on growing plants. The key to successful horticulture, whether the goal is better chrysanthemums or better vegetables, is the ability to supply a balanced diet to the plants.

There are four basic components of all natural soils that determine their ability to support plant life. The first component, from the standpoint of origin and volume, includes all of the particles derived from the erosion of rocks, and they vary in size from coarse grains of sand to the microscopic specks of colloidal clay. Sand is composed of silicates which are very stable chemical compounds, but clay particles are composed largely of compounds of aluminum that break down through the intricate chemical processes that occur in soil. The mineral content, so important to plant life, is largely dependent upon the amount of clay contained in the soil, although too high a clay content will lock up these minerals in a soil which cannot be worked.

Organic matter is a second basic component of soils, and perhaps its importance can be best illustrated by a consideration of the growth cycle of a forest. In a forest all of the leaves, dead branches, and dying trees eventually fall to the forest floor, where they decompose to give increased vigor to the living trees. A forest is constantly growing in a soil which is self-replenishing, without the aid of man.

The inorganic chemicals contained in the soil particles and the organic chemicals contained in leaves, manure, or any substances mixed with the soil which have gone through the plant growth cycle are useless without the action of the most complex group of animal and plant forms found in the world. These denizens of our soils are the third important component of soils and they occur in numbers beyond the range of human comprehension. They include protozoa, nematodes, rotifers, algae, fungi, actinomyces, bacteria, and many other smaller organisms, as well as larger insects and worms that can be seen with the naked eye. These are the chemists of our soils which, by a process of digestion, break down organic matter into a substance we call humus. The humus products in the soil, including hormones, vitamins, and chemical compounds, are unavailable to the roots of plants in the dry form, but in solution they make a source of plant nutrients that are readily absorbed. Every ounce of plant food obtained by a plant from the soil requires many gallons of water that pass through the plant stem to the leaves and into the air through the process of transpiration. Water, the fourth essential component of soil, thus becomes very vital to the proper growth of plants.

The chrysanthemum plant, which weighs several ounces when set out in the spring, increases to a weight of several pounds at blooming time. Thus, a garden of a hundred plants would require the absorption of several hundred pounds of growth-producing substances. If all of this material was obtained from the soil the grower would have quite a problem in supplying it. Actually, only 2 per cent of the plant's food requirements are derived from the soil. The balance is obtained from the air through the process of photosynthesis.

SOIL CHEMISTRY IN THE CHRYSANTHEMUM GARDEN

The discussion about soils and humus has indicated that a good chrysanthemum soil is one which provides the many small roots in the top layer of soil with a solution of chemical compounds. These produce the healthy leaf structure needed to carry out the process of photosynthesis. All reactions of chemicals in solution are controlled by the acidity or alkalinity of the solution. While this statement might seem to be of interest only to a chemist, it is very important to the gardener, for a soil solution which is too alkaline will lock up, or fix, certain chemicals essential to plant growth, notably iron. An acid soil solution, on the other hand, will make unavailable the important plant food, phosphorus. Scientists have measured soil acidity on the basis of its "hydrogen ion concentration" and have developed a scale designated for convenience as pH. The scale reads from 1 to 14 with 7 as the neutral point. All chemical nutrient elements in the soil are available in the range of 6 to 7. Chrysanthemums do best in a soil which is slightly acid, so a pH of 6.5 is ideal for them. As a general rule, the soil in the western part of the United States is more alkaline than in the eastern portion, but why take a chance on guessing what the soil conditions are when it is so easy to test it with a kit designed for use by amateur gardeners? Such a test takes only a few moments, but the test is only accurate if the soil sample is truly a representative sample of the soil in the proposed chrysanthemum garden.

To get a good sample, take a trowelful of soil from each corner of the garden and from 4 equidistant points near the center. Mix this together thoroughly and divide the sample in quarters. Discard ¾ of the sample and repeat the process several times with the remaining ¼ of the sample. The residual sample will be representative of the over-all garden soil and can be tested in accordance with the instructions contained in the kit.

If the soil is in the 5 to 6 pH range, it is necessary to "sweeten" it by using lime. Agricultural lime, in the form of ground limestone, is the best form to use, and 5 pounds per 100 square feet will raise the pH approximately ¾ of a point. This material is relatively slow acting; so its full effect is not apparent for nearly a year after application. Be careful not to spread lime directly on manure or commercial fertilizer, for it will react with them chemically to release nitrogen in the form of ammonia gas. This wastes the nitrogen component of the fertilizer and the gas may burn the leaves.

If the soil test shows a pH in the range of 7 to 8 it is much too alkaline for chrysanthemums. Aluminum sulphate, at the rate of 1½ pounds per 100 square feet, will lower the pH approximately ¾ of a point. If the soil is naturally inclined to be alkaline, or if it has been fertilized with plant food containing nitrate of soda, which sweetens soil, it would be better to make sure that the nitrate supplied in any fertilizer used is composed of ammonium sulphate. This will make the soil more acid.

TYPES OF FERTILIZERS

Any discussion of nitrates must include phosphorus and potassium, the two other principal chemicals which are depleted from our soils by growing plants. A standard soil-testing kit is designed to test the chemical concentrations of these elements in the soil, since they must be replenished by means of the fertilizer used. Fertilizer is used in addition to any manure or cover crop that might be applied, for the chrysanthemum's food requirements are such that it is often referred to as a gross feeder. The chemical analysis of any fertilizer appears as a 3-part number, such as 5–10–5, which means 5 parts of nitrogen, 10 parts of phosphorus, in the form of phosphate, and 5 parts of potassium, in the form of potash. In addition to the big 3 ingredients, other chemicals, in trace proportions, are required by all growing plants. Much research has been done to determine the actual chrysanthemum plant needs for calcium, boron, magnesium, iron, and other elements. Usually most soils contain the small percentages needed, or they are added when organic fertilizers have been incorporated in the soil.

In any 100-pound bag of dry fertilizer the guano, or mined mineral deposits, contains the equivalent of approximately 20 per cent of the pure compounds of nitrogen, phosphorus, and potassium. Thus, almost 80 pounds of the fertilizer are inert substances. Since these elements are not in a chemically pure form, this type of fertilizer has the advantage of containing some of the required trace elements in the form of impurities. The application of this type of fertilizer is not too easy when it must be done on a large scale; so many commercial growers have been switching to the so-called high-analysis liquid fertilizers. These fertilizers are made up of pure chemicals to make them water soluble, and the analysis is in the order of 15–30–15. These fertilizers can be of value to the amateur grower, for they can be used during watering by means of a mixing device attached to a standard hose connection.

A new development in plant fertilization that has received considerable publicity has been the foliar feeding method of plant nutrient application. By means of radiation photographs it has been shown that radioactive isotopes, contained in a solution sprayed on foliage, were absorbed by the leaves in a very short time. From this discovery it was learned that as much as 50 per cent of the nitrogen applied, and 15 per cent of the phosphorus applied, had entered the leaves within an hour after they were sprayed on the foliage.

Studies of foliar feeding at the University of Michigan have indicated that more nutrients will be absorbed through the leaves if cane sugar is added to the spray material. Also, absorption will take place during the night hours. The stomata of the leaves, through which foliage-applied nutrients must pass, are open during the dark hours; so cloudy days are ideal for applying foliar sprays. The chemicals used for foliar feeding are high-analysis compounds, designed to supply a plant's requirements for nitrogen, phosphorus, potassium, and some trace elements without burning the leaves. In using this method, the directions of the manufacturer should be followed carefully. A more recent development in the stimulation of plants to greater development is promised by the use of Gibberellic acid. This is a growth stimulant which has experimentally increased plant size up to 3 times normal. The individual grower must prove the claims of any new product in his own garden before it can gain universal acceptance, but all of these new developments in horticulture provide increased incentive in our gardening hobby.

In any comparison of fertilizers, cost is of course an important consideration. The high-analysis foliar-feeding compounds have approximately 3 times the amount of the 3 important chemicals, on a per-pound basis, than have the commercial fertilizers that are sold by the bag. The commercial fertilizers cost about 3 to 4 cents per pound, but, instead of costing about 12 cents per pound, the foliar-spray products cost about $1.00 per pound. Of course, any drip of foliar feeding solution from the leaves acts the same as any fertilizer applied to the soil. The chief advantage in the foliar-feeding method appears to be in quickly correcting deficiencies of plant nutrients whenever cold and wet, or extremely dry, conditions prevent soil-applied materials from being immediately available.

SOIL CONDITIONERS

Any supplementary feeding applied to the soil is dependent for its effect upon the ability of the soil to transmit it in chemical solution to the roots of the plants. If the soil is heavy and waterlogged, air cannot enter to provide the pumping action necessary to move the chemical solution into the plant channels. Foliar feeding will be no better, for it cannot compensate for an inefficient water circulation system within the plant. Some soils, which tend to compact and become crusted, require so much organic material and aerating substances that it is impossible to make them suitable for a chrysanthemum garden in a reasonable length of time. Fortunately, chemistry has provided the answer for such soils. The polyacrylonitrile soil conditioners have the ability to convert the very tiny flat clay particles from a tightly compact water-soaked mass into small granular particles that will drain well. The effect of these soil conditioners is more pronounced the poorer the soil is from a clay standpoint. Soils that are already in a good friable condition do not derive any benefit from application of soil conditioners, for these products contain no plant food nutrients.

CHAPTER 6

Propagation of Plants

Dᴜʀɪɴɢ the winter chrysanthemum plants remain in a semidormant condition, for, if the ground does not become completely frozen, some root growth will occur. Early the following spring many new shoots will emerge around the old stalk, some of them many inches away. This clump has long been called a "stool" by chrysanthemum growers. The growth of a chrysanthemum differs somewhat from that of many garden perennials; for, instead of a mass of small fibrous roots radiating from a central point, the chrysanthemum stool will be composed of many thick underground stems called stolons. Most of the live roots of the plant will be found along the stolons, and each stolon will terminate in a vegetative growth above ground. To allow each shoot to develop into a new plant would result in a tangle of growth that would not produce the quality of flowers that can be obtained with good cultural practice. Hence, the plant must be divided, but the procedure is different from the one used for fibrous-rooted perennials. A large delphinium clump, for example, can be divided by making two right-angle cuts at the center of the plant with a spade, then each quarter can be removed as a separate plant. This procedure with a chrysanthemum would result in too many shoots in each quarter.

DUTCH CUTTINGS

A 5- or 6-inch section of each stolon, having a healthy green shoot and strong roots, can either be planted directly in a newly prepared chrysanthemum bed, or in a flat or pot for future planting in the garden. This method of plant division has the properties of several of the recognized types of plant perpetuation. The part of the stolon which was below ground has a root system capable of supporting the vegetative growth above ground. The vegetative portion of the plant division could develop a root system of its own if it were removed to a plant propagating bench. This type of cutting is commonly called a "Dutch cutting." Often the stem and leafy portion of such a cutting is unusually long, if there has been a favorable spring period for development. It is a great temptation for the neophyte grower to plant the cutting rather deep to shorten the stem length above ground, but this is definitely the wrong procedure to use. If the stolon portion is planted much deeper than its original depth, the roots along the stolon will die. Future development of the plant will then depend upon its ability to produce roots along the stem at the normal depth. If adequate moisture is available, the softwood portion of the stem will produce roots 2 to 4 inches below the soil surface; however, such ideal conditions are much easier to maintain in a specially prepared cutting bench than they would be in the outdoor garden. The only safe way to shorten the stem of a Dutch cutting that has been planted at the proper depth is by making a hard pinch. This procedure will be covered under the section on pinching, but, since there are practical limits to the amount of stem growth that can be removed by pinching, it is far better to take cuttings to produce shorter chrysanthemum plants. This is done by making softwood cuttings from the new growth around plants that have wintered over.

SOFTWOOD CUTTINGS

All commercial growers, and those amateurs who want to get their plants off to the best possible start, use only softwood cuttings. Proper rooting conditions are then provided to produce plants ready for garden planting. Softwood cuttings are prepared by cutting off the top 3 or 4 inches of new healthy growth, making a sharp clean cut, at any time there is a minimum of 4 or 5 inches of stem above the soil line. Plants that have been wintered over in a cool greenhouse will produce suitable cuttings first; cold-frame plants will be ready a month or so later; and plants outdoors will sleep a little longer. The date at which cuttings are made will determine the over-all size of the plant, but the date of flowering will be the same for each variety, regardless of the time the cuttings are made. The more quickly the cutting can be outfitted with a root system the better are its chances for development into a strong healthy plant. Therefore, a knowledge of the rooting process, and the factors which favor it, will help the grower in providing a beneficial environment.

SUBSTANCES THAT PROMOTE ROOTING

Plant scientists have found that one of the growth substances in plants, technically known as auxin, collects at the point where the stem is cut and produces a callus to form the base from which roots develop. Efforts were made to find external substances which would hasten the natural action of the plant tissue, and indolebutyric acid was found to produce faster rooting of cuttings. It is now standard practice for commercial growers to dip cuttings in a liquid solution of this growth substance to accelerate rooting. However, it is more convenient for those who have fewer cuttings to root at any one time to use a powder made up of dry indolebutyric acid mixed with an inert carrier, such as talc powder. To prepare the cutting for insertion in the rooting medium, it is necessary to remove the lower leaves so at least an inch of bare stem will be below the surface. Some growers cut the large leaves below the top terminal growth in half to reduce subsequent wilting, but this is not necessary. After dipping the base of the cutting in rooting powder, it is ready to insert in whatever rooting material is used.

REQUIREMENTS FOR ROOTING CUTTINGS

A satisfactory rooting material must perform three functions. It must remain uniformly moist, must permit the entrance of air, and must be firm enough to hold the cuttings upright. Sterile substances such as builder's sand, vermiculite, and milled sphagnum moss are the best. Fertilizers and plant foods are of no value in the rooting medium, since there are no roots in the beginning to absorb them and later on the newly formed roots might be burned by too much fertilizer.

Uniform moisture is rather difficult to define precisely, for it does not mean a soaking-wet condition. Perhaps a look at the function of moisture will help to provide its intelligent application. The leaves alone now have the task of providing the growth foods required to produce roots. This they do by means of photosynthesis, which requires sunlight, moisture, and air. The bare stem is unable to provide as much moisture as the leaves give up to the air in transpiration on bright sunny days, so the leaves will wilt. This is a normal condition, but many growers reduce leaf wilting by shading new cuttings with light shade, such as that provided by a sheet of newspaper, for the first few days. However, the chrysanthemum cutting can take a considerable amount of direct light with no ill effects. If too much water is added to the rooting medium in an effort to prevent wilting, the stem passages that carry water to the leaves will become so waterlogged that air will be excluded. Cuttings that are kept too moist have a droopy or soggy look, and they either remain in a dormant stage until conditions are corrected or else develop a black rot below the surface of the rooting material. On the other hand, if there is too little moisture, the leaves will wilt and assume a light green, droopy appearance. If this condition is apparent in the morning, after the leaves have had all night to recover their lost moisture, it is a definite sign that the stems are either not inserted deeply enough in the rooting medium or else that the upper stratum does not remain sufficiently moist.

Temperature plays an important part in rooting cuttings because the same functions of the growth cells are required as in normal plant growth. At low temperatures, activity is slow and there is danger that plant tissue will rot. As temperature increases, plant cell activity increases up to a point where the rate of evaporation of water through the leaves exceeds the capacity of the water-carrying channels in the stem. Prolonged high temperatures will produce such dehydration that the water channels will collapse and the cuttings cannot recover. An ideal temperature range for rooting cuttings is 60 to 65 degrees, but, unless artificial conditions are provided, it is impossible to maintain such a narrow range. No harm is done if the sun increases the temperature to 80 or 85 degrees, provided there is sufficient humidity in the atmosphere around the cuttings. Conversely, the temperature may drop as low as 50 degrees at night, as long as the moisture condensed at this temperature does not create an overwatered rooting medium in the event of a period of 3 or 4 cloudy, cool days.

EQUIPMENT FOR ROOTING CUTTINGS

It is evident that some type of structure is required to maintain satisfactory rooting conditions. Those who are fortunate enough to have a greenhouse have their problem materially reduced, although, even here, more judgment and care are required than would be needed for the growing of plants having established root systems. In a greenhouse, temperatures can be controlled on the low side by the heating system, and the rise in temperature due to sun heat can be held within safe limits by means of ventilation. Most greenhouse operators maintain a cutting bench which contains a minimum depth of 4 inches of rooting material. Sand was usually the old-time favorite, but it does have a tendency to dry out more quickly than other materials. Some of the commercial growers have kept more even moisture conditions by mixing peat moss into the sand in ratios up to 50 per cent. This has a further advantage in that the new roots can obtain some nourishment from the peat moss, particularly if they are left too long in the cutting bench. If the chrysanthemum grower is available during the day to apply a fine water mist to cuttings that wilt too severely under the influence of a bright sun, there is no problem. However, many greenhouse owners have to rely on automatic temperature and ventilating controls to maintain good growing conditions while they are away all day. In such a case, a very good automatically watered bench can be easily constructed.

AUTOMATIC CUTTING BENCH

A tight bench of any convenient size, but with a 6-inch minimum depth, is constructed of cypress, or other long-lasting bench material. It is then made waterproof by coating with asphalt roofing com-

Author's automatic cutting bench, showing ball float, water feed, and root-ing medium of sand and peat moss. *(Photography by Roche)*

pound applied to the inside. A water compartment, large enough to provide free action of a float valve, is attached to the front side of the bench, either on the outside of the bench center, or inside. A ½- or ¾-inch pipe from a standard water-supply system is connected through the bottom of the water compartment directly to the inlet of the float valve. Care should be taken to insure a good tight connection at the point where the pipe comes through the water box. A 1-inch galvanized pipe is then run from the water box, at a point about an inch from the bottom of the water compartment to a galvanized tee located at the mid point of the bench. From each side of the straight-through run of the tee a galvanized pipe is run the length of the bench, with the size of pipe dependent on the length of bench to be watered. For a bench 12 to 15 feet long, a 1¼-inch pipe would be adequate. A bench large enough to root 400 or 500 cuttings at one time would only have to be about 3 feet by 4 feet, and a 1-inch pipe would be large enough. The lateral pipes are capped at the end and ⅛-inch holes are drilled at intervals of a foot along the bottom of the pipes. The pipe system should be raised an inch from the bottom of the bench to prevent clogging of the holes. Clean builder's sand can then be added to within an inch or so of the bench top. Sand in such a bench acts just as the sand along an ocean beach, for it will be almost dry on top, yet very moist several inches below the surface. As more water is absorbed into the air by evaporation from the sand surface, it is replenished by the float valve, which keeps a set level regardless of water requirements. A little experimenting will indicate the proper float level for keeping the sand barely moist at the surface.

Equally good results can be obtained from a hotbed that has an electric soil-heating cable to provide bottom heat. The standard hotbed sash is 3 feet by 6 feet in size and there are usually 5 rows of glass panes. The glass is so arranged that each pane laps over the pane below about ¼ inch to permit condensation on the inner glass surface to seep outside. A hotbed should face south to take full advantage of the sun's light and heat. To insure good runoff of condensation, the top of the hotbed sash should rest on a north wall 1½ to 3 feet above the bottom, which should be at ground level. A permanent hotbed frame can be made by using cinder blocks. However, if a wooden frame is used, it should be treated with copper naphthenate wood preservative to prevent it from rotting too quickly in the damp ground.

Before building the frame, a pit should be dug deep enough so there will be approximately 6 inches of clearance between the glass and the cuttings at the bottom, after a 6-inch layer of rooting medium has been placed in the pit. A cold frame is so much an adjunct of all types of gardening that plans should be made to make the pit large enough to accommodate both hotbed and cold frame sash. It is good practice to have twice as much cold frame space as hotbed space, since potted cuttings take up more room than cuttings in the rooting bench. There should be a partition between hotbed and cold frame sections to maintain proper temperature in the hotbed. Electric soil-heating cable is encased in a lead sheath and can be controlled either by a soil thermostat buried in the top inch or so of the rooting medium, or by an air-type thermostat. The soil-type thermostat is perfectly satisfactory for rooting cuttings. Kits are available which contain both cable and thermostat and are designed to heat the area under 1 or 2 standard hotbed sash. The cable is spread in the bottom of the pit, in accordance with the kit directions, with any suitable rooting medium placed on top. There will be little trouble in keeping a moist rooting medium because of the surrounding dampness, but care must be taken to provide ventilation on sunny days, even when the temperature is low. A hotbed permits rooting of cuttings in early March, if the old stock plants have made suitable new growth. After a normal rooting period of 2 to 3 weeks these plants would still be too tender to trust outdoors; so the cold frame makes an ideal conditioner for the change from greenhouse, or hotbed, conditions, to those in the garden. A cold frame itself can be used for rooting cuttings later on in the season. The only difference between a cold frame and a hotbed used in rooting cuttings is the absence of a heating cable.

Some rather interesting experiments have been conducted to find out more about the process of rooting, and uninterrupted growth seems to be the key to quicker rooting. In a sunny greenhouse chrysanthemum cuttings remain turgid until about 2 o'clock in the

A commercial propagating device with a timed mist system. *(Mist Methods Co.)*

afternoon. Wilting then closes the leaf pores, so the exchange of carbon dioxide, the raw material of photosynthesis, cannot take place. Prevention of wilting and more rapid rooting and growth are made possible by using a mist spray of water over the cuttings. This mist propagation method has been worked out for commercial growers so that a fine mist is produced by spray nozzles for 4 seconds of each minute during an 8-hour daylight period. Rooting time is cut almost in half by the use of this method. Amateur growers may now obtain a unit which incorporates a timed spray device inside a plastic unit that absorbs light and heat from the sun.

ROOTING PROCEDURE

After the equipment for a satisfactory rooting system has been obtained, the actual rooting procedure is relatively simple. Enough cuttings should be made so that a few spares of each variety will be available to fill in unforeseen gaps, or to trade with other growers. Only strong-growing, disease-free growth should be used. Just enough leaves should be removed by cutting close to the stem with a sharp knife to prevent the remaining leaves from resting on the rooting medium. Dipping the bases of the cuttings in liquid or dry root-promoting substances is such an aid to better rooting that it pays to use it. The rooting medium should be compacted by light tamping before a straight furrow for the cuttings is made in it by drawing a knife blade along a straight board. Space the cuttings close enough together to help reduce evaporation from the surface, but not so close that air cannot reach each leaf surface. With the cuttings set several inches deep, the rooting medium should be pressed firmly around each stem.

To keep plant names in order, wooden labels can be placed in front of the first cutting in the row, with the date the cutting was made and the variety name marked on it with a waterproof pencil. It will usually take from 10 days to 2 weeks for roots to form. Cuttings that do not root in 3 weeks under good conditions are apt to make poor plants. It does no harm to examine the cuttings for signs of roots, although when cuttings no longer wilt in direct sunlight it is a good indication that roots have formed. Cuttings should be removed when the roots are about ½ inch long. Rooted cuttings

Rooted cuttings which have been placed in pots and plant bands in a cold frame for conditioning before planting in the garden. *(Photography by Roche)*

then need a period of protection in a cold frame before being planted outdoors. If the plants are to be grown in pots they can be potted directly in 2¼- or 3-inch clay pots, using only moderately rich potting soil, and shifted to larger pots when necessary. For plants that will be set out in the garden, either fiber pots, clay pots, or plant bands can be used. Plants in bands or fiber pots may be planted at the proper time without removal of the container.

CHAPTER 7

Insects, Diseases, and Other Troubles

CHRYSANTHEMUMS make such rapid growth under good cultural conditions that they have considerable resistance to insects and diseases. However, they do have as many potential enemies as most garden plants. The list of harmful insects, pests, and diseases contained in this chapter will undoubtedly make it appear hopeless for any chrysanthemum to survive the season. Fortunately, however, it is doubtful if the average chrysanthemum hobbyist will encounter more than one quarter of these enemies in a lifetime of mum growing. A good preventive war on insects and diseases, as described in Chapter 8, may make reference to this chapter unnecessary, but, should trouble occur, early recognition of the symptoms will expose the culprit. From this point on the tide of battle will be in favor of the grower.

Scientists are waging a constant battle of wits against nature's law of survival of the fittest in their efforts to develop new insecticides and fungicides. In time, plant enemies build up a resistance to the various materials which formerly have controlled them. Approximately 30,000 registered brands of insecticides, fungicides, and rodenticides have been approved for sale, although many of them use the same active ingredient in their formulation. The control measures given in this chapter will usually specify the active ingredients required, but a list of trade names and sources of these materials will be contained in Appendix B.

WHAT MATERIAL TO USE

So much has been written about new miracle insecticides and fungicides that many gardeners are confused and resigned to the fact that the equipment required for an adequate control program would make the garden spray material shelf resemble a well-stocked drugstore. While it is true that colleges and agricultural experiment stations have recommended many products for the control of specific insects and diseases, it is also true that there is considerable overlapping of effectiveness against many conditions by the use of but one combination material. For this reason the recommended control methods in this chapter will be based upon combinations of basic ingredients which should be effective. However, where insects, pests, and diseases are discussed in detail in this chapter, a material known to be a specific control for the trouble will be listed.

Insecticides may be in the form of dusts, sprays, fumigants, and aerosols, or combinations of these types. Dusts can be effective by contact action, stomach poisoning, or fumigating action. They are relatively easy to use in a good dust gun, and in some cases are easier to handle than sprays. They give good distribution where plantings are thick, although dusts are quite easily washed off the leaves. When dusts are applied a respirator should be worn and pets should be kept away from the dusting area. Sprays are generally better for hard-to-kill insects such as spider mites. Sprays, when mixed with a material that is referred to as a spreader or sticker, adhere to leaves better than dusts. Both sides of the leaf surface should be reached by the active ingredient, although this is often difficult to accomplish in a thick planting. Many spray materials are corrosive, so extreme care should be used in handling them. Sprays are sold either as emulsified solutions or wettable powders. The emulsified solutions are generally formulated with solvents such as xylene or kerosene, which may be somewhat harmful to plant tissue. Wettable powders are compounded with inert carriers such as talc, which will not be injurious to plants. Emulsified solutions do not leave a residue, but the carrier used in the wettable powders may leave an unsightly residue on the leaves. Wettable powders tend to be somewhat less effective in killing insects and mites, although they do have a longer residual action. Insecticide sprays should not be used after the blooms show color, for some spray materials tend to bleach the petals. If an insect or pest should prove troublesome at this season, one of the commercial dust preparations may be used. When emulsified solutions are stored on the shelf they may corrode the containers. Where such solutions are sold in cans, it is better to transfer any remaining solutions to plainly marked bottles for winter storage. Wettable powders are usually packed in containers made of paper. These packages tend to absorb moisture on the shelf, so they should be stored in cans which have tight-fitting covers.

Fumigants are formulations of active ingredients combined with materials which will give off a dense smoke when ignited. The poison-laden smoke will reach every insect hiding place, but it is only effective in a confined space. Fumigants give excellent results in a greenhouse or under a tight frost cover.

Aerosol bombs are pressure vessels which contain the active ingredients in a volatile solution. Small units are available for use on house plants, and larger units are used by florists and commercial greenhouse operators. The small units are handy for limited use in controlling a specific insect, although the cost for an equivalent amount of active ingredient is greater than it would be for a spray material.

Fungicides differ from insecticides, for they are designed to control diseases caused by pathogenic agents such as bacteria, fungi, or viruses. They also are obtainable in the form of dusts and wettable powders. Usually a fungicide is compatible with an insecticide so that the two may be combined for application. However, since the method of control is different in each case, neither will be effective alone against both types of chrysanthemum enemies.

The discussion of insecticides has included materials which either kill on contact or provide a protective poison coating on the leaf surfaces. There is an additional method of insect and pest control called systemic poisoning which is based upon an entirely different principle. This method also has a bearing on the disease problem, for often insects are the agents by which virus diseases are transmitted from plant to plant. This control method has gained wide acceptance commercially, but its use by amateur growers is very limited. The hazards involved should be clearly understood before it is used.

SYSTEMIC POISONS

Plant pathologists have known for some time that it is possible to make plants poisonous to insects by injecting poison into the sap stream, or by having it absorbed through the roots or leaves. Since the plant fluids reach every portion of the system, such a poison would be a systemic poison. However, there is always the danger that the material might be poisonous to higher forms of life as well, and for this reason the development of systemic poisons has proceeded slowly and with extreme caution.

A German chemist named Schrader developed the first commercially available systemic poison, using an organic phosphate. Two such types of materials, Ompa and Systox, are used by commercial growers today on ornamental crops, although in Europe materials containing the same chemicals are used on a variety of edible crops. Recently the state of California has permitted the use of Systox on certain crops of the cabbage family, but the application must be relatively weak and must be made at least 21 days before harvesting the crop. Systox is absorbed very quickly by the plant tissues, but it breaks down rapidly, leaving no harmful residual compounds. For use on chrysanthemums, in areas where no food crops are grown, Systox could be used in the ratio of 1 pint for each 1000 square feet of bed area. The easiest way to apply the material is by means of a ground drench with a proportioning device attached to the garden hose. Several applications a season will give good insect control, and the first application should be delayed until the mums are making good growth. In view of the studies made in California, the land used to grow chrysanthemums should be suitable for food crops after one year during which no systemic poison was used. However, a check should be made with a local agricultural agent before any systemic poison is used.

The United States Department of Agriculture has developed a systemic poison using sodium selenate as the toxic agent. This poison is also used by commercial growers of ornamentals in greenhouses, but it does render the soil *unsuitable for food crops for many years.* A dry form of this poison, called "P40" is a 2 per cent solution of sodium selenate impregnated upon superphosphate. An application of P40 at the rate of 3 pounds per 100 square feet of bed area will provide chrysanthemums with the most complete protection against insects it is possible to obtain; however, as pointed out before, it is dangerous to use, due to possible contamination of food crops. One application will usually be effective for a year, and it, too, should be used after the plants are well established. The best indication of the effectiveness over the season is the lack of aphids on the tender terminal growth of chrysanthemums. As explained in the section devoted to specific destructive insects, aphids are the most persistent of the chrysanthemum enemies.

COMBINATION DUSTS AND SPRAYS

It is impossible to give one formulation which will be effective for all chrysanthemum growing areas. Some insects, pests, or diseases are more prevalent in some sections than in others. In general, however, one of the following basic combinations will be found suitable for a particular area. Whenever an insect or disease condition is known to exist in an area the basic spray which contains a specific control ingredient for that condition should be used. Since strengths may vary between trade-name brands of active ingredients, manufacturers' directions should be checked against the following recommendations. In case of conflict the directions of the manufacturer should be followed.

BASIC COMPOUND NO. 1

To make 1 gallon of spray

Sulfur — 2 level tablespoonfuls (use wettable powder designed for spraying)
Ferbam — 2 level tablespoonfuls
Malathion — ½ teaspoonful (25% emulsion)
Spreader — 1 tablespoonful of Dreft (or other suitable detergent agent which will spread the spray and cause it to stick)
Water — 1 gallon

Malathion is a powerful organic phosphate insecticide which is related to Parathion, the insecticide which is widely used in commercial greenhouses. However, it is much less toxic to warm-blooded animals, thus making it much safer for use by amateur growers. It has a wide range of toxicity for many types of harmful insects. It is available in 50 per cent emulsions and 25 per cent wettable powders.

Sulfur and Ferbam are fungicides which have no noticeable toxic effect on warm-blooded animals.

BASIC COMPOUND NO. 2

To make 1 gallon of spray

Zineb — 2 tablespoonfuls (wettable powder)
Lindane — 1 tablespoonful (wettable powder)
Aramite — 1 tablespoonful (wettable powder)
Spreader — 1 tablespoonful of Dreft or other recommended spreader
Water — 1 gallon

Lindane is an excellent contact poison having considerable residual insect-killing potential. This latter property makes this a good weapon against larvae hatched from eggs laid on the foliage. Lindane is sold for spraying in emulsions of 5, 10, or 20 per cent strengths and wettable powders containing 25 per cent of the active ingredient. It also may be obtained as a 1–5 per cent dust.

Aramite is a new specific insecticide for mites. It is relatively nontoxic to warm-blooded animals and to plants. It also is harmless to beneficial insects.

Zineb is a potent fungicide which is harmless to insects and higher forms of life.

BASIC COMPOUND NO. 3

Multi-Purpose Dust

Lindane	1%	Aramite	1%
Ferbam	10%	Sulfur	20%
DDT	5%	Inert Carrier	63%

DDT is the powerful insecticide which gained such popularity in World War II. It acts as a stomach and contact poison with excellent residual properties. It is not very toxic to warm-blooded animals and is safe to use on plants. It is sold as 1–10 per cent dusts and 25–33 per cent emulsions or wettable powders. It has one disadvantage, however, for it will kill beneficial insects as well as parasites and predators.

BASIC COMPOUND NO. 4
Proprietary Spray

Isotox Garden Spray M
contains Lindane, DDT, Malathion
To be combined with Orthocide Garden Fungicide
contains Captan

This spray material is ready to mix with water and it may be obtained at most garden supply stores. The recently discovered Captan fungicide is particularly useful in combating rusts and other spore diseases.

INSECTS AND PESTS WHICH ATTACK CHRYSANTHEMUMS

During the course of a season many insects will be seen on the plants in a chrysanthemum garden. Some may be harmful, and a great many are actually helping the grower by eating the harmful insects. Before rushing for the sprayer every time a bug is spotted, check for any sign of injury. Harmful insects will either suck the plant juices or chew the leaves or stems. There are also insects that lay their eggs on chrysanthemum foliage, but it is the young who actually do the damage. In addition to insects that can be seen, there are some who are too small to be seen with the naked eye. These are often the most troublesome, for by the time symptoms are noticeable the invasion is well under way.

APHIDS

Aphids or plant lice of several species can become particularly troublesome in chrysanthemum plantings. Both black and green aphids may be found on the terminal growths of mums where they are busily engaged in sucking the plant juices. They can be very persistent, for they are usually carried to the plants by ants. Ants, in their organized living that appears almost human, have learned how to extract a honeylike secretion from the aphids, just as humans have learned to milk cows. The ants may carry aphids up to the green pastures of chrysanthemum terminal growth at any period during the growing season. One additional type of aphid, the root aphid, is sometimes found sucking the root juices. A serious infestation of this species can be disastrous, for the injury may not be discovered until the plant is damaged beyond recovery.

Symptoms — When black or green aphids are present they may be easily seen in the terminal growths of the plants. A serious invasion causes the plants to become stunted. The leaves curl inward, and when the bloom is infested it may be deformed. The green aphids are more difficult to kill than the black aphids.

Control — Malathion will kill both types of aphids. Root aphids may be controlled by Systox, sodium selenate, or a chlordane soil drench.

Chlordane is a complex chlorinated hydrocarbon stomach or contact poison. It also has slight fumigating properties. Chlordane is an excellent killing agent against most soil insects and pests. It is available as a 50 per cent wettable powder, or as a 5 per cent dust. One half pound of the dust should be used for each 100 square feet of bed and it should be well mixed in the soil. As a soil drench it should be used according to the manufacturer's directions.

CUTWORMS, CORN-EAR WORMS, AND SOW BUGS

These pests are grouped together because the type of injury they cause is similar and the same control methods are applicable to all of them. The first two pests are greenish brown or dull brown caterpillars, while sow bugs are scaly bugs which roll into a ball when disturbed. All of them may girdle newly planted cuttings at the soil line so that they topple over. Later in the season the corn worms may climb the stem and feed on new tender growth or open blooms.

Symptoms — A cutting neatly cut off at the base is a sure sign that a cutworm or sow bug has been at work the night before. Later in the season, chewed leaves or petals, together with little brown or black droppings, are an indication that corn-ear worms have been active.

Control — Circular cardboard collars or plant bands set around the plant stems will discourage cutworms and sow bugs. Worm injury late in the season may be controlled by dusting with DDT.

LEAF MINERS

The leaf miner larvae disfigure and weaken chrysanthemum plants and they may do considerable damage if they are not checked.

Symptoms — The larvae make irregular winding tunnels between the upper and lower leaf surfaces. The leaf surface above and below the tunnels turns white, and the leaves may later die and turn brown.

Control — A lindane spray will give good control.

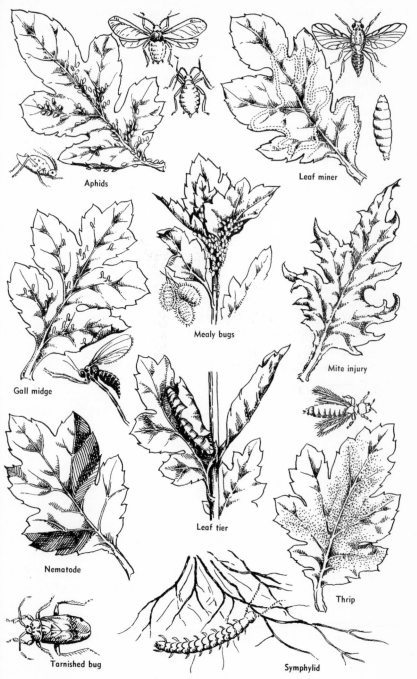

Aphids

Leaf miner

Mealy bugs

Mite injury

Gall midge

Leaf tier

Thrip

Nematode

Tarnished bug

Symphylid

Fig. 3 — Chrysanthemum enemies

55

LEAF TIERS

The leaf tier is a very agile caterpillar which will often lower itself out of sight on a silklike strand when knocked off a leaf. The larvae eat the undersides of the leaves, while the adults spin webs which tie the edges of the leaves together.

Symptoms — The larvae do not break through the upper leaf surface, but they may skeletonize a leaf from the underside. Frequent examination of the underside of chrysanthemum leaves will reveal this enemy. The adults' curled-leaf hiding place can be easily spotted.

Control — If 1 or 2 adults appear, they may be caught or killed with a DDT aerosol. When an infestation is well started, it will be more economical to provide protection with a DDT powder mixed with water.

MEALY BUGS

Mealy bugs are small, sluggish, soft-bodied insects which cover themselves with a white waxy protective coating. They suck plant juices and deform the foliage.

Symptoms — The small white bugs or their waxy coating can be easily seen in the young leaf axils or other tender parts of the plant. They are usually much more of a nuisance in a greenhouse.

Control — A mild infestation may be controlled by touching each bug or white coating with a toothpick which has been dipped in alcohol. Where the problem is greater use a malathion spray.

MIDGES

The adult midge is a small-winged insect which is usually not noticed in a chrysanthemum planting. The reddish orange eggs which are deposited under the top leaf surface produce larvae that feed on new tender growth. The light-colored leaf surfaces over the eggs are raised as much as $1/16$ of an inch, thus producing the swellings commonly referred to as galls. The life cycle of the midge requires a little over a month, so considerable damage can be caused in a short time.

Symptoms — There can be no doubt about a midge attack when little galls or warts are seen on the leaves.

Control — Lindane is effective against young and adults. Most attacks occur in a greenhouse where stock is being propagated. Fumigation will give good control here.

MITES

The extremely small cyclamen mite and the slightly larger broad mite both attack chrysanthemums. Usually they are rather difficult to kill.

Symptoms — Infested leaves become deformed, curl from the outside, inward, and wrinkle so that pockets and pitlike depressions are formed. Mites may also deform the buds.

Control — Aramite is a specific poison for mites.

NEMATODES

There are many types of nematodes, many of which do not harm chrysanthemums. However, there are two specific groups of these unsegmented worms which do cause considerable damage to mums. The harmful nematodes which spend their entire lives in the soil are referred to as root knot nematodes, for they bore into chrysanthemum roots and cause cancerlike swellings. The plants then become weak and stunted in growth. The foliar nematodes are very minute species which migrate from the soil to the foliage of the plants. They can only reach the leaf surfaces by swimming up a wet surface. Then they enter the leaves through the stomata and feed on the plant cells. This pest has become much more serious throughout the country in the past few years.

Symptoms — The injury to chrysanthemum leaves by the foliar nematodes might easily be mistaken for a disease except for one distinguishing characteristic. The nematodes destroy plant cells between the veins but do not cross the vein barriers. Thus, a newly infected leaf will have a triangular brown patch with its base at the leaf margin. Examination of the brown area will indicate that the sides of the triangle coincide with the leaf veins. As the invasion proceeds the entire leaf will turn brown, and usually the leaves become infected evenly around the stem of the plant. A disease, on the other hand, may cause uneven browning of the leaves on one side of the plant only. Of course, as plants grow taller, some of the basal leaves will be so heavily shaded that they will turn brown.

This is a natural condition, but nematodes should be suspected whenever leaves turn brown early in the season and the telltale triangular patches appear.

Control — All infected leaves should be removed and burned. This step, along with the preventive spray program, may check the spread of foliar nematodes, but they are difficult to kill once they have entered the leaves. Either Systox or P40 will give absolute control of both types of nematodes if the invasion becomes serious. Nematodes will remain dormant in dead chrysanthemum leaves and reappear the following year; so good garden housekeeping is an important step in checking this pest. The soil should also be sterilized before the start of a new chrysanthemum season if either type of nematode becomes a problem.

RED SPIDERS

Red spiders are actually several species of very small spiders that vary in color from yellow to red. They hide on the under surfaces of the leaves and suck the plant juices. They thrive in a hot dry atmosphere.

Symptoms — The fine silken webs spun by these insects are their distinguishing trademark. They damage the leaves to some extent, but the chief danger lies in their rapid reproduction rate.

Control — These insects are easily discouraged by syringing the plants with water, although they are difficult to kill. An aramite spray will be necessary for a heavy infestation. The problem is more often encountered in a greenhouse. Here a dithio fumigation will control them. This is a formulation of 15 per cent ditho contained in tetraethyl-ditho-pyrophosphate.

SYMPHYLIDS

Symphylids are small white creatures about ¼ of an inch long. They inhabit the soil and feed upon the tender root hairs. A serious infestation may kill the plants, and even a mild attack will stunt the plants.

Symptoms — If the plants seem to be growing slowly and have yellow leaf margins, dig up 1 or 2 plants. If symphylids are present they may be seen running for cover.

Control — Lindane is a specific poison for symphylids, but it must be used as a soil drench to be effective. Six ounces of 25 per cent lindane wettable powder for each 100 square feet will give good control.

TARNISHED PLANT BUGS

The tarnished plant bug is a ¼-inch-long beetle which is often called a sting fly. It is particularly troublesome because it injects a saliva into the plant tissues, which kills the plant cells in the immediate area.

Symptoms — The loss of plant cells at the point of the sting causes the stem to bend at that point. Often the terminal growth becomes malformed because of the injury.

Control — DDT is the best remedy if this pest is not controlled by the preventive spray program.

THRIPS

There are several species of thrips which injure chrysanthemums. They are greenish black winged insects about ½₂ inch long which infest the foliage and open blooms. They scrape the surface of the foliage and petals.

Symptoms — The upper leaf surfaces will have whitish blotches, while minute black specks will appear on the lower leaf surfaces.

Control — The lindane spray should control these insects, but if they do persist, DDT should be used.

DISEASES WHICH AFFECT CHRYSANTHEMUMS

Disease is a greater problem to the grower than the insect menace on three counts. First, disease is more difficult to detect because the causative agent often cannot be seen and the trouble may exist for some time before detection. Second, disease is more difficult to eradicate because it often cannot be reached by control materials. Unfortunately the third phase of the problem is the most heartbreaking, for certain diseases show their effect only at blooming time. There are some diseases specific to chrysanthemums and some which may be transmitted from other flower species. All of them are caused by pathogenic agents such as fungi, bacteria, or viruses.

Fungus diseases are the most numerous, most readily detected, and fortunately are the most easily controlled of the chrysanthemum diseases. Fungi increase by means of spores that are air-borne between plants. These spores vary in color for the particular disease and may be white, gray, pink, red, or black. Often they can be seen with the naked eye.

Bacterial diseases are caused by the smallest living organisms that can be seen with the aid of a microscope. They cannot penetrate the surface of leaves or stems, but can enter the plants through the stomata or a tissue wound. Once inside a plant they live as parasites or saprophytes.

Virus diseases are similar to those of warm-blooded animals in that they are infectious. A virus is a protein which requires the presence of living cells for multiplication, and it causes changes in the structure and functions of living cells. Once a plant has been infected its chances for recovery are slight; so any plants showing virus-disease symptoms should be rogued out to avoid possible spread of the disease. The control for each group of diseases is essentially the same, so it will follow the lists of diseases.

FUNGUS DISEASES

Chrysanthemums may become the hosts for any of the following fungus diseases:

Ascochyta — This is a gray mold condition which is present only on open blooms. It is often referred to as ray blight or flower spot, since the petals first show little brownish spots covered with gray spores. Eventually the entire petal will rot, along with other petals in the same area of the bloom.

Botrytis — The gray spores of this fungus disease are quite similar to Ascochyta, but are more easily spread by splashed water. Here again the bloom is the only portion of the plant which is affected, and the disease may be apparent on widely scattered petals on the same bloom.

Fusarium — This is a pink fungus disease which is often called aster wilt, since it usually is more of a problem on asters. The spores of fusarium are not readily seen, but the toxins produced by this parasite cause yellowing and wilting of the foliage.

Mildew — The white or grayish spores of this disease are developed

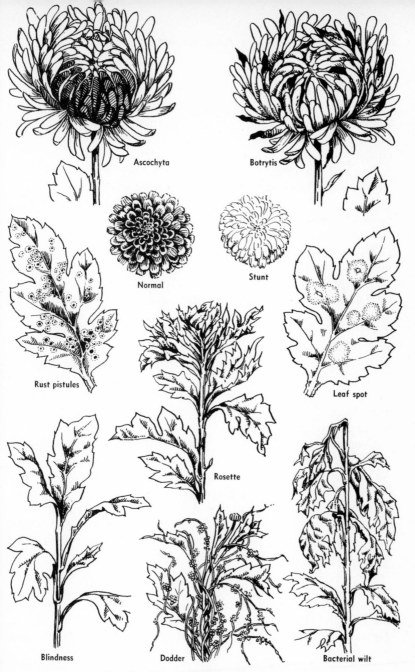

Ascochyta

Botrytis

Normal

Stunt

Rust pistules

Leaf spot

Rosette

Blindness

Dodder

Bacterial wilt

Fig. 4 — Chrysanthemum diseases

61

superficially on the leaves and stems of the plants. Thus, they do not produce toxins which affect normal leaf growth. However, a severe infestation will make the foliage unsightly and will inhibit the leaf functions. The spores spread rapidly under humid conditions; so mildew becomes a problem late in the season when humid conditions exist in the greenhouse or under a frost cover.

Rust — These fungi are obligate parasites which must develop on living hosts. The condition is usually noticed when the rust pistules develop as reddish brown spots on the leaves. Later these pistules burst and discharge brown powdery spores which carry the disease to other plants.

Septoria — This is the leaf-spot disease of chrysanthemums. It might be mistaken for foliar nematode destruction, except that these spots are generally round. The spots are yellow at first, but then turn dark brown or black. The white spores may be seen under a hand lens.

Verticillium — Often this disease is called wilt or seidewitz disease. The margins of the leaves turn yellow, then wilt, and eventually the leaf will die. This disease usually starts at the base of the plant and works up the stem, but unlike an attack by foliar nematodes, the wilting often proceeds up one side of the plant only. This disease usually results from cuttings which have become infected at their point of origin.

Control — A good fungicide used in the regular spray program will kill the spores and prevent spread of many fungus diseases. Any leaves which exhibit signs of spot or rust infections should be picked and burned. Any cuttings that are obtained from a questionable source should be immersed in a solution of Ferbam diluted in accordance with the manufacturer's directions. If verticillium has been a problem in a chrysanthemum planting it is advisable to sterilize the soil with steam or chloropicrin.

BACTERIAL DISEASES

The parasitic types of bacteria cause abortion of the plants, while saprophytic types cause decay or putrefaction of nonliving tissue. Thus, the latter types usually appear after damage to plant tissue by insects.

Bacterial Wilt — The cuttings appear healthy and grow to a height of 10 or 12 inches before there is indication of trouble. Then the top of the stem becomes soft and jellylike. The top leaves turn black and exude drops of liquid. This condition may appear after pinching, in which case it is probable that the bacteria entered the damaged tissue around the pinch and caused its decay.

Collar Rot or Stem Rot — This condition is usually caused by damp-off organisms such as rhizoctonia. The area just above the soil line turns dark, and the spread of the rot around the stem eventually topples the plant.

Fasciation — This is a bacterial disease which causes abortion of the plant. The stems become short and thick near the crown, and the leaves are small and misshapen. As the plant develops it remains dwarf, with the small leaves close together on the stem. An unusually large number of inferior buds may also be formed.

Control — Usually when the condition is apparent it is too late to save the plant. Any diseased plants should be removed and burned. A well-worked friable soil into which the cuttings are set no deeper than they were in the cutting bench is the best preventive measure for collar rot. A hard pinch below a terminal growth which exhibits signs of bacterial wilt may save the plant. Any plants showing signs of fasciation cannot be saved.

VIRUS DISEASES

The same methods used to prevent spread of human virus infections may be used in the garden. Thus, isolation of healthy plants is most important. Plants which show signs of infection should be removed and burned. New plants should be purchased only from reliable dealers.

Mosaic — This is not a serious disease in a chrysanthemum garden, although it may be easily identified if it does appear, for the leaves will exhibit light and dark areas in a mosaic pattern. In this case the light portion does not turn brown late in the season, but the plant does not achieve normal growth.

Rosette — The leaves of a plant having this disease look normal, but they grow very close together on a stem which does not elongate. It is possible for the plant to appear to outgrow this condition, but once infected it will transmit the infection to subsequent cuttings. Poor blooms will always follow an attack of rosette.

Stunt — As the name implies this disease causes stunted growth. The plant itself will be ½ to ⅔ the size of a normal plant, and the blooms will be small and off-color. This disease has become more of a problem in recent years because some inexperienced growers have mistaken the different color of the blooms for a sport of the parent variety. Thus, the disease has been passed on in cuttings from infected plants.

Yellows — This disease also is descriptively named, for the basal foliage of an infected plant becomes bright yellow. The blooms become aborted and often have a greenish color in the central portion.

Control — If stunt in particular has become a problem it is desirable to sterilize the soil and start the season with fresh cuttings from a reliable source. Under no circumstances should cuttings be taken from any plant which has shown any symptoms of virus diseases.

OTHER TROUBLES

There are several other minor conditions which might not belong in a section devoted to insects or diseases. However, they can be just as annoying to the grower.

Blindness — A plant is called blind when it does not form flower buds. If temperatures are too low at the bud-forming stage the plant will not bloom. This is rarely a problem when chrysanthemums are grown outdoors in the usual mum-growing areas. Sometimes blindness will occur on a very few plants in a chrysanthemum garden. This is a condition which occurred many years ago in a particular variety. Since that time the trait has been passed down through hybridizing of the variety which contained the blind trait. It rarely affects many plants in even a large garden, but it can be annoying. The top of the plant ends in a leaf rather than in a terminal growth.

Control — The top of the plant should be pinched out as soon as the blind growth is apparent. The subsequent breaks may then grow normally. While this condition may not appear in future cuttings from affected plants, it is safer to take cuttings from plants which behaved normally the previous season.

Dodder — This is the only parasitic plant which can become a real problem in a chrysanthemum garden. It is a leafless, orange, twining vine that lacks chlorophyll. Thus it is incapable of producing its own food. The orange tendrils puncture the chrysanthemum stems, and the parasite then develops rapidly at the expense of its host. The plant produces white flowers which are capable of perpetuating the species through the seeds that develop.

Control — All plants on which dodder is growing must be pulled out, for even the smallest piece of tendril left in a chrysanthemum stem will start growth anew.

CHAPTER 8

Planting and Summer Care

A LOT of the ultimate success of any gardening venture depends upon the right start at planting time. Fortunately, nature has combined all of the factors required to promote good growth in the spring of the year. There is adequate moisture; chemicals required for plant growth are available in solution; and the temperature is moderate so that new growth is stocky. However, spring can be a season of contrasts and it varies as to the date of its appearance in different parts of the country. All plant growth ceases below 43 degrees Fahrenheit; so until that temperature is exceeded for the major portion of the day, it is better to delay planting. Chrysanthemums are always considered rugged plants and it is a temptation to plant them early. However, they will get off to a much better start if they are conditioned in pots or plant bands in a cold frame until conditions in the outdoor garden are favorable.

In this chapter devoted to basic chrysanthemum culture the information applies to all mums grown outdoors; however, the differences in cultural practice required to grow the large blooms outdoors will be covered when we discuss advanced culture. These differences do not occur until long after planting.

PLANTING

The soil should be in a well-worked condition that will permit a handful of it to just hold together under hand pressure on the day planting is undertaken. If the plants have been hardened by a period in plant bands or pots they can be firmed into the ground with no subsequent evidence that they have been transplanted. Be careful to place the plants no deeper than they were in the bands or pots. Plants set too deep are subject to stem rot and they will not start off as quickly into active growth as those planted properly. The same advice applies to Dutch cuttings or bare-rooted cuttings, except that they will show the effects of transplanting. If the ground has been prepared by turning under manure the previous fall, no additional organic material is required at planting time. If it is difficult to obtain manure, the dehydrated manure product obtained at garden centers may be used. Thoroughly mix a handful of it with the soil around each plant at planting time. When the plants are better able to assimilate richer food additional fertilizer should be used. Careful attention, particularly during warm sunnny days, as to watering and shading of these plants is required until they become established.

SPACING

Where plants are to be used primarily for display the ultimate height of the plant will have a lot to do with the proper spacing needed for good development. Low-growing Azaleamums can be spaced as close as 12 inches, but taller Korean hybrids should be placed 15 to 18 inches apart. Where the quality of the blooms is more important, as it would be in a garden where mums are grown for cut flowers, adequate room for development becomes more necessary. A more detailed discussion of spacing and planning various types of mum gardens is contained in the section covering uses of chrysanthemums.

MULCHING

Since the chrysanthemum is a relatively shallow-rooted plant it is more dependent upon sufficient moisture in the topsoil layer than many of the perennials having taproots. Usually in the spring the ground remains moist enough to supply the plant's water requirements, but during the hot days of summer the ground becomes progressively drier. At the same time the increasing growth of the chrysanthemum plants demands a greater water supply.

A mulch for use with chrysanthemums which combines sheet composting with leaves and a top covering of peat moss. *(Photography by Roche)*

A surface mulch can help considerably to regulate the availability of water by preventing the caking of the soil surface which causes water to run off too quickly. Water which can penetrate the soil surface will not evaporate quickly and will be stored in the subsurface soil for future delivery as needed. Almost any type of organic material that is not too coarse can be used for a mulch. Sawdust, buckwheat hulls, pine needles, ground corncobs, straw, tobacco stems, peat moss, and other products locally obtainable have been used with good results, although there are some disadvantages in some of them that have to be compensated for. Sawdust particularly, and other types of mulch to a lesser extent, are decomposed by bacteria that remove nitrogen from the soil. This is a temporary nitrogen loss, since it eventually returns to the soil after decomposition is complete. To compensate for this loss during the active growth period of the chrysanthemum it is advisable to use a high nitrogen fertilizer, as described later in this chapter. Tobacco stems tend to discourage some insect pests, but this mulch is obtainable at a reasonable price only in tobacco-growing areas. Peat moss of the horticultural grade is considered the best all-purpose mulch and it is obtainable at all garden centers.

Sheet composting is a method of incorporating organic matter into the soil that is gaining in popularity with gardeners. Since this consists of a layer of organic material which is spread on the soil surface, it is in effect a mulch. This is nature's own method of returning organic material to the soil, for all fallen leaves will decompose into humus if allowed to remain where they fall. The use of leaves for sheet composting chrysanthemum plantings is an excellent way of following nature's example. To do this, leaves should be stored in a crib or enclosure open to the elements over the winter. Here they will compress and start the process of decomposition. After the chrysanthemum plants have become established, the leaves, which will be in wet layers after a winter in the open, can be placed around the plants to a depth of several inches. If left in this condition, however, they will dry up and blow loose, and invariably a beautiful crop of weeds will spring up from the seeds picked up in the leaf-raking process. To offset these disadvantages a thin layer of peat moss spread over the top will minimize weed growth and present a well-kept appearance in the garden.

PINCHING

As the plants develop, a process called "pinching" is required. Pinching means removal of the top ½ inch of terminal growth, usually by cutting the soft stem between the thumb nail and index finger. A clean cut rather than mashing is desired. Pinching serves two purposes; it controls the vertical growth by forcing the plant's energy into side branches which develop in the leaf axils immediately below the pinch, and it affects the stem length and spray formation of the flowers. The grower of hardy chrysanthemums is concerned largely with the first effect.

The other effect resulting from a "time pinch" will be discussed in the section on advanced chrysanthemum culture. The objective in growing hardy chrysanthemums is to obtain a well-developed symmetrical plant with as many flowers as the plant can produce.

Breaks which have developed from a pinch

In Chapter 2 it was shown that the early buds which were formed produced natural branching. The grower merely carries out nature's plan more quickly by abruptly stopping the upward growth. Not only can the grower pinch earlier than the date on which a given variety would produce a normal break bud, but he can also pinch more times than the plant would normally form branching buds. The normal branching of chrysanthemums varies widely between varieties. For example, Azaleamums usually branch sufficiently with no pinching, while some of the late pompons, unless they are pinched, tend to grow tall and leggy. In a bed it is advisable to pinch all plants of the same variety at the same height. This will make the main stems of all the plants equal in length. After lateral branches have formed, the longest ones can be pinched to induce further branching. The resultant symmetry of the bed at blooming time depends to a large extent on the pinching by the grower, but pinching should not be done so often that too many stems of short length are formed. If pinching is started by June 1 and is stopped approximately 3 months before the blooming date there will be ample time left for development of good terminal stems having well-spaced flowers.

There is no hard and fast rule about the amount of terminal growth to be pinched off, although a "soft" pinch made in the top ½ inch or so of growth is preferable to a "hard" pinch which removes the top 3 or 4 inches of growth. As the chrysanthemum plant grows, the portion of the stem from the ground up becomes progressively harder and more woody. The ability of the stem to force out new branches decreases as the stem becomes harder; so branching from a hard pinch is delayed. Often the branches grow out more nearly at right angles to the stem from a "hard" pinch, thus producing an awkward-looking plant. Only to correct a drastic height differential is the gamble of a hard pinch worth taking. In foundation plantings, wall plantings, and perennial borders it is better to pinch at different times to create the desired banked effect at blooming time.

WATERING

The amount of water lost by transpiration from the leaves of a chrysanthemum plant on a hot summer day is considerable. Unless the shallow roots of the plant receive sufficient water from the surface soil layer the upward growth of the plant will be curtailed. Like all plants whose function it is to flower and perpetuate itself, the chrysanthemum, if denied sufficient water, will reserve what strength it has to produce flowers. However, these blooms will not be such as to compliment the skill of their grower. The chrysanthemum tries to check the loss of water by letting its leaves hang limp along the stem, thus reducing the surface exposed to the sun. Usually during the night the leaves return to their position at right angles to the stem, but *if they are limp in the morning it is a definite danger signal.* Water should then be supplied immediately.

When it is necessary to water during spells of dry weather it is much better to water for 4 to 5 hours once a week than to sprinkle lightly every day. Light applications of water tend to make the shallow roots of chrysanthemums reach up for water, whereas thorough soakings at longer intervals more nearly approximate natural rainfall conditions and send the roots deeper in the soil. The best method of applying water, when it is required, is by means of units that spread water horizontally, or by ground soaking hoses that are perforated along the area to be watered. This is of course contrary to the effect of natural rain, but it will help prevent the spread of disease and will not wash insect sprays from the leaves.

SPRAYING

Adequate spacing of plants and sufficient organic material to promote strong growth of chrysanthemums will be the best insurance against spread of disease and infestations of insects. However, the grower must be alert to recognize any of the danger symptoms discussed in Chapter 7 and to apply the proper control methods. In the field of human medical practice the trend is toward preventive medicine to ward off disease. The same reasoning may be applied to a chrysanthemum garden, for a preventive spray program will often be the difference between a trouble-free garden and a constant battle against a stubborn pest or disease. One of the combination dusts or sprays described in Chapter 7 should be applied once every two weeks. If a heavy rainstorm washes off the spray it is advisable to repeat the spraying rather than take a chance until the next regular spraying date.

A typical sprayer for use in the average home garden

A good garden sprayer should be used, and the spray should reach both surfaces of the leaves. When mixing spray materials carefully estimate the amount required for one complete application. Always wash out the sprayer after each use to avoid corrosion and clogging. Also, manufacturers' directions should be carefully checked, particularly the strength of the poison emulsion to use.

FERTILIZING

It has been stated before that chrysanthemums are gross feeders, but this does not imply that they must be fed too heavy a diet. If the chrysanthemum beds were prepared by turning under a layer of manure, or by the addition of dehydrated manure at planting time, no additional fertilizer will be required until midsummer. Also, if superphosphate was added at the same time it should supply the plant's phosphorus requirements for the season. As indicated earlier, the big three chemical components required in gardening are nitrogen, phosphorus, and potassium. Organic fertilizers such as manure are usually quite complex in their chemical components, but an inorganic fertilizer which is usually sold in bags is composed of these three chemicals in the proportions printed on the label, with an inert compound to reduce the potency.

The chrysanthemum grower has a wide variety of dry or liquid fertilizers from which to choose. It is relatively unimportant which product is used so long as some feeding program is carried out to supplement the nourishment already provided by organic fertilizers in the soil. The old-time experts relied on manure water made by dipping a bag of manure in a barrel of water. This was diluted to the color of weak tea and applied at weekly intervals, but, since this is a messy operation, the trend today is toward the use of chemical fertilizers. The proper scheduling of the feeding program is the key to success, for no plant does well when subjected to alternate periods of overfeeding and starving. It is better to feed as often as every week in small doses than to make large applications at longer intervals. Unfortunately there can be no printed instructions which will apply to every chrysanthemum planting in each section of the country. The growth of the plants and particularly the color and texture of the leaves are the most important indications of a plant's food requirements. Plants in a healthy condition have firm-textured dark green leaves that can be snapped like a ripe string bean.

The phosphorus applied in the form of superphosphate is relatively slow acting and will not burn the roots. It is much faster acting than bone meal which is a good source of phosphorus, if applied a year in advance. Plants require considerable amounts of phosphorus; so any temporary excess due to the initial application of superphosphate, plus subsequent additions from application of commercial fertilizers, will do no harm and will remain available for future use.

Potash in excess will burn the roots of chrysanthemum plants and cause browning of the leaf margins, while plants starved for lack of potash will have yellow leaf margins. Too much nitrogen will cause poor growth with bright yellow leaves at the top of the plant, while pale green leaves on the entire plant usually indicate lack of nitrogen. A weekly application of a balanced dry fertilizer such as 5–10–5 at the rate of ½ pound per 100 square feet, starting about the middle of July, will supply the plant's requirements for the rest of the season. The total amount applied should be limited to 6–8 pounds per 100 square feet for the season. All feeding should stop when the buds show color.

If plants seem to require a pickup late in the season, nitrate of soda or ammonium sulphate, which are concentrated nitrogen compounds, may be applied at the rate of 1 pound per 100 square feet. Any nitrogen fertilizer should be applied while the buds are still green, for too much nitrogen in the soil after the buds show color will soften the flowers and decrease their keeping qualities. All dry fertilizers should be applied when the soil is moist. If there appears to be an excess of fertilizer in the soil at any time the planting should be thoroughly watered to leach out the excess.

SUPPORTING

The necessity for some method of support for chrysanthemums increases with the height of the plants. Azaleamums and the low-growing hardy chrysanthemums will probably require no supporting during the entire season; medium tall chrysanthemums will probably require supporting at blooming time; while tall varieties will definitely require a support system at blooming time. In addition to a method of protecting the blooms from the effects of driving rain and fall gales it may be necessary to support the main stems of tall chrysanthemums during the growing period. This is particularly desirable if they are not protected from winds by walls or shrubbery. Stakes of wood, bamboo, or galvanized iron adjacent to the main stem are satisfactory for use in perennial borders, or where few plants are to be grown; but in mass plantings or beds a wire system will be more satisfactory.

On estates, or where public displays of massed chrysanthemums are grown, the common practice has been to use birch branches with the butt end placed in the ground. Birch was chosen because the growth is naturally branching with many short twigs. The branches were placed among the plants before the bud-forming stage, and any ends which were visible after the buds showed color were cut off. This method is still one of the best where plants are irregularly spaced and of different heights, but it is not always easy to get suitable branches. In lieu of branch supports in such a planting, green twine may be tied to the central plant stakes and looped around the branches of the chrysanthemum plants.

In regular beds or borders the same system used by florists in supporting bench crops, such as snapdragons and carnations, may be used. In this system posts are set at the corners of the beds. Then a single strand of galvanized bench wire is strung around the posts, outlining the bed, a short distance above the point where the plants begin to branch out. Strings are then tied to the wire at 6-inch intervals and stretched to the wire at the opposite end. The same procedure is repeated from side to side, so that the bed is divided into 6-inch squares that will support the initial branch growth. Later in the season a second such support with a wider string spacing may be used to support the terminal branches. This is a laborious job, but it provides support on all sides of the branches without restricting or deforming future growth. A somewhat simpler method substitutes bench wire for the string, with one wire running the length of the row just below the point where the plants begin to branch. Later in the season two wires are run at a higher level, with the wires about 12 inches apart and parallel to the ground. At the bud-forming stage a third pair of wires about 18 inches apart are added. This provides a V-shaped support for each row which will cradle the outer branches. To prevent the plants from moving to one side or the other along the row, individual branches can be attached loosely to the wires with raffia, or one of the patented wire-type plant ties. If the posts used at the corners of the beds are to be moved every year it is advisable to use locust, redwood, or cypress that will resist decay when buried in the ground. To extend the life of these posts, or any wooden posts used in the ground, they should be dipped in a copper naphthenate solution. If the beds are permanent it is better to use ½-inch galvanized pipe set about 12 inches deep in a well of concrete. Each grower will find it best to experiment until the best type of supporting system is found for his particular planting.

Fifteen-inch spacing of bush-type mums to allow ample room for development. Note the type of support provided for the blooming season

CHAPTER 9

Autumn Activities

CONSIDERABLE anticipation has built up in the mind of the chrysanthemum hobbyist by the time autumn arrives. Other flowers have come and gone, but until that time the mums have not returned any dividends to the grower for his months of work. Then, as if to compensate for such a long growing season, the chrysanthemums burst forth in a long and colorful season of bloom that provides a fitting climax to the outdoor growing season.

COMPARISON WITHIN THE GARDEN

If the grower has been interested in growing chrysanthemums for use as cut flowers, comparison of color, quality of bloom, and suitability for use in arrangements will assume the most importance. On the other hand, if he has incorporated chrysanthemums in a landscape plan there is an added pleasure if he has succeeded in duplicating the mental picture with which he started the year. Bare spots and irregularities can be corrected by transplanting from a reserve bed if one was planned, but if the over-all picture is bad there is always the opportunity to check the causes and resolve to do better next year.

Where plants are too tall they should be compared individually with others of the same variety in different parts of the garden, as well as with other tall-growing varieties. A leggy plant usually has been starved for light or forced to grow tall because it has been crowded. The point at which the first pinch was made might have been either too high or made too late in the season. On the other hand, a plant which is lower than expected may have been pinched too often. A plant with many short branches, and particularly with short, weak terminal branches, has been pinched more than necessary early in the season. Also, the last pinch was made so late that there remained insufficient time for proper elongation of the terminal stems. Considerable work has been done with the pompon chrysanthemums grown by commercial growers to determine how often they should be pinched — particularly the exact date for the last pinch to produce a good stem length and a well-proportioned spray of terminal blooms.

Much less work along this line has been done with the hardy varieties that are largely raised outdoors by amateur growers. The diversity in the branching habits of the hardy varieties also makes it more difficult to give time-pinching data. The catalogues which list commercial varieties usually specify the most favorable date for the last pinch, but many retail catalogues omit this data, even where it is available. Fortunately, more and more of the improved growing techniques employed by commercial growers are being made available to amateur growers in the catalogues exclusively devoted to them.

OUTSIDE COMPARISONS

Perhaps the best road to success as a chrysanthemum hobbyist is one that detours slightly through other chrysanthemum gardens. A comparison with other growers or with test gardens is bound to be instructive. Many of the commercial growers listed in Appendix A maintain display gardens that are open to the public. Also, there are many state and civic test gardens that are interesting as well as educational. A committee of the National Chrysanthemum Society has checked the following list of display, test, and trial gardens and recommends them to all those interested in chrysanthemums:

California: Oakland Park Department, Lakeside Park, Oakland
Hawaii: Agricultural Experiment Station of the University of Hawaii, Honolulu
Kansas: Branch Experiment Station, Kansas State College, Colby
Louisiana: Southeastern Louisiana College, Hammond

Michigan: Michigan State College, East Lansing

Hidden Lakes Garden Farms, Michigan State College, Tipton

Montana: Montana Agricultural Experiment Station, Bozeman

Nebraska: University of Nebraska, College of Agriculture, Experiment Sub-station, North Platte

New Jersey: Essex County Park Commission greenhouses, Branch Brook Park, Newark, Rutgers University, College of Agriculture, New Brunswick, Highway U. S. #1

New York: Brooklyn Botanical Garden, Prospect Park, Brooklyn, Long Island Agricultural and Technical College, Farmingdale, Long Island

New York Botanical Garden, Bronx Park, New York City

Ohio: Parks Department, City Hall, Columbus

Kingwood Center, Mansfield

Oregon: Lewis and Clark College, Portland

Oregon State College, Corvallis

Pennsylvania: Arthur Hoyt Scott Arboretum, Swarthmore College, Swarthmore

Longwood Gardens, Kennett Square

Rhode Island: Roger William Park, Providence

Washington: Irrigation Experiment Station, State College of Washington, Prosser

Public Parks, Spokane

Local chrysanthemum shows provide a real comparison of results, for each entrant will display only his best blooms. With a large number of blooms in a wide diversity of bloom types the grower will find much to whet his appetite for succeeding chrysanthemum years. The state and regional shows sponsored by the chapters of the National Chrysanthemum Society are particularly good and the national show of the Society has entries from all sections of the country each year.

RESULTS FROM YEAR TO YEAR

In addition to visual comparisons made in the garden and with other growers, it is good practice to maintain adequate records so that results can be compared from year to year. The human memory can often minimize poor horticultural practices and exaggerate average results, but a written record will serve as a constant guide to a better chrysanthemum garden. The best type of record is usually the simplest, for anything complicated is apt to become boring to keep and review. A loose-leaf binder with cross-ruled paper is ideal for tabular use as well as for sketches. A scale drawing of the bed or border on one sheet is useful in locating varieties, while a listing of all varieties on an adjacent sheet may be followed by 5 or 6 columns of information. Each grower will keep in his records the information he deems most important; however, there are certain statistics that are particularly useful for planning from year to year.

If the height, color, and blooming date of each variety are copied from the catalogue in columns at the time the plants are ordered, it is a simple matter to record the actual results in adjacent columns at blooming time. The actual height, compared to the listed catalogue height, is a good indication of whether proper pinching and feeding have been done. Color comparison is important because it is possible to have color variations which result from differences in soils. The chrysanthemum is such a long-blooming flower that it is difficult to pick an exact blooming date.

The cushion chrysanthemums, for example, start the blooming season with scattered flowers in late August and reach their height of bloom in early October. After that they continue with presentable although somewhat faded blossoms into November. The taller-growing hardy chrysanthemums as a rule have a more definite blooming date. Also, since their colors are more true there is a shorter interval between the time all blooms on a plant are fully opened and the time that fading of the colors is apparent. The date of maximum flower development and purest color is properly considered the blooming date. The difference in the blooming date caused by latitude variation between the source of plants and the grower's garden should also be considered. Every chrysanthemum record should have a column for remarks. Here is the place for notation of those qualities which make a particular variety more useful or appealing than others of the same color and blooming time.

PHOTOGRAPHIC RECORDS

There is an ancient saying that "one picture is worth more than ten thousand words." That is indeed applicable to flowers, for there is no better way to compare results from year to year than by photographic records, particularly if they are in color. Often the chrysanthemum grower who is willing to take infinite pains in caring for his plants will not be as painstaking when it comes time to photograph the results of his efforts. Rare indeed is the person who is an expert at both raising chrysanthemums and taking pictures of them. One of the best ways to obtain the maximum photographic results with a minimum of attention is by use of a reflex camera. This 2-lens camera will show an image on the ground-glass plate that is a duplicate of the picture obtained by the taking lens. Of course, some photographic knowledge is necessary, but this can be obtained from an instructive book entitled, *Photographing Your Flowers,* written by two of the foremost flower photographers, Jack and Mary Roche.

CUTTING AND KEEPING CHRYSANTHEMUMS

The long lasting quality of chrysanthemums in comparison to more fragile blooms makes any special care in cutting seem unnecessary; however, there are several ways of prolonging the flowering life. Research has indicated that carbohydrates are manufactured by chrysanthemum plants during the daylight hours and are utilized in respiration or translocated to other parts of the plant at night. For this reason, flowers cut in the afternoon will last longer than those cut in the morning. This also provides a factual basis for the old-fashioned practice of adding sugar to the water used in flower containers. When the stem of a blooming chrysanthemum is placed in water the growth cells react the same as those in the stem of a chrysanthemum cutting. They begin to form a callus over the surface of the cut as a base from which new roots can develop. Of course there is insufficient growth energy to produce roots, but the callus plus the hard woody growth of the stem make it difficult for water to enter the channels which carry food and water to the top of the stem. If the stems are crushed with a hammer for several inches above the cut these channels will remain open. It is also beneficial to plunge the stems in moderately hot water for several hours before the blooms are arranged.

While good foliage is an effective complement to a colorful spray of chrysanthemums, it should not remain on the stem below the water line of the container or it will decay and sour the water. Changing the water every 2 or 3 days is added insurance for longer bloom life. While cutting chrysanthemums it is good practice to strip off the leaves which would normally be below the top of the vase and place them in a covered pail or box. In this way any nematodes or disease spores which might be present in the leaves can be carried away from the garden. Even though these leaves might seem to be ideal material for the compost pile it is safer to burn them in an incinerator.

PROTECTION OF FLOWERS

Properly grown chrysanthemums will withstand storms that would be ruinous to more fragile flowers. However, direct hits by hurricanes and early frosts are becoming factors with which the eastern chrysanthemum grower has had to contend. Plants that are supported by wooden stakes are more apt to suffer damage from wind than those supported by galvanized wire stakes or by wires stretched the length of the bed. Such measures will probably bring a chrysanthemum garden through a near miss by a hurricane with only superficial damage.

The effect of frost on unprotected chrysanthemums can be disastrous, yet both flowers and plants can stand temperatures several degrees below freezing. In fact, chrysanthemum blooms will come through a freezing rain much better than a frost, provided that the weight of ice does not break the branches. Frost occurs on still nights when the upper stratum of moist air condenses into droplets of moisture that form ice crystals on the top petal surfaces. Since wind is not a factor on nights when frost occurs, a covering of newspaper over low border chrysanthemums will provide temporary protection. For taller growing and later blooming mums it will be better to provide one of the types of structures discussed in Chapter 12.

CHAPTER 10

Winter Protection

Weather conditions at the end of the chrysanthemum-blooming season are usually not too inviting for outdoor garden activities. However, there are a few things left to do in order to provide winter protection for the plants and beneficial conditions for the start of next year's garden.

GOOD HOUSEKEEPING IN THE GARDEN

Good housekeeping in a chrysanthemum garden is important at any season of the year, but it is most important at this season, for any disease or insect infestation in the old leaves will remain over winter and reinfect the garden the following year. After the plants have finished blooming, all of the stalks should be cut off close to the ground. Then all leaves, stems, and faded flowers should be disposed of, preferably by burning. While good cultivation, adequate control measures against insects and diseases, and good housekeeping are the best insurance for a trouble-free mum garden it is always possible for one of the virus diseases to gain a foothold. This is particularly true where the same soil is used for many years of chrysanthemum culture. If this should happen, and it is not convenient to change the location of the garden, the soil must be sterilized.

SOIL STERILIZATION

Commercial growers use steam for soil sterilization, but the average amateur grower has neither the steam capacity nor the equipment for this operation. There are several chemical compounds which may be used to eliminate virus diseases, soil insects, and, in some cases, weed seeds.

The oldest chemical soil sterilization material is formaldehyde, also used as an embalming fluid. The commercial product for soil sterilization is a 40 per cent solution called Formalin. This material offers no problem in application, for a drench in the ratio of 1 gallon of Formalin to 50 gallons of water may be poured on the soil to be treated. One-half to 1 gallon per square foot should be applied to the plot after the soil has been turned over and raked. A cover of tarpaulin or plastic should be placed over the plot to prevent escape of the gas. After 2 weeks the cover may be removed. This treatment will kill soil insects and eliminate virus diseases, but it will not kill weed seeds.

The bromide formulations are only slightly more disagreeable than formaldehyde to use and they have about the same sterilization affect. Ethylene dibromide is sold as Nemex; and methyl bromide is sold for soil sterilization under the name Bromex or Larvabrome. These materials may be used in the presence of living plants and at low soil temperatures. This makes them particularly useful for soil sterilization after the chrysanthemum blooming season. They, also, require a gas retention cover.

Chloropicrin or tear gas will destroy all living organisms as well as weed seeds. It is more expensive to use and requires a special applicator for best results, but it is the most effective method of chemical sterilization. Two to 3 c.c. of the commercial product, Larvacide, should be applied at points 12 inches apart either way in the plot to be sterilized. This can be done without the applicator if a gas mask is used, but, without one, it can be an uncomfortable job. A tight cover is essential for good results and the effectiveness of the material decreases as the temperature decreases.

OVER-THE-WINTER CARE

Since many of the chrysanthemums grown in the outdoor garden are listed as hardy varieties in the catalogues it is a natural tendency to let them shift for themselves over the winter. If the plants became frozen in December and remained in that condition into

March there would be no loss of hardy chrysanthemums. Even many of the so-called tender varieties would survive this treatment. This condition exists in Minnesota and New England where many of the hardy varieties were developed, but unfortunately, in many other areas, along the Atlantic coast garden plants are subjected to alternate thawing and freezing. The shallow rooting habit of the chrysanthemum is its own undoing under such conditions, for when the ground freezes to a depth of several inches, and then thaws and freezes alternately over the winter, the thin crust cracks and heaves. This breaks the roots of the plants and in some cases actually pushes the plants out of the ground. The greatest damage occurs in soggy soils that contain little organic matter. Good cultural practice with regard to drainage and the use of a summer mulch will help to prevent loss of plants over the winter.

Another factor which takes its toll of chrysanthemum plants in many areas is the early spring thaw which may be followed by freezing conditions in March or April. Often plants that have lived over the winter will start into growth during an early March warm spell. If this tender new growth is subsequently frozen the plants will probably be unable to make a second start.

A good winter mulch is adequate protection for most varieties of chrysanthemums. Such a mulch should be loose and resistant to packing. The advantage of a winter mulch lies in its ability to keep the ground from thawing, hence it is applied *after* the ground has become frozen. A combination of old chrysanthemum stalks and leaves is the poorest kind of mulch, even though it may be the easiest to obtain and apply. In addition to the disease hazard old chrysanthemum plants present, they either pack tightly or blow away. Salt hay, field hay, or straw will make a good mulch, but salt hay is preferred because it is free of weed seeds. The mulch should be examined periodically to be sure mold doesn't get a start around the crowns of the plants. Toward spring the mulch should be gradually removed.

Many growers who raise the greenhouse varieties of mums outdoors have the beds conform to the size of standard hotbed sash. When the plants have finished blooming the sash is mounted on frames placed around the beds. The space between the sash and the plants is packed loosely with salt hay. In March the sash is removed and as the weather becomes warmer the hay is gradually removed. Such care gives both excellent protection and earlier growth of cuttings.

The chrysanthemum bed that has orderly rows of plants all summer and fall can often become an unrecognizable tangle of growth in the spring, for the underground stolons may travel several feet before poking up their leafy cuttings. This can cause a lot of cases of mistaken identity at cutting time unless varieties are carefully segregated in the garden. An accurate plan of the bed and careful measurement of the spacing between plants will locate the stubs of the old stalks. However, it may be necessary to trace the stolons back from the cuttings to the parent plant by digging them up.

COLD FRAME STORAGE OF STOCK PLANTS

Cold frame storage is an excellent method of protecting and segregating chrysanthemum stock plants. Sufficient plants to provide spring cutting stock are dug up and placed in a cold frame. If the cold frame has a soil bottom the plants of a given variety can be placed closer together than they were in the garden. Soil should

A suitable frame for winter storage of stock plants or conditioning of young plants

then be packed tightly around the roots. Six-inch-wide boards may be used between each group of one variety to keep the stolons separated. A loose packing of salt hay or straw over the plants will carry them safely through the winter. If the cold frame has a sand bottom it is better to place the stock plants in boxes which can then be buried in the sand. The standard grape box which may be obtained from fruit stores is ideal for this purpose. Each box will hold

A fruit crate used to hold old chrysanthemum clumps for winter storage in a cold frame

4 plants. If these boxes are treated with a copper naphthenate preservative they will last 4 or 5 years. A covering of salt hay should also be used over these plants.

In addition to the advantage of variety segregation, the stock plant storage system permits rejuvenation of the chrysanthemum garden with fresh organic material. After the stock plants have been transferred to the cold frame and all excess plants removed from the garden, the procedure described for the start of a chrysanthemum garden may again be employed. With the soil turned over and allowed to freeze and thaw through the winter it will be in much better condition for planting earlier the following spring.

CHAPTER 11

Big Mums in the Garden

THE large commercial chrysanthemum blooms that are an autumn tradition in florists' windows and at football games, together with the exhibition blooms in all their regal splendor, can be grown in the outdoor mum garden as easily as any chrysanthemum. The only cultural difference is in the control of growth to direct all of the plant's flowering energy into the production of but 1 or 2 blooms. The selection of varieties of the different types to grow will depend upon the ultimate use of the blooms and the amount of frost protection which can be given. Varieties for exhibition in chrysanthemum shows should be selected with an eye to the classes in which they will be entered and the dates of the shows. On the other hand, mums grown for home arrangements without frost protection will be selected on the basis of earliness of bloom. Many of the large incurves, reflexes, spiders, quills, anemones, and large singles may be grown outdoors. There are also a few of the pompons which will respond to the culture of big mums outdoors by producing a single perfectly ball-shaped bloom, equal in size to a baseball.

PLANTING AND SPACING

Preparation of the ground and planting is the same for growing big mums as it is for any of the bush types. However, the spacing may be closer because the horizontal growth of the plants is restricted by the grower. Cuttings of the big mums for the outdoor garden should be started in April. They are then grown in pots or plant bands in a cold frame until mid-May in the 40 to 45 degree latitude. At planting time the different varieties should be kept together in rows spaced 12 inches apart. The 12-inch spacing gives adequate room for plant development; and it is possible for the grower to handle 2 rows from each side of a 4-row bed. If the plot is a large one, it is advisable to leave a 2-foot spacing every 4 rows to allow easy access to every plant. The spacing between plants depends upon the number of blooms permitted to develop on each plant. Best results from the standpoint of bloom size will be obtained by allowing only 1 bloom to a plant. The spacing then should be a minimum of 8 inches. If a good ball-shaped bloom is desired — but increased quantity of flowers will offset a slight decrease in maximum bloom size — 2 blooms should be permitted on each plant. In this case the spacing should be 12 inches. It becomes difficult to provide adequate support for more than 2 blooms per plant. After planting, a mulch should be applied as soon as the plants are making good growth.

SUPPORTING AND TYING

Support for the taller growth of big mums must be provided before the plants become tall enough to require a restraining influence against a natural tendency to sprawl. Until these mums reach a height of 2½ to 3 feet the growth is soft and the stems require training upward. After the plants reach the 3-foot height in late July the lower stems are woody and stiff, but the new terminal growth being produced remains soft until the blooms develop.

If only a few large mums are to be grown outdoors, 7-foot wooden stakes or galvanized iron stakes will provide adequate support, but where a considerable number of plants are to be grown, stakes become troublesome to work with and store. Heavy posts at the row ends provide the basis for several support systems. Some growers run galvanized bench wire of the type used by florists for supporting bench crops at intervals between the posts. As long as all plants in the row are the same variety and the same height at planting time this system will work fairly well. However, where there is a difference in plant height some plants will either need support above or below the existing wires, or else an excessive number of wires must be used.

By far the best system of support consists of heavy twine run

String-support system at the start of the season and supported rows of large-bloom chrysanthemums in September vertically between 2 wires. The wires are run between the posts at the row ends, one 3 or 4 inches above ground and the other at a height of 7 feet. White cotton mason's twine stretched under slight tension between the wires is an ideal material. The twine may be tied around the lower wire at each plant with a loop slip knot. The proper tension can then be provided when the second slip knot is tied to the top wire. When it is time to remove the strings a pull on the free end will untie each knot. There is a flexibility to this system that does not interfere with plant growth and yet there is sufficient support to keep the plants growing straight. If a frost-protection cover is to be used it is advisable to design the supporting structure for the cover in such a way that it can also be used as a point of attachment for the support wires.

The plants need tying to whatever plant-support system is used. For many years raffia was the favorite of professional gardeners. Raffia will not cut tender growth, but it is not uniform in size and is very time-consuming to use. Modern substitutes for raffia that are a vast improvement consist of steel or copper wire inclosed in a covering of paper or plastic. The paper-covered products last 1 or, at the most, 2 seasons, but the plastic covered wires can be used over and over again. The plants require tying of the new succulent growth at a point approximately 2 inches below the terminal. Once the growth has become woody it needs no further tying, but the new growth will require training to the supports until the blooms are cut. When string supports are used it is a good plan to have sufficient plant ties, cut about 3 inches long and bent in the form of a horseshoe, ready for the first tying. As soon as a plant has made several inches' growth above the lower support wire a plant tie should be placed loosely around both the plant and string, with a single twist to hold it in place. Later, as the plants make upward growth, a second tie can be made when the plants are 15 to 20 inches tall. From this point on it is a simple matter to remove the lower tie and move it to the top of the plant when required. At blooming time the top tie should be close to the bloom. This is particularly true if there is no frost cover over the bed, for the weight of water in a 6-inch bloom after a rain may be sufficient to break an unsupported stem at a point near the top of the plant. The rest of the cultural program, with regard to spraying and fertilizing, will be the same as that discussed in the basic chrysanthemum culture section.

TIME PINCHING AND DISBUDDING

For many years growers of exhibition blooms made a final soft pinch of the terminal growth on a specified date and one or two of the resultant breaks were permitted to develop blooms. Each grower had his own preferred date for each variety, and there was quite a variation between the dates used by different growers. Later on a time-pinching system was worked out by Cecil Delworth which was based upon the blooming date. When this system was used all varieties that bloomed on a given date were pinched at the same time, approximately 3 months before blooming.

The natural growth of a chrysanthemum was discussed in Chap-

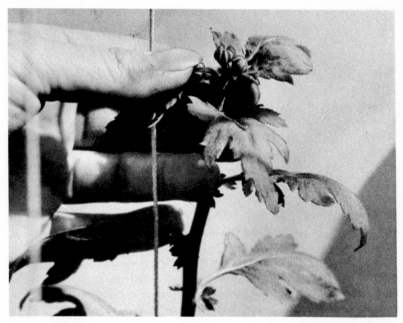

Removal of side buds in a terminal bud cluster. (*Photography by Roche — courtesy* Flower Grower Magazine)

ter 2. Chapter 8 described the effect of pinching to produce properly proportioned bushes. Here we are concerned with only 1 or 2 blooms on each plant.

If no pinching is done and only one shoot is permitted to develop from each break made by the plant there will be a short length of stem between break, crown, and terminal buds. The time pinch will produce a straight stem from the point of the pinch to the bloom. The time pinch performs the function of the crown bud but delays the formation of side shoots slightly longer. The bud cluster which next appears on the shoot permitted to develop will be either a late crown bud or a terminal bud. If it is a crown bud it will be formed late enough in the season to produce a good bloom when the leaf buds surrounding the central bud are removed. If a terminal bud is formed the flowering buds around the central bud are removed (*Page 93*).

The pinching dates given in Chapter 22 are taken from the catalogues of the various chrysanthemum propagators, but there may be some variation in the pinch date for a given variety in the different catalogues. Since these dates have been compiled over the years by many people there will be differences. However, the best date to use for all varieties of chrysanthemums will occur between 90 and 110 days before the normal blooming date. The date at which the plants are set out will determine whether a break bud will form, but this will not affect the pinch date.

The axillary growths which develop along the stem below the top of the plant should be removed systematically as they develop. This is part of the disbudding required to produce one large bloom. If these growths are cut while they are short and succulent they may be removed by pinching out with the fingernails. Once they become hard a knife or shears must be used. The last disbudding operation occurs when the side buds around the blooming bud are removed. This is best done when the side buds have developed individual stems a fraction of an inch long. The easiest way to do this is to roll the buds away from the central bud with the thumb, while the fingers support the main stem. A little practice makes this a pleasant after-dinner task as the days grow shorter and cooler.

There is so much confusion about time pinching that it might be well to summarize the steps required to grow large chrysanthemums:

For Latitude 40–45 Degrees

1. Set plants out between May 15 and July 1.
2. If a break bud appears before the pinch date allow as many shoots to develop as the number of blooms desired.
3. Make a soft pinch on each shoot on the pinch date specified. If no date is given subtract 100 days from the normal blooming date.
4. Remove all axillary shoots below the terminal growth.
5. When a bud cluster forms remove all but the central bud.

THE END OF THE SEASON

The grower who finds he can grow large mums outdoors usually derives so much satisfaction from his accomplishment that he keeps extending the season with later varieties each year. In the 40 to 45 degree latitude a frost cover will be required for varieties which bloom much later than October 15. Even with a frost cover it is not practical to attempt flowering varieties that bloom later than November 15, because the night temperature at the bud-forming stage for late varieties will be below the desired 55 to 60 degree temperature range. After the flowers have finished blooming the stalks should be cut and burned. The plants may be carried over the winter by using the same procedure outlined under basic chrysanthemum culture.

ENGLISH PLUNGE-PIT MUMS

The English growers who were largely responsible for the chrysanthemum shows which have become a part of the hobby of growing mums in America had a unique way of growing large mums outdoors. The English growers started their cuttings in a greenhouse as early as January and shifted them from their original 2-inch pots into successively larger pots, until they were placed in 8- or 10-inch pots in July or August. The final flowering pots were plunged in sand or soil outdoors. Thus the chrysanthemums received all of the advantages of outdoor culture, but they could be moved indoors in the fall. These plants required 3 or 4 pinchings to control the stem length. Then the last pinch was made on a specified date for each variety to produce a crown blooming bud.

Each English grower was jealous of his own secret soil formula, but in general all of them preferred a chrysanthemum potting soil made by composting alternate layers of pasture sod and manure. Special chrysanthemum fertilizers were compounded by many English firms, the most famous being Clay's. Many growers watered each pot with soot water to promote better bloom color. At exhibition time the crown blooms were entered on boards. Since the stem fitted through a hole in the board, only the bloom was visible. Thus judging was based upon size, color, and bloom formation only. Adjustment of the petals with tweezers was also permitted. The typical lack of leaves on the crown blooms did not detract from this type of exhibit. With a few modifications the plunge-pit system may be used by American chrysanthemum hobbyists.

AMERICAN PLUNGE-PIT MUMS

It is possible for American growers to produce in a shorter growing season mums equal to those grown in England. A greenhouse is not essential for this method of culture, but it does provide an ideal place to exhibit the blooms in the fall. A sun porch or other cool protective enclosures may also be used to display mums which have been grown outdoors in pots.

Cuttings for plunge-pit plants should be started any time between mid-March and mid-June. The earlier cuttings will produce plants 6 to 7 feet tall, depending upon the variety, while the later cuttings will produce shorter plants that will give a banked effect to the flowering display. Early cuttings should be potted in 2-inch pots and placed in a cold frame. A shift to 4-inch pots will be required before the final shift to the 6- or 7-inch flowering pots in June. When the plants show a firm network of roots against the inside of the 4-inch pots they are ready for the final shift. At this potting the soil mixture should contain approximately ⅓ composted manure or other rich organic material. With the plant potted so that the soil level is equal to the lower edge of the pot rim there will be room for a collar of peat moss. This will serve as a moisture-retaining mulch.

If a cold frame with a 6- or 7-inch sand base is used for conditioning tender plants and winter storage of stock plants, it can serve the chrysanthemum hobbyist the year round by holding the plunge-pit mums during the growing season. The pots should be firmly buried in the sand up to the lower edge of the pot rim. The actual spacing between plant stems for single bloom plants should be approximately 8 inches. This leaves an inch spacing between pots when 7-inch pots are used. An 18-foot cold frame will hold 26 plants in each row. A good arrangement for such a cold-frame area consists of 3 rows of large mums spaced 8 inches apart at the back. Then 2 rows of late-blooming pompons with 12 plants in each row may be spaced 18 inches apart in front. There will be sufficient room to reach the 3 rear rows by standing between the pompon plants.

A different type of support will be required for plunge-pit mums since they will be moved indoors at blooming time. Seven-foot gal-

The author's plunge-pit mums in late summer. *(Papas Studios)*

vanized iron stakes are ideal for the purpose because they can be pushed into the pot at the final potting and do not need to be disturbed until the plants have finished blooming. To keep the stakes rigid during the growing season, each row of stakes in the pots of large mums should be fastened to a wire stretched the length of the

Plunge-pit mums displayed in the author's greenhouse

row. Wire clips may be obtained which wrap around the support wire and clamp to the stake in one easy motion. Three-foot stakes will suffice for the pompons. These may be arranged three or four to each pot at an angle which will give support to the main branches produced by the first pinch. These stakes will require no bracing at the top.

Feeding of plunge-pit mums is best done by applications of fertilizer every 2 weeks, starting in mid-July. Either dry or liquid fertilizer may be used. However, foliar feeding will tend to enrich the sand by dripping to an extent which will permit a lavish crop of weeds to grow. Dry material such as 5–10–5 fertilizer may be sprinkled on top of the peat moss at the rate of ¼ teaspoon to each pot. Sodium selenate, in the form of P40, may be mixed with the fertilizer in the ratio of approximately 5 parts of fertilizer to 1 part of P40. This will give good control of most insects harmful to chrysanthemums.

WARNING! *Sodium selenate is a deadly poison!*

When frost threatens, the plants may be moved into a greenhouse or sun porch and staged in accordance with height to give a long display period (*Page 98*). After blooming is over, the stalks should be cut and burned or removed from the garden area. Then the potted plants may be returned to the cold frame for winter storage.

CHAPTER 12

Frost-Protection Covers

Mention has previously been made of the need for a frost-protection cover for late-blooming mums. Also, the hardiness of chrysanthemums has been stressed; so it might appear as though a discrepancy existed between the two references. Actually the need for frost protection has no bearing on the hardiness of the *plants,* for only the blooms are affected by frost. The leaves of the plants will be undamaged by frost and will stand considerably colder weather than can be endured by many other plants. Before discussing any particular frost-protection cover it might be well to determine the conditions under which it should be used. In the area near New York City frost may occur any night during early October. At this time the night temperature may fall to 40 degrees or slightly below; but moisture condensed in the higher air strata can freeze into icy crystals that form on the open blooms. This condition in itself might not cause damage if the frost melted before being struck by the rays of the morning sun. However, by focusing the burning power of the sun on the petals, frost is responsible for the brown discoloration that appears. Usually a period of frosty nights is followed by an interval of warmer weather, during which the day temperature may climb to 80 degrees or more. There may be 2 to 3 weeks of good chrysanthemum-growing weather after the first frost. Mums under a tight enclosure during this period would be heated above the desirable growing temperature. Also, mildew can become a serious factor if the plants are subjected to high humidity with little air movement. From the above conditions it is evident that a frost cover should place a barrier between the petals and falling ice particles; it should be easily removed or ventilated during hot days, and it should not shut off light during the daylight hours.

TYPES OF FROST COVERS

Human ingenuity, which reaches a very high point within the ranks of amateur chrysanthemum growers, has provided the answer for many a hobbyist. To describe all of the types of covers now in use would require a full-length book; but readily available materials and the number of plants to be protected will often be the deciding factor for each grower. The following types have been selected as the most satisfactory to meet the requirements of the average grower.

A temporary shelter will suffice for most varieties which bloom in mid-October. The partially opened blooms of early October varieties may be cut on any night that frost threatens, for they will open fully indoors in a pail of water. Thus the cost and labor involved in erecting even a temporary shelter can be saved. A temporary shelter for later-blooming varieties can be made like a tent, with stretched wires and any type of cloth having a reasonably fine mesh. Proof against water penetration and resistance to wind are two factors which do not have to be too greatly considered in this type of cover, for frost only occurs on still, cloudless nights. Such a cover may be made in 2 sections, if the bed is large, so that it may be pulled from each end to the center when required. It is advisable to provide some method of support which will keep the top portion of the cover reasonably tight so it will not become wet with dew and sag against the blooms. This can be accomplished by placing weights on the cover where it touches the ground. A piece of 2-by-4 lumber along each side makes an ideal restraining influence. It is also possible to attach guy ropes and support the cover in the same manner a tent is kept taut. The cover should extend a few feet on either end of the bed so that it will not shade the plants when pulled back. The extension will also give protection to outer rows of plants if the ends of the bed are not covered. The temporary structure is the least expensive to construct and easiest to erect; but the cover must be pulled back after each night's use. However,

Large-bloom chrysanthemums under the author's frost cover.

an unexpected rain- or windstorm might raise havoc when the cover is in use.

When the mum garden is larger and devoted primarily to later-blooming commercial and exhibition types of chrysanthemums, it is much more satisfactory to make provision for a permanent structure to hold the frost cover. Where it is desirable to combine the facilities for protecting blooms against frost, providing winter protection to stock plants, and starting cuttings earlier in spring, a sash house is ideal. This can be constructed with standard 3-by-6-foot hotbed sash for the roof. They should be pitched both sides at a 25- to 30-degree angle to give a house width of approximately 10 feet. The sides may be constructed of either additional sash or re-movable wooden sections that rest on a cinder-block footing. During the summer such a structure is open on top and all sides. In October the roof sash are put on and by November 1 the sides are added. Similar-sized panels covered with plastic fabric are easier to handle and require less maintenance, but they will not last as long.

One of the best protection systems combines the flexibility of the temporary structure with the ruggedness of a sash house, at less cost than a glass-covered unit. A good permanent framework is a basic requirement for this type of cover. A wooden framework may be used; but protection against rotting of the posts at the soil line is difficult, and the wood members are unsightly during the growing season. However, if wood is used, posts of redwood or locust set in concrete footings will last a long time. Galvanized iron pipe will make a more attractive, longer-lasting unit.

One-half-inch-diameter pipe will be adequate for a 20 by 40 foot chrysanthemum garden, provided no unsupported span is longer than 10 feet. To erect the structure a certain amount of plumbing knowledge is required, in addition to the standard pipe stock and die, pipe cutter, 3-legged vise, and pipe wrenches found in any plumber's kit. Cutting and threading pipe is laborious but not too difficult. However, the pipe and any connections used must continue from a fixed starting point in order to avoid too many union joints. Union couplings are relatively expensive, but they are required whenever 2 pipes fixed at one end meet. To join horizontal members together, a type of clamp joint used in building pipe-frame greenhouses may be used in place of a union. This may also be used to attach the horizontal members to the vertical supports at the same time.

A detailed plan of the framework should first be drawn to scale. The number of fittings, such as unions, elbows, tees, and greenhouse pipe-support connections should be kept to the minimum. The standard length of galvanized pipe is 21 feet; so 2 lengths will be needed for the top member across the 40-foot length of the garden. With spans kept at 10 feet, 5 supports equal to the peak height will be required. For ease in erection and strength against lateral pressure, these supports should be attached with unions near the ground level to pipes 2 to 3 feet long set in wells of concrete. The top spans may be joined to the supports with elbows on the ends and tees at the 2 central supports. The entire assembly may then be connected to the buried pipes. The use of unions also makes possible the replacement of a support member if it becomes necessary.

The roof pitch should be such that water will drain easily; but the height at the eaves should be enough to avoid interference with the blooms. Either a 7-foot eave height may be used or, if it seems better to keep it lower, several rows of pompons may be grown on each long side. The greenhouse type of clamp which can be set at any angle should be used to join the pitched roof members to the horizontal peak. Where these members meet the lengthwise spans at each eave they may be connected by a single socket clamp. This

Top sections of the vinyl frost cover ready to unfold on the framework

type of greenhouse fitting is used by florists to connect pipe supports for bench crops. Connection of the uprights at the eaves is similar to that of the central support members. A horizontal tie span running from eave to eave at each support point will give much greater rigidity to the structure. These horizontal spans will be at an ideal height for attachment of the support wires which run along each row. In addition to the support from the galvanized pipe, florists' galvanized bench wire should be run both ways over the top to keep the cover from sagging between supports. Three-foot spacing of these wires will provide a reasonably smooth roof.

Vinyl plastic is the most durable of the translucent flexible plastics. When this material is stretched over the framework described above it can easily support a 3-inch blanket of wet snow. The tear strength of vinyl however, like that of most plastic fabrics, is rather low. This material is used by commercial growers for temporary structures, and for steam sterilizing covers. It may be obtained in either a 4 mil. or 8 mil. thickness. The 8 mil. material is heavy enough for a good frost-protection cover, but is light enough so that it can be put on and removed by one man. For a 20-by-40-foot area it is advisable to make 2 pieces to cover the sides and roof. Each piece will be easier to handle when the cover is put on. Also, the smaller size will take less ground space when it is being folded for winter storage. Each section would be about 36 feet by 21 feet to permit a center overlap of 1 foot. The firms who make covers for commercial growers can make any size cover by joining together combinations of 2 standard widths of plastic. The heat-seal method they use produces a strong joint. There is a plastic cement which will give an equally good seal but, for the amount of joining required for a cover of this size, it is much better to have it done at the factory. Any shape other than square or rectangular is more costly; so it is advisable to buy rectangular pieces for the ends. The extra material may either be lapped over, or the excess may be cut off.

To reduce the chance of tearing, any plain edges should be folded over ½ inch and sealed. In order to attach the cover it is possible to heat-seal a hem in the edge so ⅛- or ¼-inch rope can be run through. However, it is better to use grommets at each point of attachment. The area around grommets should be reinforced with 6-inch squares of plastic cemented to the cover. An inexpensive grommet kit can usually be purchased at any large hardware store. At high temperatures vinyl becomes more flexible and tends to stretch slightly. This is the one weakness in an otherwise perfect protection cover; for if pockets form at the eaves during a warm spell, they can fill up with water during a rainstorm. If this occurs the plastic will continue to stretch. The ever-increasing pockets will collect more water until something has to give. Invariably the pipe will break before the plastic, although as soon as the pressure is removed the plastic will return to its original shape. To avoid this condition the sides must be kept under tension. Pieces of 2-by-4

The end section of the frost cover in place

The completed frost cover with the end raised during mild
weather

lumber attached to the sides of the cover will provide sufficient tension. A piece of lumber, equal in length to each section of the cover, may be attached to the bottom at each side. To equalize tension and avoid damage to the plastic, the nails should be driven through strips of shingle lath which hold the plastic against the pieces of 2-by-4 lumber. When assembled, the wooden weights should hang suspended 2 to 3 inches from the ground. A more protective structure may be made if the weights hang suspended in ditches dug along either side of the enclosure.

When the cover is first put on the ends may be left open. If the weather becomes very warm the sides may also be rolled up. It is advisable to delay addition of the ends as long as possible. This will help avoid mildew which thrives in tight enclosures where the humidity is high. Once cold weather becomes a daily occurrence the cover may be kept closed all day, with possibly the top portion of each end left open for ventilation. A properly installed cover will be tight enough to permit fumigation for insect control. Also, the pickup of ground heat will keep the inside temperature as much as 5 degrees above the low night temperature. It would be possible to install portable heaters under the frost cover to extend the blooming season a week or two; but the danger of a heavy snowfall is too much of a gamble to compensate for the few blooms which would remain. In the 40- to 45-degree latitude it is not worth while growing mums which mature later than November 10–15 under a frost cover.

A bright sunny day should be chosen when the cover is removed, so it may be spread out on the ground and allowed to dry thoroughly. Careful folding of each section, first in 2-foot widths one way, then with the completed 2-foot pile folded each end toward the middle, will make a small bundle. The cover should be stored in a dry place until it is needed the following year.

CHAPTER 13

Chrysanthemums under Glass

A GREENHOUSE is a natural progression as interest in a chrysanthemum hobby increases. It not only makes it possible to start the growing season earlier and extend the blooming season later, but it is useful for special cultural techniques. This chapter will cover only the greenhouse culture of mums for their normal period of bloom, since the special requirements for producing out-of-season bloom will be covered in Chapter 15. There are many fine amateur greenhouses available today; and for those who wish to construct their own greenhouses, using hotbed sash, there are complete instructions contained in *Farmers Bulletin No. 1378* and *Leaflet No. 24,* both obtainable from the U. S. Department of Agriculture.

Many greenhouses designed for amateurs are made lower than commercial greenhouses to achieve a more graceful appearance in residential surroundings and to reduce the heating cost. This is somewhat of a restricting factor if the greenhouse is to be used primarily for growing chrysanthemums; for tall varieties of pompons may grow too close to the glass in side benches; and taller-growing commercial incurves and exhibition blooms may become too tall for the center bench. For this reason it is advisable to add an extra foot to the foundation of any standard amateur greenhouse. The increased over-all height does not materially detract from the appearance, and the extra cost for heating is very small.

LIGHT

The light requirements for the culture of chrysanthemums in the greenhouse are much greater than those for such plants as orchids;

so a difference in shading will be required. A greenhouse facing south could house both mums and orchids if the orchids were grown at the north end under relatively heavy shading, while the chrysanthemums in the south end received little or no shading. Proper light conditions for both types of plants are almost impossible to maintain in a greenhouse which faces east or west. Where shade-demanding plants are grown in the greenhouse during the summer, it is possible to make use of the chrysanthemum's resistance to the damage of transplanting by moving outdoor grown mums into the plant benches in October or early November. By this time the shade required on the greenhouse will be less and the chrysanthemums will have completed their vegetative growth. The plunge-pit method described in Chapter 11 is an even better way to provide greenhouse mums in late fall. Pot-grown mums are best kept in a healthy moist condition if the pots are buried up to the rim in moist sand in the plant benches. The soil for transplanted plants may be any composition which will absorb water readily, for the plants have made their growth before they are moved into the benches. Where mums are grown from cuttings in greenhouse benches it pays to provide the growth-producing medium best for the restricted growing area of a greenhouse.

GREENHOUSE SOIL PREPARATION

Some growers who use the greenhouse primarily for chrysanthemums grow the large types in a ground bed instead of a central bench. The 6- to 7-foot stems then make a well-proportioned picture with pompons grown in the side benches. A ground bed should have a 6-inch drainage layer of crushed stone or gravel placed 2 feet below the surface. Good soil is then put on top, with a peat moss mulch added after the plants are set out. Greenhouse soil should be composed of approximately 1 part good topsoil, 1 part sand, 1 part peat moss, and 1 part well-rotted manure. Since soil is such a fundamental part of greenhouse operation it is well to make provision for a readily available supply. Three or four bins constructed of 4-inch cinder blocks are very handy for storing sand, manure, compost, and mixed soil. A 3-foot by 6-foot screen made from ¼-inch mesh wire is a useful adjunct in mixing soil; for proportionate shovelfuls of the ingredients can be mixed together through the screen. The soil composition described above will be satisfactory for chrysanthemums grown in standard greenhouse benches. However, watering can be made much easier by means of a subirrigation type of bench.

SUBIRRIGATION GREENHOUSE BENCHES

A standard greenhouse bench is first coated inside with asphalt roofing compound. Then, a layer of coke or large-sized crushed stone is placed in the bottom to a depth of several inches. If the bench extends the length of the greenhouse, ⅜-inch copper tubes should be spaced 3 to 4 feet apart on top of the drainage material. One end of each tube should be sealed; and ⅛-inch holes should be spaced 6 inches apart along the bottom. Each tube should be connected to a common manifold which extends along the side of the bench. The manifold is connected to a valve at the greenhouse water supply. Soft copper tubing and expansion fittings make the simplest method of connection for the various parts of this system. Subirrigation is ideal for chrysanthemums as well as other benched crops, since it avoids both caking of the soil and splashing of the foliage.

BENCH CULTURE OF CHRYSANTHEMUMS

There is no noticeable difference in size or quality of chrysanthemums grown in benches or ground beds, so the choice is a matter of individual preference. Cuttings of early-blooming pompon mums should be benched by the middle of May, although it does seem a waste of greenhouse bench space to raise early-blooming chrysanthemums that would bloom satisfactorily outdoors. Later-blooming varieties of pompons, which would supplement an outdoor planting, should be benched about July 1. Standards grown in a center ground bed should also be planted about May 15, but the same varieties grown in a raised center bench should be planted about July 1. Pompons should have a 12-inch spacing each way to provide good air circulation, but standards may be spaced as close as 8 inches each way. In a greenhouse where space is at a premium and the factors which affect good blooming are under more careful control, the spacing may be closer than it would be in an outdoor garden. Pompons grown in the greenhouse would be used solely for cutting; so a single pinch, given at the time recommended in the catalogue for the variety being grown, would produce the 3 or 4 sprays per plant to produce maximum bloom for a minimum of space. Standards with an 8-inch spacing should be allowed 1 stem from a single pinch on the specified date. However, greater production can be obtained if 2 stems are permitted to develop. Quality will be slightly less, but not enough to affect any but chrysanthemums grown for show purposes. If quantity of bloom is most important, the spacing may be made 6 by 9 inches, with 3 blooms per plant. Where number of blooms and quality are of equal importance to the grower it is advisable to pinch inside rows once and allow 2 stems, while the outside rows which receive more light can provide 3 blooms of equal quality from a single pinch.

Inadequate support for greenhouse mums is more noticeable than it would be in an outdoor garden; so a support system that does not detract from the pleasing sight of a well-grown bench of chrysanthemums should be installed early in the season. Single-stem standards in a center ground bed may be supported with the galvanized iron stake and wire support system discussed in the section on plunge-pit mums. Pompons and multiple stem standards do best with the bench-support system used by commercial florists. This is a galvanized wire and string system held rigid by ½-inch galvanized pipe at the bench ends. The wire is run down both sides of the bench and across the ends, at the 1-foot level, with wires run between the ends along each row. The main stems are attached to the wires with plant ties. As the plants grow taller and the stems branch, a single wire around the edge of the bed provides a point of attachment for the strings. These are spaced between the wires at 6-inch intervals. A similar support may be required above, if the plants grow above the 3-foot mark.

Only the time pinch specified in the catalogue should be used for greenhouse-grown mums; and, to give top quality blooms, all side growths along the resultant flowering stems must be removed.

Watering in the greenhouse requires a little more judgment on the grower's part than it does outdoors because of the restricted

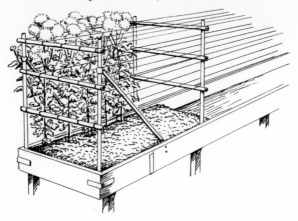

Fig. 5 — Standard system of bench support

growing area. Mums require enough water to prevent excessive drooping of the leaves during warm sunny days, yet the soil should not remain soaking wet. Subirrigation makes it quite easy to strike a happy medium. A month after the plants have been set out, weekly applications of a balanced fertilizer should be started. A 10–6–4 formulation is widely used by commercial growers, but the importance in any chrysanthemum-feeding program is a regular schedule for application. All feeding should be stopped when the buds show color.

Insects and diseases are easier to control in a greenhouse than they are in an outdoor garden, although an infestation once started is likely to be more disastrous. The sprays recommended for outdoor mums are satisfactory for use in the greenhouse, but fumigation is an easier method. A nicotine-smoke generator is adequate to control aphids and the more easily killed insects, but smokes containing tetraethyl dithopyrophosphate, asobenzine, or lindane are more lethal. Smoke generators come in two sizes, one which treats 5000 cubic feet and a large size which treats 20,000 cubic feet. For preventive application, fumigation should be used once every 1 or 2 weeks in summer and less often in winter. Should an infestation of white fly, red spider, or mite start in the greenhouse, it is advisable to fumigate 3 times at 3-day intervals to eliminate all of the adult insects and those hatched from eggs laid before the original fumigation. Mildew and other fungus diseases may be eliminated by use of a Ferbam or Captan spray. If foliar nematode becomes serious, and cannot be controlled by removing infested leaves, it may be necessary to use a systemic poison. *Sterilized soil in the greenhouse benches is the best defense against soil-borne insects and diseases.*

Commercial growers steam soil directly in the greenhouse benches, but an amateur will find chemical sterilization easier. One of the soil bins previously described makes an ideal container for soil which is being sterilized. The open front of the bin may be closed with spare cinder blocks. After the sterilizing agent is applied to the soil, the top of the pile may be covered with a non-porous material. It is not necessary to replace chrysanthemum bench soil every year, provided it is enriched by replacing an inch or two of the old soil with a mixture of ⅔ peat moss and ⅓ manure. The above culture is suitable for all of the standards and pompons normally grown in the greenhouse, but it is also possible to grow specimen plants and cascade mums within the controllable environment of a greenhouse.

SPECIMEN PLANTS

Specimen plants used to be a feature at chrysanthemum shows held years ago, but they are not so popular today, since they re-

Fig. 6 — Specimen plant

quire considerable bench space during the growing season. Usually one of the white commercial incurves or spider varieties of chrysanthemums which will bloom on a particular show date is chosen for this type of culture. A well-grown plant is usually seen as a semihemisphere of a hundred or more blooms. Cuttings must be started as early as possible. December cuttings will produce sufficient growth to cover the wire frame required for bloom support.

The rooted cutting is started in a 2-inch pot; and will probably require shifting to a 4-inch pot before the pinching required to produce the ultimate shape is started. When the plant has reached a height of 12 to 15 inches the first pinch is made. All of the resulting shoots from this pinch are retained. In order to get 3 or 4 equally spaced shoots around the main stem it may be necessary to start half a dozen plants. The objective in this type of culture is vegetative growth at as high a rate as possible; so repotting in successively richer soil before the plants become potbound is the secret of success. By the time the side shoots have made 6 to 8 inches of growth the plant will be in a 6-inch pot. The single galvanized-iron plant stake used to keep the main stem straight will have provided sufficient support, but from now on the wire support, made to conform to the blooming shape, will be necessary. At this stage, experience — with a lot of luck added — will determine the ultimate shape of the blooming plant. Pinching must be done often enough to keep each original side shoot radiating outward with an increasing number of lateral growths. They should reach the outer curve of the wire support by October 1. All side growths below the retained shoots from each pinch must be removed. The first buds formed after the desired vegetative shape has been obtained are used as the blooming buds. By this time the plant will be in its final 10–12-inch pot. All of the other cultural requirements for greenhouse chrysanthemums apply to specimen plants.

CASCADE CHRYSANTHEMUMS

There are only a few of the single mums which will produce a good cascade shape, but their informal ripples of bloom make a striking picture as they hang 5 or 6 feet below the pot in which they are grown. Just as in the case of specimen plants, the earlier the cuttings are taken, the larger will be the blooming plant. A December cutting will make a plant of 6 to 8 feet in over-all length and up to 3 feet in width. The varieties suitable for cascade development can be trained into almost any desired shape, but the simplest form is grown in a fan shape and dropped to its flowering position late in the season. The various steps necessary for development of the standard shape are required for all other forms. Rooted cuttings are grown to a 6-inch height and pinched back to 4 or 5 leaves. This will produce 3 or 4 laterals. As the laterals continue to grow, one is selected as the continuation of the main stem. One shoot is retained on either side of the main stem. These side shoots are pinched back to 2 or 3 leaves and the sublaterals resulting from this pinch are also pinched, after they have made several inches of growth. Pinching is continued approximately each week on all new shoots which develop. This will produce a plant with a broad base of many short stems. The main stem is allowed to grow up straight to a height of approximately 1 foot, at which time training begins. A 7-foot galvanized wire stake is placed in the pot alongside the main stem, and it is bent 45 degrees from the vertical at the 1-foot height. The end of the stake should always point north to keep the vegetative face of the plant toward the greatest light. Then, the main stem should be tied to it at frequent intervals. Cascade varieties normally produce a long pliable central stem and numerous side branches. All side branches are permitted to develop, and additional branches from these laterals are induced by several pinchings at the tips of this side growth during the season. To achieve best results all pinching must stop by September 1. Frequent repotting of cascade mums is also a necessity. When the plants require shifting to the larger-sized pots the operation becomes a two-man job. In August the plant stake should be gradually bent so that it will be horizontal by September 1. The stake is further bent until it is 45 degrees below horizontal by October 1. This is the most difficult part of the procedure; since the greatest strain will come in the stem below the first pinch, at a time when it has become rather hard and woody. A pad of foam rubber may be fitted over a curved piece of wood and placed against the stem. With the wood braced against the pot rim, there should be no breakage when the stem is bent. However, if the stem does crack it may be bound with adhesive tape. Slight cracking of the main stem will not affect the quality of the display. During the gradual lowering of the main stem, the lateral growths will automatically arrange themselves to the desired two dimensional curvature. When the stake has reached the lower 45-degree point it should be removed. The potted plant should then be turned so that it faces south. A light weight, which will just keep tension on the plant, should be tied to the main stem, at a point where it has become hard. This will pull the stem to the vertical flowering position, with each terminal spray facing up and to the south.

Cascades which are displayed in a hanging basket are very effective, for 3 plants per basket will completely circle it with bloom. These plants are started later than the cascades which bloom in pots. Cuttings started in February will produce plants which have the proper width and length to make a well-proportioned basket display. In all other respects, the culture is the same until October 1. At this time the plants are removed from their 6- or 7-inch pots and placed in the basket. Protection of the basal stem against breakage is again important. Further lowering of the stem toward the vertical position may be accomplished by tying a thin rubber strip between the bottom of the basket and the plant stem. Sufficient tension must be maintained to cause a slow inward movement of the stem. During this period before blooming the basket should be suspended in its final display position. Each day thereafter the basket should be turned 120 degrees to give each plant an equal period of southern exposure.

An odd shape, such as a chair, may be produced from an early rooted cascade variety. A wire chair form is required for final training. The rooted cutting is grown to a height equal to that of the chair bottom before the first pinch. After this first pinch, the culture is the same as it would be for a normal cascade, until the plant stake has been bent to the horizontal position. The plant pot is then buried in the ground in front of the wire form. However, if the exhibit has to be moved, the pot may be placed on a platform to which the front legs of the form are secured. Part of the horizontal portion of the plant at the 15-inch height will now form the chair bottom. The balance of the growth should be bent upward to form the back and side arms. The last few pinches must be carefully made to produce flowering sprays which conform to the chair outline. The main stem should also be pinched to terminate the length of the plant at the top of the chair back. As in the case of other cascade plants, the chair should face south.

STOCK PLANT CARE

After blooming, greenhouse-grown chrysanthemums may be carried over the winter using the methods previously described, or they may remain in a cool greenhouse. Potted plants should be given bench space rather than be left to struggle along under the plant benches. If these stock plants demand too much bench space it is possible to root any strong basal cuttings and carry them through the winter for stock plants. These rooted cuttings may be grown in pots or flats. They should be pinched during the winter to produce bushy plants from which the cutting stock may be taken in the spring.

CHRYSANTHEMUMS IN THE SUNPIT

A gardener who desires the advantages of a greenhouse for mum growing, but who does not wish to spend the money required to erect and heat one, will find the sunpit an ideal supplement to the outdoor chrysanthemum garden. A sunpit is a modified greenhouse, although it actually is the forerunner of our present-day greenhouses. George Washington, during his quieter days at Mount Vernon, operated a type of sunpit which used brick insulation and a slanting glass roof. The conventional type is an east-west structure with an even span roof. Glass is used on the south side of the roof, with an insulated roof on the north side. The glass area must have a 45-degree pitch to allow the maximum amount of air to be heated by radiation from the sun, and to permit the rays of the sun to reach every corner of the enclosure. In order to get adequate headroom, without having more than the gable ends exposed, it is necessary to dig a pit to a depth of 5 or even 6 feet. One foot of this depth will be required for drainage, since this can be a problem, even in a well-drained location. For this reason, a slope facing

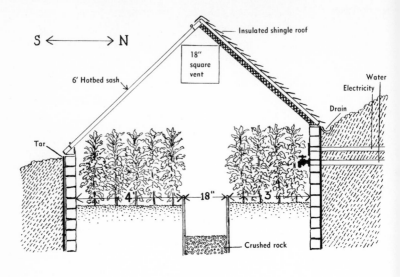

Fig. 7 — A typical sunpit

south is the ideal location, because it simplifies construction of the pit and assures positive drainage. One foot of crushed stone, or similar material that will drain easily, should be used in the bottom of the pit. This will be better than a solid concrete floor, for a considerable part of the heat for the pit will come from the ground. It is possible to construct a sunpit with just the walk dug out, but such a unit does not heat up as well, nor is it as adaptable to chrysanthemum culture. The walls below ground may be made of any standard foundation material, but, since the weight to be supported is low, 4-inch cinder blocks have an advantage in ease of construction and insulation value. Any foundation should be treated with tar or other waterproofing on the ground side to prevent water seepage. Bolts 4 or 5 inches long should be embedded thread end up in concrete every 3 feet along the top of the foundation. This will make it easier to attach the roof framework.

During construction of the wall, provision for water and electricity should be made by installing two ¾-inch galvanized pipes below the frost line. One pipe should be connected to the house water supply and 2 No. 12 or 14 electric wires should be run through the other pipe. When the wires are run through pipe they may be replaced if it becomes necessary. The heavy current-carrying capacity of No. 12 or 14 wire will make possible the use of emergency electric heaters should they be required. No additional heat should be required for late-blooming chrysanthemums at their normal blooming season. Out-of-season mums are a little more difficult in the sunpit because it is difficult to maintain the 60-degree average night temperature required during the bud-forming stage. This condition can be corrected with auxiliary heating for this critical period only, although the low night temperature in a well-constructed sunpit rarely goes below 40 degrees, even when the outside temperature is zero.

Atop the foundation a solid wood base of 2-by-4-inch redwood should be bolted. The roof and gable ends are then nailed to this framework. For a permanent structure, standard insulated frame construction may be used, with shingles or clapboard on top of tongue-and-groove sheathing for the gable ends and roof. Four-inch glass wool or similar insulation should be placed between the sheathing and the inside wall face. The inside sheathing should be made of cypress or redwood for greatest resistance to moisture deterioration. A variation of this construction makes an even better sunpit for chrysanthemums, for it involves a removable insulated roof.

A removable roof may be constructed of sections, sized for easy handling and storage, using an oblong frame of 2-by-3 redwood. A layer of aluminum-foil vapor-barrier insulation is then nailed to the top and bottom. The weather side should be covered with waterproof plywood panels to keep weight to a minimum, but the inside foil may be left uncovered to give added reflection of sunlight. When the sections are in place a capping strip should be placed over each joint to keep water from running into the cracks.

The glass section of the roof may be made of standard hotbed sash. However, the new Fiberglas corrugated panels may prove to be better, for they are lighter in weight than glass, require no maintenance, and permit construction of a larger sunpit. Since their standard length is 12 feet an 8-foot panel at a 45-degree angle will make a sunpit wide enough for a 5-foot center bench and two side benches 18 inches wide. It will be necessary to buy the standard length and cut it to fit. Three-foot-square vents should be provided in each end wall, with a similar-sized skylight in each 10 feet of insulated roof. If removable panels are used, several of them may be opened slightly during sunny days to avoid overheating. Insulation of the glass side of the pit is required during the night in winter; although it may not be required for December-blooming chrysanthemums in moderately cold sections of the country. The material used as an undercushion for rugs makes a reasonably good insulation cover. One end may be nailed along the top of the glass, with the other end fastened to a round pole so that the cover may be rolled up on sunny days.

Benches are installed on either side of the central walk, or in the center and sides of a wide pit. Bench construction is the same as it would be in a standard greenhouse. Also, the culture of mums in the sunpit is much the same. Watering is required less often in the sunpit, but it should be done more carefully to avoid splashing the leaves. The higher humidity in the sunpit makes mildew more of a problem, and careless watering causes the spores to spread.

Chrysanthemums may be either moved into the sunpit or grown directly in the benches. If removable panels are used for the insulated roof the latter method is ideal, for the mums will have the advantage of outdoor growing for most of the season. The spacing of the plants and their care are the same as described for greenhouse mums. About October 15 the roof is assembled and conditions within the pit become more like those in the greenhouse. Ventilation at this time is extremely important because the design of the sunpit to obtain maximum heat from the sun's radiation makes overheating a definite problem.

WINTER OPERATION OF THE SUNPIT

In the morning, as soon as the sun is up, the insulation over the glass should be rolled up and watering should be done if it is required. The type of hose nozzle that has a hand-squeeze valve and a 3-foot extension to the water outlet is ideal for use in the sunpit. If the temperature goes above 60 degrees the end vents should be opened; and, if the day is unusually warm, the roof vents, too, should be opened. The vents should be closed early in the afternoon. The insulation should be rolled down over the glass about an hour before dark, although on cold gray days the insulation on the glass may be left down, with no ventilation required. In fact, it is possible to leave the sunpit closed and unattended over a weekend if desired, regardless of the outside conditions.

Lights will be required for evening work in the sunpit. A well-designed lighting system may also be used to supply light for the plants during long spells of cold dark weather. Daylight-type fluorescent tubes give the most effective light at the least operating cost. Three 40-watt tubes equally spaced on the insulated roof are adequate for each 6 feet of sunpit length. An electric heater placed at each end will give additional protection during extremely cold weather. A thermostat may be used to turn the heaters on and off. The above equipment will make it possible to have chrysanthemums in bloom all winter long if they are grown under the lighting procedure described in Chapter 15.

As basal growths develop, they may be rooted and carried through the winter in flats for next year's stock. After blooming, the old plants may be replaced with annuals to provide cut flowers until late spring. A little experience in operating a sunpit will enable the grower to plan a crop-rotation schedule which will supply cut flowers, equal to those grown in the greenhouse, all winter long. All plant growth in an unheated sunpit will be slower, however, because the night temperature is lower than it would be in a greenhouse.

CHAPTER 14

Hybridizing and Growing from Seed

THE amateur horticulturist receives one of his greatest gardening thrills when he watches the progress of his first seedlings, from cross-pollination of the parent plants to mature blooming plants.

Chrysanthemums are ideally suited for hybridization, since nature has endowed the Compositae family with 2 seed-production systems. Both the ray florets and the disk florets have stigmas which connect with ovaries deep in the cup-shaped receptacle at the base of the bloom. Only the disk florets, however, have stamens which support the pollen-carrying anthers. The stigmas in the ray florets become receptive to pollen first; the stigmas of the disk florets do not become receptive to pollen until much later. Also, the pollen of the disk florets is not formed until after the stigmas of the ray florets have passed their receptive stage. Thus a chrysanthemum bloom is first receptive to cross fertilization by pollen from an earlier blooming plant. Then, as though nature intended it as a last resort, the disk florets become susceptible to self-fertilization.

Such a guaranteed seed-production system should make chrysanthemum seed very plentiful. Many so-called volunteer seedlings may spring up in a chrysanthemum garden, but rarely do offers of perennial chrysanthemum seed appear in seed catalogues. It is necessary to go back to the laws of heredity expounded by Mendel to discover why seeds which are produced so freely by nature are so difficult to obtain commercially.

Gregor Mendel, an Austrian monk, discovered through his work with peas that characteristics of the parent plants were passed on to their offspring in pairs. Mendel started his experiments with purebred strains of peas, such as a tall variety which, crossed with itself, always produced tall peas and a dwarf variety which produced only dwarf peas. His first cross between a tall and short variety produced seed which grew only tall peas. When these tall-growing plants were self-pollinated they produced peas that would grow into both tall and short plants, in the ratio of approximately 3 tall plants to 1 dwarf plant. These tests were made many times by Mendel and carried through several more generations.

The basic discovery of Mendel, however, was the existence of the hidden characteristic of dwarfness in his first generation of tall peas. He reasoned that the tall characteristic was dominant and that the dwarf characteristic was recessive, since it showed up in subsequent generations. There is a definite ratio which has been worked out for pairs of inherited characteristics in many of our food crops, such as corn and tomatoes, so that accurate predictions regarding crosses can be made. Mendel's work has been checked many times and found to be accurate, although in the case of some of our flowers the parents may contribute equally to the offspring. Thus, a purebred red flower crossed with a purebred white flower may produce first-generation offspring which will have only pink flowers. It is customary to identify a first-generation cross as F1, with subsequent generations numbered F2, F3, etc. When these pink flowers are intercrossed they will produce seed that will cause a 1–2–1 ratio in the F2 generation. There will be 1 white, 2 pink, and 1 red. This adds to the knowledge of plant heredity without upsetting Mendel's ratio findings. Introduction of other characteristics, such as hardiness, time of blooming etc., complicates the arithmetic involved but does not change the ratios.

To see how these inherited characteristics affect the supply of chrysanthemum seed we must go back hundreds of years, for chrysanthemum breeding began over 2000 years ago. So many crosses have been made in the intervening years that the cumulative effect of dominant and recessive characteristics makes it impossible to predict the probable outcome of any cross. Perhaps only one seedling out of a thousand would produce flowers equal to or superior to either parent. The work of crossing is still being done, but largely by professional hybridizers who are trying to develop new varieties that can be introduced for sale and reproduction from cuttings. The seed produced in these crosses never reaches the market. Of course, it might be possible to obtain seed that has resulted from natural cross-fertilization by insects, but such seed will produce only single varieties because the construction of double blooms will not permit pollination by insects.

Since chrysanthemums are so easily propagated and can be obtained from many reliable sources there is no need for the amateur grower to raise plants from seed; however, there is always the thrill of discovery for those who enjoy growing plants from their own seed. This can be a most interesting part of the over-all hobby of gardening; and the fact that mums produce the most unpredictable offspring shouldn't prevent anyone from trying to develop new varieties. While the actual mechanics of cross-fertilizing crysanthemum plants are not too difficult, it might be well to devote only a small portion of the chrysanthemum garden to seedlings, for the named varieties will put the seedlings to a disadvantage until success in raising that one outstanding new variety is achieved. One such experience in a chrysanthemum grower's lifetime can make up for a lot of mediocre seedlings.

Either of the two types of florets might be used for seed production, but the space within the disk florets is so small that it is difficult to remove the anthers. This would have to be done to avoid self-fertilization. For this reason it is much better to place pollen from another plant on the stigmas of the ray florets of the seed parent. Even though it is impossible to plan the results of any cross it is good practice to strive for certain desired characteristics. For example, if there is a good hardy white variety with small flowers and the purpose of hybridization is to increase the size of flowers while retaining the desirable characteristic of hardiness, it is well to cross this plant with a large-flowered variety that may not be as hardy. The essential requirement in making the cross is the application of the pollen from the anthers of the pollen-parent plant to the stigma of the seed-parent plant at the proper time for fertilization.

This requires a little planning to assure good results. The stigma remains receptive only a relatively short time; so the plant selected for the seed parent should have the stigmas of ray florets ready for pollination at the right moment. This is done by cutting all the ray petals off around the bloom at a point which will just avoid injury to the recessed stigma. If this is done when the bloom first unfolds the stigmas will project beyond the cut petals by the time they are ready for fertilization. Covering the bloom with a very fine mesh cloth bag will avoid accidental fertilization by insects without completely shutting off air to the flower head.

Pollen should then be gathered from the pollen parent by shaking the flower head over a clean piece of wax paper, as soon as grains of pollen are evident in the disk florets. This pollen can be stored in the folded wax paper for several weeks on the bottom shelf of a refrigerator, but should be warmed to room temperature before use. The prongs of the stigma will enlarge and become sticky when the seed parent is receptive to fertilization, but to be on the safe side it is good practice to pollinate three or four florets each day for a period of a week. Be careful to mark the starting point and continue around the flower head until all ray florets have been pollinated. A small brush dipped in pollen makes the best transfer medium; and it should be thoroughly cleaned before making additional crosses.

A label of plastic or wood, with copper wire for attachment to the plant, should be filled out for each cross. The following information should be indicated: date crossing was started and the names of the parents. For brevity on a label, this is written, for example, as follows:

C. Silver Sheen
X C. Mrs. H. E. Kidder

with the name of the seed parent always appearing first and the name of the pollen parent last. This keeps the lineage correct for future hybridization. The cloth bag is removed to make the cross, but is replaced and kept on for a few days after the last pollination. Effective crossing will be evidenced by enlargement of the seed capsules; and the flower head should be allowed to ripen normally on the plant. As the plant foliage begins to die, a small bag may be tied around the flower head to avoid accidental loss of seed. The seed should be stored in a small envelope over the winter in a cool dry place, with all of the data transferred from the label to the envelope. The following spring the seed should be started as early as practicable.

It may have been noticed that the foregoing discussion dealt with single varieties only. The elements involved in crossing double and spider types are the same, but the procedure is a little more difficult. The degree of doubleness varies so much with chrysanthemums that it is possible to find a normal disk center within a loose interlacing of ray florets in one variety, while in another variety the ray florets may be so interspersed among the disk florets that there is no discernible disk.

Cutting off all the ray petals as close to the base of the bloom as possible, without injury to the tiny disk section on the pollen par-

Fig. 8 — An incurved chrysanthemum with ray petals cut to expose the stigmas for pollination

ent, will expose the disk florets (*Fig. 8*). The pollen which develops in these florets could never be reached by insects in the normal bloom, but now it can be easily shaken out or removed with a brush. When the bloom of the seed parent first unfolds, cut back the ray florets on one side of the bloom, a little at a time, until the stigmas can be seen. From this point on the procedure is the same as it is for crossing the single varieties.

SPORTS

There is one characteristic of the chrysanthemum which through the years has had as much effect on the introduction of new varieties as the development from seeds. Mutation involving a change in color or form of blooms from that of the other blooms on the plant occurs sometimes with chrysanthemums. This is a chance occurrence *within the plant itself.* It becomes apparent in a flowering branch which has blooms identical in every respect to others on the same plant, except for color or, more rarely, petal formation. Such flowers are called "sports," and it is possible to fix the characteristic so that future plants will continue the new color or form. The chrysanthemum catalogues contain many varieties having the same name with sometimes as many as three or four color variations. All are examples of sports that have been propagated vegetatively (i.e., from cuttings) and introduced commercially.

CHRYSANTHEMUMS FROM SEED

It is very easy to raise chrysanthemums from seed, for the seeds germinate quickly and under good cultural conditions develop well. Unlike many perennials, chrysanthemums will bloom inside of one year from seed. This is an advantage to the chrysanthemum hobbyist who likes to see the results of his own hybridizing efforts. The key to success in raising chrysanthemums from seed is an early start; for a seedling requires a longer growth period before blooming than does a cutting.

The grower who has a greenhouse will be able to start seeds as early as January without danger of getting weak, spindly growth before it is safe to trust the plants outdoors. Anyone using a hotbed to raise seedlings should wait until the end of February before starting seeds; and a window gardener who has sufficient space on a sunny window ledge may also start seeds at this time. Many indoor gardeners are now using fluorescent lights to grow African violets and other house plants, but the light requirement for these plants is considerably less than it is for seedlings. The apparently bright light from fluorescent lights is deceiving, for the actual intensity at the plant level in a good installation will be about 300 foot-candles. Several times this amount would be required for good results with seedlings.

Seedlings have two enemies that cause more poor results than all other causes put together. Damp-off fungus and the careless grower, working together, can ruin any seed's chances of survival. In order to minimize the chance of damp-off, the soil used for seedlings should be sterilized. Commercial growers use steam sterilization, but the amateur will find chemical sterilization or oven heating easier. Chemical sterilizing can only be done outdoors when the ground temperature is above 50 degrees; so unless a supply of sterilized soil has been prepared during the summer it is necessary to sterilize it in an oven. The soil mixture best suited for seedlings is one that has been made loose by the incorporation of sand and organic matter. Peat moss is admirable, for it has a high moisture-retention capacity. The plant-food content of the soil is relatively unimportant, since seedlings do not require any outside food until after they have sprouted. A mixture of ⅓ sand, ⅓ peat moss, and ⅓ compost or leaf mold is ideal if the seedlings are to remain in the seed flat for a considerable period of time. Sufficient soil mixture to fill the number of seed containers required should be heated for 2 to 3 hours in an oven set at 350 degrees Fahrenheit. This will sterilize as well as kill weed seeds. Of course, vermiculite or other sterile seed-starting mediums may be used without oven heating, but liquid plant foods will be required after the seeds have germinated.

The containers in which seeds are to be sown may be wooden flats, such as those used by commercial growers, or smaller receptacles such as cigar boxes, low clay pots, or bulb pans. A good container for seedlings should permit drainage of excess moisture, but should be capable of absorbing moisture by immersion after the seedlings have sprouted. The soil mixture should be moist but not soaking wet when it is firmed in the seed containers. The soil mixture may be too dry after oven heating, so it should be moistened and thoroughly mixed before the seeds are sown.

If seeds from several crosses are to be sown, or if the seeds are from several sources, it is best to make shallow drills in the soil surface with the edge of a wooden label or other convenient straight edge; otherwise seeds may be broadcast over the surface. To keep records straight, the seed information and planting date should be marked on a wooden label at the beginning of each row. A waterproof pencil should be used to mark the label. Chrysanthemum seed is large enough so that it may be planted individually.

This will permit sufficient spacing so that the seeds may remain for a long time in the seed container without crowding. In order to avoid subsequent damp-off after planting, it is good practice to use the method found best by the U. S. Department of Agriculture at Beltsville, Maryland. This consists of a light sprinkling of dry sphagnum moss over the seed flat. This can be obtained as a fine milled product; or else dry sphagnum moss obtained from a florist can be rubbed through a ¼-inch mesh screen. Sufficient dry moss should be sprinkled over the seeds to cover them with a ⅛-inch layer.

The above procedure will guarantee germination of viable seeds, but from this point on carelessness on the part of the gardener, particularly with regard to proper watering, is the reason for loss of plants. With adequate moisture in the seed container at planting time there probably will be no need for additional watering until germination is completed. If water is needed it is best applied with a bulb atomizer or other misting device. After the seeds have germinated the moisture requirements are best supplied by immersing the seed container in water until the surface is barely moist. This should not be done until there is a definite need for watering. More seedlings are lost by overwatering than by underwatering.

While the seeds are germinating the temperature should be between 60 and 65 degrees. After the seeds germinate, a day reading of 65 to 70 degrees in a sunny location, with a night temperature of 55 degrees, will help promote healthy, stocky growth. If the seeds were spaced an inch or so apart they may remain in the original container until it is time to transplant to pots or plant bands; otherwise the plants should be transplanted to a flat of richer soil after their true leaves have formed. Seedlings should never be permitted to crowd each other. As soon as practical the plants should be transferred to a cold frame to harden them before they are planted in their permanent position.

To conserve space in the garden, since these plants are grown to test blooming only, they should be spaced approximately 12 inches apart and pinched once. At blooming time any poor seedlings should be pulled out, but worth-while plants may be perpetuated by taking cuttings the following spring.

CHAPTER 15

Out-of-Season Mums

In Chapter 2 the effect of day length on the flowering bud formation of chrysanthemums was discussed. There does not seem to be an exact day length that causes an immediate change from vegetative growth to flower bud development, for this change takes place gradually. Early-blooming varieties begin to form flowering buds when there are about 10 hours of darkness; midseason varieties make the change when the nights become 10½ hours long; and late-blooming varieties require 11 hours of darkness. This phenomenon led commercial growers to seek methods of artifically creating longer than normal dark periods to produce earlier blooming. How this condition could be obtained became a trial and error experiment for college agricultural staffs and commercial propagators. The results of more than a decade of testing have been extremely beneficial to both growers and florists. The usual autumn glut of chrysanthemums on the market has been greatly reduced by spreading the blooming period over the entire year. Perhaps no chrysanthemum hobbyist could maintain interest in his hobby if he had plants in bloom every month, but there are two phases of out-of-season mum production which have particular significance to the amateur grower. There are many hobbyists who enjoy raising chrysanthemums for show purposes. For them, earlier blooming of good late varieties is a distinct advantage. Also, the greenhouse owners who are looking for good dependable winter cut flowers will find out-of-season chrysanthemums ideal for this purpose.

SHADING FOR EARLY BLOOMING

The artificial conditions required to produce early blooming may be obtained by means of either black cloth or black plastic shade. A framework to hold the material must be built; and the shade must be put on and removed on a definite time schedule each day. Before discussing the exact procedure to follow it might be well to see how the chrysanthemum reacts to a man-made daylight schedule in the 40- to 45-degree-latitude area. Let us assume that a chrysanthemum variety which normally blooms on November 5 is desired for entry in an October 24 show. We must convince the chrysanthemum that it is time to bloom by artificially producing the proper day length which would be in effect for its normal blooming date. Tests which have been made indicate that the short days required to initiate bud formation in a November 5 variety must commence August 15. In other words, a minimum night length of 10½ hours must be maintained from August 15 until buds have formed. Usually by September 19 buds have developed to such a degree that it is unnecessary to continue shading. On the other hand, to have varieties that normally bloom on November 24 ready for an October 24 show date it will be necessary to start shading August 1. This is two weeks earlier than necessary for the November 5 varieties, although it is logical, since it takes a longer period of short days to make these varieties set buds under normal conditions.

The above results indicate that it is possible to group chrysanthemum varieties that require a definite period of short days. This has been done by placing all varieties in numbered response groups from 6 through 15. Thus, a 6-week response-group variety would bloom 6 weeks after shading started. Those varieties that normally bloom between September 25 and October 1 are placed in the 6-week response group, while those that bloom between December 25 and January 5 are in the 15-week response group. The arbitrary schedules set up for commercial growers may seem confusing, but it must be remembered that the above discussion is an explanation of proven results which were obtained over a long period of trial-and-error experiments.

Chrysanthemums are extremely sensitive to light during the bud-initiation stage. For this reason, the shading material must provide almost complete darkness. A light intensity of only 2 foot-candles in a shaded chrysanthemum planting will cause uneven blooming. Commercial growers usually purchase specially prepared black shading cloth or black Saran plastic. Black cloth has a tendency to bleach and admit more light after several years' use, while the plastic cloth will last at least twice as long. The amateur grower will probably wish to shade only a relatively small area; so the weight of shading material to support is not as much of a problem as it is with commercial growers. For this reason, almost anything that will provide complete darkness for the area occupied by the few plants grown by the chrysanthemum hobbyist will suffice.

Naturally those plants grown under shading will be separated from those intended for normal blooming. Also, only those plants in the same response group should be placed in the same shaded bed. If a grower wants varieties of 9-, 10-, 11-, and 12-week response groups in bloom at the same time he can plant them consecutively in one 3-foot bed. Then the shading structure can be erected so that it will provide shade in the sequence given in Table 1. With the plants spaced 8 inches apart, there will be room for 4 rows of plants and a 6-inch clearance on each side. Pompon varieties that are grown with 3 terminal sprays from a single pinch will require 12 inches between rows. Only 3 rows of pompons can be grown in a 3-foot-wide bed. A framework having a flat sloping or peaked top should be erected early in the summer. The height of the framework will depend upon the planting date of the varieties being grown. Some varieties of standards set out in late June will require 6 feet of headroom. Pompons will require 4 to 5 feet of headroom, depending upon the planting date.

In late July the end opening of the frame at the start of the 12-week response group, and the vertical area at the other end of this group, may be covered with the shading material. Enough shade material to cover the entire bed from ground level on one side over the top to ground level on the other side should then be placed on the frame. With the top shading material pulled back to the start of the 12-week response group, the entire bed will receive normal light. When the shading date for this group arrives the top should be pulled to the end of the 12-week response group of plants.

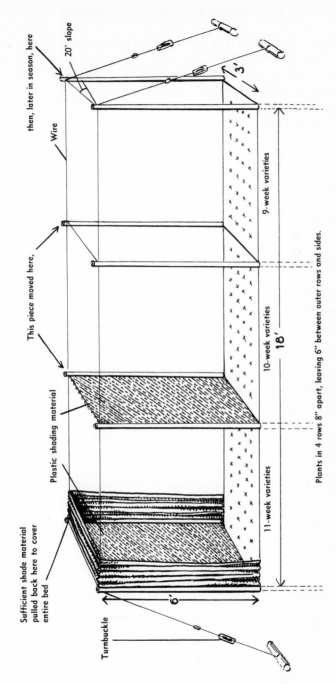

Fig. 9 — A shading method which will produce coincidental blooming for chrysanthemum varieties in different response groups

Twelve hours of darkness should be given each night from this date until the blooming bud is the size of a marble. When the shading date for the 11-week response group occurs, the vertical shading piece between the 11- and 12-week response group should be moved to the end of this group. The top shade is then pulled over both groups each evening. This procedure is then repeated with each group until the whole bed is receiving shade.

The recommendations given commercial growers for shading call for 12 to 14 hours of uninterrupted darkness. The longer period actually deprives the plants of several hours of good growing weather, but it is designed to permit handling of the shade material during a normal working day. The amateur grower is not concerned with labor problems; so he can arrange the schedule to fit his convenience. In order to avoid overheating in the enclosed bed it is best to apply the shade as late in the day as possible. The cooler morning weather makes it possible to leave the shade on until 8 o'clock. The time that the shade is put on and removed is not important as long as the plants receive 12 hours of uninterrupted darkness. All of the other cultural requirements remain the same as for normal blooming mums, with just one additional word of caution; mildew and fungus diseases are more apt to occur in the close atmosphere of a shaded mum bed than they would in the open garden.

The following condensed tables are designed to correlate the information required to produce earlier blooming chrysanthemums during the fall months only. The varieties best suited for this purpose will be found in Chapter 22. It will be noted that the varieties used for shade culture are in the 8- through 12-week response groups. Most of the experimentation has been done with the varieties on these groups, principally because they contain the largest and most perfectly formed blooms.

TABLE 1

SHADING SCHEDULE (40–45 DEGREE LATITUDE)

Response Group	Normal Blooming Date	To Bloom Sept. 15		To Bloom Oct. 1		To Bloom Oct. 15	
		Pinch Date	Shading Date	Pinch Date	Shading Date	Pinch Date	Shading Date
8-week	Oct. 15–Oct. 23	June 16	July 21				
9-week	Oct. 25–Nov. 1	June 16	July 14	July 2	July 31	July 9	Aug. 13
10-week	Nov. 5–Nov. 12	June 16	July 7	July 2	July 23	July 9	Aug. 6
11-week	Nov. 15–Nov. 23			July 2	July 16	July 9	July 31

Response Group	Normal Blooming Date	To Bloom Oct. 20		To Bloom Oct. 31		To Bloom Nov. 10	
		Pinch Date	Shading Date	Pinch Date	Shading Date	Pinch Date	Shading Date
9-week	Oct. 25–Nov. 1	July 14	Aug. 18				
10-week	Nov. 5–Nov. 12	July 14	Aug. 11	July 18	None		
11-week	Nov. 15–Nov. 23	July 14	Aug. 4	July 18	Aug. 15	July 28	Aug. 25
12-week	Nov. 25–Dec. 3	July 14	July 28	July 18	Aug. 8	July 28	Aug. 18

TABLE 2

SHADING SCHEDULE (25-40 DEGREE LATITUDE)

Response Group	Normal Blooming Date	To Bloom Sept. 15		To Bloom Oct. 1		To Bloom Oct. 15	
		Pinch Date	Shading Date	Pinch Date	Shading Date	Pinch Date	Shading Date
8-week	Oct. 25-Nov. 1	June 23	July 21	July 9	Aug. 7		
9-week	Nov. 5-Nov. 12	June 23	July 14	July 9	July 31	July 16	Aug. 13
10-week	Nov. 15-Nov. 23	June 23	July 7	July 9	July 23	July 16	Aug. 6
11-week	Nov. 23-Dec. 3			July 9	July 16	July 16	July 31

Response Group	Normal Blooming Date	To Bloom Oct. 20		To Bloom Oct. 31		To Bloom Nov. 10	
		Pinch Date	Shading Date	Pinch Date	Shading Date	Pinch Date	Shading Date
9-week	Nov. 5-Nov. 12	July 21	Aug. 18				
10-week	Nov. 15-Nov. 23	July 21	Aug. 11	July 25	None		
11-week	Nov. 23-Dec. 3	July 21	Aug. 4	July 25	Aug. 15	Aug. 11	Aug. 25
12-week	Dec. 5-Dec. 13			July 25	Aug. 8	Aug. 11	Aug. 18

The bench lighting method used in the author's greenhouse for winter-blooming chrysanthemums. (*Photography by Roche — courtesy* Flower Grower Magazine)

137

LIGHTING FOR DELAYED BLOOMING

Since even a small amount of light in a shaded mum bed will prevent bud initiation, it would seem natural that even a small amount of light should delay blooming. This is indeed true, for some chrysanthemum hobbyists have found that light from a street light may be sufficient to prevent blooming. As little as 7 foot-candles of light at the plants will cause this effect. The chrysanthemum grower with a greenhouse may thus have blooms throughout the winter, simply by using incandescent lights. In essence, this procedure involves a growth period under lights with bloom occurring after the lighting has been stopped. Here again the plants will react to the short days after the lights are turned off the same as they would for normal blooming. As might be expected, the light period does not need to be continuous, since delayed bud initiation is the reverse of accelerated bud development where continuous darkness is required. In actual practice it is better to split the night period into two relatively equal dark periods.

An inexpensive time switch that will turn the lights on for 3 to 4 hours each night, starting about 10 o'clock, will be the simplest way to control the procedure. Seventy-five-watt lights spaced 4 feet apart along the bench will produce about 10 foot-candles of light, provided they are kept approximately 2 feet above the plants. This requires adjustment of the lights as the plants elongate; so they should have adjustable suspension. The plants may be grown directly in the bench with a 7-inch by 4-inch spacing for standards and an 8-inch by 8-inch spacing for pompons, or they may be grown in pots. More work is involved in growing mums in pots, but it is possible to rearrange pots of mums in the greenhouse to obtain a beautiful display.

Insect control by means of fumigation, staking, feeding, and disbudding are carried out in the same manner described for plants grown in the greenhouse for normal blooming. Pinching is reduced to one pinch by commercial growers, or it may be eliminated entirely.

The commercial grower is concerned only with salable blooms that have a minimum stem length. For this reason he follows a schedule which requires the minimum use of valuable bench space during the poorest growing months of the year. Standards grown under lights with no pinch will produce one large flower in 4 months on 3-foot stems. Plants that are pinched once should be planted 3 weeks earlier than those grown for a single bloom. They will produce 2 or 3 acceptable blooms that are slightly smaller. Pompons will do best if they are pinched once to produce 3 terminal sprays. The amateur grower can afford more time than the commercial grower. Thus, he may continue lighting over a longer schedule to give his plants a longer period to develop into good blooming specimens. As long as the lighting is continued the plants will make vegetative growth, but lighting cannot be carried on into early spring without encountering long-day conditions after the lights are turned off. Once the day length exceeds 12 hours the effect of the night length on bud initiation decreases rapidly. In order to have chrysanthemums in bloom during the spring months, commercial growers have to start plants off under lights and obtain bud initiation by the use of shade. By the time spring arrives, the chrysanthemum hobbyist who has grown mums during the winter will be too busy with plans for the outside garden to bother with this refinement. Any amateur interested in combination lighting and shading should consult one of the commercial growers for the proper schedule.

The amateur may encounter one problem in growing winter mums that can be easily overcome, but only if he realizes how difficult it is for a chrysanthemum plant intent on blooming to provide good cuttings at the same time. During the spring season all of the growth energy of the plant is concentrated in the new green shoots on the stolons; and they are making vigorous growth under ideal conditions. As summer approaches, the stem between the pairs of leaves elongates and the growth energy is spread over the entire plant. Also, the natural tendency of the plant is toward production of vegetative growth to support flowers rather than toward manufacture of roots. For this reason, it is more difficult to obtain a cutting with a good root system at this time than earlier in the season. Commercial propagators maintain special beds of plants with many short growths to provide cuttings at this season. These cuttings are propagated under lights and shipped to growers for planting on a specified date. Unless the amateur is willing to reserve some plants for cuttings he will be forced to use the lateral growths from his standard plants and the tops of some of his pompons for winter-grown plants.

Six-inch-long lateral cuttings from the leaf axils of standard plants will root in 2 to 3 weeks, provided they are kept in a moist, shaded cutting bench. If the cuttings wilt to such an extent that the stems begin to droop, it is probable that the water-carrying channels are damaged beyond recovery. Four-inch tops of pompons will root with a little more difficulty than lateral growths from standards. Since a 4-inch cutting from a pompon is equivalent to a hard pinch, the plant from which it was taken will product an awkward spray of bloom if the time interval to the blooming date is too short.

The foregoing has been a rather general discussion of the problems faced by the amateur who wishes to grow winter-blooming chrysanthemums. In actual practice it is not too difficult to get good results if certain limitations are understood and methods are used to compensate for them.

Cuttings in the rooting bench will initiate buds the same way the plants from which they were taken will do, if the days are short enough. For this reason, the cutting bench must be lighted, or else cuttings must be taken early enough to allow 3 weeks' rooting time before the night length equals the day length. Since the summer heat intensifies the problem a chrysanthemum cutting has in forming roots, any method which will reduce the transpiration rate is beneficial.

A mist-spray cutting bench will reduce cutting mortality considerably, although medium shading over the bench may be sufficient to provide 1 good rooted plant out of 2 original cuttings. A fluorescent-lighted cabinet will increase the percentage of rooted cuttings to over 90 per cent. Such a cabinet should have 2, 3, or 4 40-watt fluorescent lights, depending on size, to produce 600 foot-candles of light, 16 hours a day, at the cuttings. This value of light intensity was determined by Rutgers University as adequate for most foliage plants; and it also gives good results with chrysanthemum cuttings. Of course, the rooting medium under the lights must be kept uniformly moist.

The discussion of normal-blooming chrysanthemums did not stress temperatures, since prevailing summer temperatures average

60 degrees or more wherever mums are grown. Studies of winter-blooming chrysanthemums have indicated that temperature as well as day length has an effect on both quality and time of bloom.

Varieties tested may be divided into 3 temperature classifications: thermozero, thermopositive, and thermonegative. Those varieties in the first group are least sensitive to temperature. They will set buds and develop flowers normally at any temperature between 55 and 70 degrees. Thermopositive varieties require heat. They will not reliably set buds at any night temperature below 60 degrees, although, once buds are set, flowering will take place at any normal greenhouse temperature. The thermonegative varieties will set buds at any reasonable temperature, but will not flower at any temperature above 60 degrees.

Most of the horticultural studies result in charts, tables, or classifications that tend to confuse nature's attempts to adjust plant growth to existing conditions. Thermo classifications have their explanation in the outdoor chrysanthemum garden. Early and midseason varieties develop their buds in temperatures which average 60 degrees or more, yet temperatures at blooming time may be 60 degrees or less; hence the 8- and 9-week response-group varieties are thermopositive when grown naturally, and this fact has merely been confirmed by the studies. Similarly, the 11-, 12-, 13-, and 14-week varieties under controlled experiments were proven to be thermonegative. This bears out the garden conditions for these late-blooming varieties which may form their buds in temperatures above 60 degrees, but by blooming time the temperatures would consistently be below 60 degrees. Best results can be obtained by the amateur greenhouse operator who maintains a minimum night temperature of 60 degrees from the cutting stage until buds are well formed. If buds form but blooms do not develop in a reasonable time, the night temperature should be lowered to 55 degrees.

The length of the light period should be 3 hours during September and October, 4 hours during November and February, and 5 hours for the months of December and January. The lighting schedules for winter bloom are given in the following tables.

Important: For best results, rooted cuttings should be planted a minimum of 3 weeks before the pinch date. If planted later than this do not pinch. In any case, cuttings rooted after August 15 should be lighted before planting to avoid premature budding.

TABLE 3

LIGHTING SCHEDULE (40–45 DEGREE LATITUDE)

Response Group	Normal Blooming Date	To Bloom Dec. 19 Pinch Date	To Bloom Dec. 19 Lighting Period	To Bloom Jan. 1 Pinch Date	To Bloom Jan. 1 Lighting Period	To Bloom Jan. 15 Pinch Date	To Bloom Jan. 15 Lighting Period	To Bloom Jan. 30 Pinch Date	To Bloom Jan. 30 Lighting Period
10-week	Nov. 5–Nov. 12	Aug. 22	Aug. 8–Oct. 10	Aug. 28	Aug. 8–Oct. 23	Sept. 4	Aug. 14–Nov. 6	Sept. 19	Aug. 29–Nov. 21
11-week	Nov. 15–Nov. 23	Aug. 22	Aug. 15–Oct. 3	Aug. 28	Aug. 15–Oct. 16	Sept. 4	Aug. 14–Oct. 30	Sept. 19	Aug. 29–Nov. 14
12-week	Nov. 25–Dec. 3	Aug. 22	Aug. 22–Sept. 26	Aug. 28	Aug. 22–Oct. 9	Sept. 4	Aug. 21–Oct. 23	Sept. 19	Aug. 29–Nov. 7
13-week	Dec. 5–Dec. 13	Aug. 22	Aug. 29–Sept. 19	Aug. 28	Aug. 29–Oct. 2	Sept. 4	Aug. 28–Oct. 16	Sept. 19	Aug. 29–Oct. 31
14-week	Dec. 15–Dec. 25	Aug. 22	None	Aug. 28	Sept. 5–Sept. 25	Sept. 4	Sept. 4–Oct. 9	Sept. 19	Sept. 5–Oct. 24

Response Group	Normal Blooming Date	To Bloom Feb. 13 Pinch Date	To Bloom Feb. 13 Lighting Period	To Bloom Feb. 28 Pinch Date	To Bloom Feb. 28 Lighting Period	To Bloom Mar. 15 Pinch Date	To Bloom Mar. 15 Lighting Period
10-week	Nov. 5–Nov. 12	Oct. 3	Sept. 12–Dec. 5	Oct. 18	Sept. 27–Dec. 20	Nov. 3	Oct. 12–Jan. 5
11-week	Nov. 15–Nov. 23	Oct. 3	Sept. 12–Nov. 28	Oct. 18	Sept. 27–Dec. 12	Nov. 3	Oct. 12–Dec. 26
12-week	Nov. 25–Dec. 3	Oct. 3	Sept. 12–Nov. 21	Oct. 18	Sept. 27–Dec. 5	Nov. 3	Oct. 12–Dec. 19
13-week	Dec. 5–Dec. 13	Oct. 3	Sept. 12–Nov. 14	Oct. 18	Sept. 27–Nov. 28	Nov. 3	Oct. 12–Dec. 12
14-week	Dec. 15–Dec. 25	Oct. 3	Sept. 12–Nov. 7	Oct. 18			

Cascade chrysanthemums displayed in specimen form in a wooden tub. *(Photographed by the author at Longwood Gardens)*

A cascade chrysanthemum displayed in a wire basket. *(Photographed by the author at Longwood Gardens)*

A skillful blend of colorful chrysanthe

leasing landscape display.

ABOVE — Chrysanthemums in an aluminum greenhouse. *(Orlyt Greenhouse — courtesy Lord & Burnham)*

BELOW — A chrysanthemum display in the author's greenhouse in February. (*Photography by Roche — courtesy* Flower Grower Magazine)

For each degree of south latitude below 40 degrees the pinch date should be advanced 2 days. The lighting period remains the same for any latitude. For the 25- to 30-degree latitude belt it is not advisable to grow 14- and 15-week response-group chrysanthemums, since they are definitely thermonegative.

The preceding schedules represent the minimum amount of time required to produce average-quality blooms on medium-length stems. If the growth at the end of the lighting period is not adequate to provide a good standard bloom, or a good spray of pompons, a longer lighting period may be given. However, lighting should be stopped in time to provide the required number of weeks of short days for bloom development on those varieties in the highest numbered response group. In the shading program it is necessary to shade each response group a different length of time, but in the lighting program all groups may be grown together and lighted for the same length of time. Sequence of bloom then becomes automatic as each response group receives its quota of short days.

It is only natural that an amateur grower who is growing winter mums for the first time will try to root as many cuttings of as many varieties as he can cram into his greenhouse. Some blooms will be almost as good as those grown in the outdoor garden, but many may be somewhat disappointing.

There are two reasons for this. First, the color-producing material in chrysanthemums is a carbohydrate that develops best under warm sunny conditions. Thus, some winter mums will be lighter in color than they would be if grown for the normal blooming season. Second, the degree of doubleness varies between varieties of incurved blooms. Some varieties which hide the central disk during normal season blooming will exhibit it during the less favorable winter growing season. The varieties which have given good results under a lighting schedule are listed in Chapter 22, but this should not discourage a grower from trying any variety which produces healthy cuttings.

CHAPTER 16

Landscape and Display Planting

THE ability of chrysanthemums to fit into any gardening scheme makes them most useful landscape and display plants. The modern varieties of hardy chrysanthemums were developed with this purpose in mind. For this reason they embody the informal grace of growth habit and bloom arrangement required for this application. The more formal pompon and exhibition blooms, on the other hand, are more properly used for cut flowers or in arrangements.

A book can illustrate and suggest various methods of using mums, but each individual gardener will have to plan his own garden to fit the contours of his property, using the colors and types of chrysanthemums which have the greatest appeal for him. Since there is such a wide choice in colors, heights, and blooming dates, planning is a most important part in chrysanthemum growing. This planning should not be confined merely to a filled-out order form; for this alone will not transfer a plant in all its rich colors from a page in the catalogue to a spot in the garden. When chrysanthemum plants arrive they are approximately 6 inches high and have a leaf spread of about ½ their height. In 5 months of normal growth taller varieties will increase as much as 6 times in each direction; so, obviously, careful planning is required to achieve the proper effect at blooming time. It is far better to have this work done before plants are ordered than to end up with too few plants to do an effective job, or too many that will grow straggly due to crowding.

An excellent method of laying out a chrysanthemum garden is to draw a sketch on cross-ruled paper having 6 to 10 squares to the inch. Then all dimensions can be based on a convenient scale, such

144

as 1 square on the drawing equal to 6 inches either way in the garden. For larger plots the scale might be 1 square for each foot. With such an accurate plot plan it is easy to place a circle, whose diameter is equal to the plant width, wherever a chrysanthemum plant is desired. If it is kept in mind that low-growing mums should be spaced no closer than 12 inches, while taller-growing varieties require a minimum of 18 inches, it will be possible to plan a garden accurately in a short space of time. For those who like to sketch, it is a good idea to make an elevation drawing of the garden which will show the height of each plant. The colors of the varieties selected can be approximated by crayons. Thus it is possible to get a preview of the garden before the plants are ordered. Such 2-dimensional planning makes interesting winter work and helps avoid those empty gaps at blooming time.

The public displays of chrysanthemums, and the field exhibits at nurseries and agricultural experimental stations, have done much to bring these flowers from their former place in the back yard to a more prominent position along walks or between property lines. In fact, chrysanthemums are very adaptable in these situations.

BORDERS

When chrysanthemums are used to create a symmetrical color effect along each side of a walk, or as a border in any location that is visible to the passing public, much more careful planning is required than is necessary for a cutting garden. Here the matter of height with relation to width of the border becomes much more important. Also, stem length is much less important, although there must be sufficient elongation of the stem from the main trunk to spread the flowers over a wide area. The stem length is controlled by the natural growth habit of the plant and by the amount of pinching by the grower. For a pleasingly proportioned border the height should be limited to about 3 feet. To achieve a rounded effect that elevates the border from a mere row of plants to the compliment-inspiring category requires a selection of plants in 2 or 3 height classifications. Where a wide border is indicated, a center row of medium-tall mums may be flanked on either side by a row of shorter ones. Then a row of the so-called cushion mums along each outer side will carry the color to ground level and hide the stems and lower branches of the inside rows. For a narrow border on each side of a walk, a center row of medium-height varieties, flanked on either side by a row of cushion mums, would produce a more properly proportioned appearance.

In borders, the blooming dates of the plants also assume greater importance; for nothing detracts more from a planned color display than gaps resulting from differences in flowering sequence. In planning perennial borders containing various species of plants, color combinations become quite important. Here color clashes should be carefully avoided. With chrysanthemums this is rarely a problem, for it is possible to mix all of the colors of the chrysanthemum, with the possible exception of purple, to achieve a bold display of color that blends perfectly. This is undoubtedly due to the absence of blue in the chrysanthemum color range. It is difficult, however, to use one color in a chrysanthemum border, unless all plants are of the same variety, because there is such a variation in color shadings between varieties that are nominally the same color. There is also a definite fading of color as the flowers become older. The red- and bronze-colored flowers hold their colors better and provide a longer color display than do the lighter shades. The petals of white flowers tend to show the effects of frost first and, as they become older, they often become tinged with pink.

BEDS

When grown in beds, chrysanthemums are principally used for cut flowers. This use demands plants that will produce fairly long branches with a well-developed head of blooms, in colors that will blend well together. A secondary consideration is the over-all picture of the beds at blooming time. A bed having tall and short varieties mixed together will spoil what could have been, from a color standpoint, an outstanding display. Generally speaking, long narrow beds are better than square beds as far as easier culture and a better display are concerned. Since at blooming time each plant may measure as much as 2 feet across, 3 rows of plants across the narrow side of the bed are the most that can be conveniently handled from either of the long sides of the bed.

In planning such a bed the tallest varieties should occupy the center row, with medium-height plants in each of the outer rows. Where only 1 bed is involved, the different varieties may be placed so that a progression of bloom occurs from one end of the bed toward the other end. Where more than 1 bed is involved it is best to have the blooming dates of all varieties in each bed fairly close together. If it is possible to locate the latest-blooming bed on the south side of a garage, or similar protecting wall, it will be possible to attach an emergency frost-protection-cloth cover to the wall. This may then be spread over the flowers if frost threatens.

In selecting varieties on the basis of blooming time, it must be remembered that the dates published in the catalogues apply to the locality of the nursery supplying the plants. There will be approximately 1 to 2 days' difference in flowering time for each degree of latitude between the nursery and the planting location. Southward distance delays flowering and a more northerly latitude hastens it. Of course, the effect of drought and prolonged spells of either cloudy or sunny weather will also affect the flowering date; but changes due to the vagaries of nature will affect all of the plants in a bed equally.

In certain areas where there is natural protection against early frosts, or where chrysanthemum beds are ideally situated, it may be possible to extend the blooming season beyond the range of the available hardy types of chrysanthemums. Actually there is no sharp line of division between varieties considered to be tender greenhouse perennials and those known to be hardy in New England or Minnesota. Hardiness in chrysanthemums is relative. There are many early-November-blooming greenhouse chrysanthemums that will bloom outdoors in the 40 to 45 degree latitude and live through the winter without more than normal protection. The listing of many of these varieties in the "100 favorite varieties" poll conducted by the National Chrysanthemum Society is an indication that they can be grown outdoors by the amateur.

EDGING

Chrysanthemums formerly were dismissed as candidates for a front-row position in a floral plan because of their height, but out

Mums in the perennial border. *(Photography by Paul E. Genereux)*

Chrysanthemums in a planned landscape setting. *(Photography by Paul E. Genereux—courtesy Bristol Nurseries)*

of the constant hybridizing efforts to extend their versatility have come the low-growing cushion mums. The various nurseries that have developed these types have applied patented names, such as Ameliamum or Azaleamum to indicate their growth habit. The word cushion mum covers all of these low-growing types. As the word implies, they form a mound of flowers on a plant that is 10 to 12 inches high. Such plants are ideal for edging because their foliage is attractive all season long; they bloom from August until the first killing frost; and they make an exceedingly compact plant.

LANDSCAPE BORDERS

The lighter shades of the hardy chrysanthemums contrast well with the evergreens most commonly used in landscaping, but, here again, height and location are important. The chrysanthemum plants should never be higher than the shrubs, nor should they be used so lavishly that they destroy the purpose of the shrubbery. Rather, they should be located in groups of varied height that tend to accentuate the shrubs in the planting.

TERRACE BORDERS

The gardener who has a wall running from east to west on his property is indeed a fortunate person. There are so many ways that sun-loving chrysanthemums can be grown on the southern side of such a setting to contribute their bold colors to a fall display. If the wall forms part of a terrace, so that the ground level on the north side of the wall is at wall-top height or slopes above it, a distinctive chrysanthemum display may be made. A single row of cascade chrysanthemums may be planted in the earth behind the wall so that graceful sprays of color will hang over the wall to mingle with medium-tall chrysanthemums which are planted at the lower ground level. To complete the picture, an undulating front row of cushion mums will project the color to the ground and provide a varying width to the planting at the base of the wall.

Increased height and depth can be given to a planting of this type by using additional hardy chrysanthemums in a row in back of the wall. Care must be taken to allow enough of the wall to

A shady retreat made inviting with colorful chrysanthemums. *(Photography by Paul E. Genereux — courtesy Bristol Nurseries)*

show through the planting to create a pleasing landscape picture; and the plants at the base of the wall should never be taller than the wall itself. One exception to the last statement could be made if large incurved or exhibition types of chrysanthemums are to be used, with the wall as a background. In this case it is desirable to plan and plant the wall garden as described above, with a little wider spacing of the plants at the base of the wall. Then potted plants, grown as described in Chapter 11, may be buried in the ground among the lower-growing pompons. The potted plants, with 1 large bloom 5 or 6 feet above the ground, should be placed in such a position that they are complemented by, rather than hidden by, the smaller-flowered plants. For this reason they will be most effective if they do rise above the wall; and the only way to be sure of successful results is to have the plants available in pots so they may be moved to just the right spot.

SUCCESSION PLANTINGS FOR AUTUMN DISPLAY

Chrysanthemums may be considered fast-growing plants, based upon their sixfold enlargement in a 5-month period. However, they are relatively slow growing when compared to perennials that come into bloom in 3 months and are dormant by the time the chrysanthemums bloom. If enough room is allowed for chrysanthemum development in a perennial border the planting looks skimpy until fall, while a closer spacing shuts off light to the chrysanthemum plants. This makes them grow leggy and perform poorly at blooming time. Chrysanthemums, along with their many other good qualities, can be moved at any stage of their development. Thus they may be grown in a separate garden bed and moved into the perennial border in time to provide a fall display. In fact, the Dutch growers of commercial flowers for the cut-flower market raise most of their pompons in open fields during the summer and move them into greenhouse benches for blooming. If the plants are dug up with a spading fork and watered well after transplanting they will scarcely show the effects of moving.

The time-honored rule of planting in groups of 3 or in drifts applies to chrysanthemums as well as to other perennials. Also, a better over-all effect can be obtained by selecting the plants to be moved, rather than trusting to luck on plants set out in the border in the spring. Transplanting chrysanthemum plants just before the blooming season is being practiced more and more by municipal governments and commercial establishments. The inner courtyard of the Lever building and the Rockefeller Plaza in New York City, for example, each fall contain beautiful displays of chrysanthemums that have been moved in.

CHAPTER 17

Arrangements

Just as certain baseball stars are referred to as ballplayers' ballplayers, so the chrysanthemum has earned a similar distinction as the arranger's flower. The size range of mums makes them adaptable for all styles of arrangements; the color range blends with a wide variety of containers and accessories; and the variations in form permit many types of arrangements.

A floral arrangement might well be defined as a combination of flowers and foliage arranged in a container in such a manner as to make it pleasing to the eye and suitable for the space where it is to be displayed. All flowers have their own particular type of beauty and many containers are capable of enhancing this beauty, but skillful handling is required to make their combination an arrangement. When a separate base is used with the container it is considered as part of the container. However, when an accessory is added the combination of component parts is referred to as a composition.

CONTAINERS, HOLDERS, AND ACCESSORIES

A good floral arrangement must begin with the container. In fact, the container often suggests the individual style of the arrangement. A list of containers could never be complete, for almost any receptacle that will hold water has possibilities for some type of an arrangement. Often an unusual container will attract considerable attention at a flower show, and there is a mad scramble to buy an identical piece. So often subsequent arrangements never seem to live up to the expectation engendered by the original exhibit, thus indicating that an arrangement is the product of individual inspiration. A wide variety of containers is required to match the many sizes and forms of mums. In general, low containers of brass or pottery should have sufficient length and width to provide the proper expanse required to show off many of the larger types of chrysanthemums. Medium-tall vases are needed for many of the small-bloom chrysanthemums; and one or two tall vases will be required to properly exhibit the large commercial and exhibition types. Since the chrysanthemum is a round flower, often a difficult shape to match with a suitable container, there should be several vases that are gracefully curved to complement the curvature of the blooms. There should also be variety in color of containers with white, red, and fall colors most suitable for pottery pieces. Brass, copper, and pewter make excellent mum containers, provided they are large enough to properly set off the arrangement.

Holders become a very important part of the mechanics of making an arrangement, for unless a firm support is available for each stem it is impossible to achieve the right effect. A satisfactory holder has two functions; first, it must be firm enough to prevent the arrangement from tipping over and, second, it must hold each stem securely in any desired position. Pin holders having sharp points which project upward from a heavy base are very satisfactory. The base may be secured to the bottom of the container with floral arrangement clay. Homemade holders are often superior to purchased ones because they can be made to fit the type of arrangement preferred by the individual arranger. Strips of sheet lead are most versatile for use in flat-bottom low containers. A 12-inch strip, an inch in width, can have alternate holes spaced close together by bending the strip around a pencil, first one way and then the opposite way. The completed strip of holes can then be adjusted to any contour desired.

When the arrangement is made in a tall vase, crumpled chicken wire may be inserted in the top to hold the stems. Also, privet or evergreen branches may be used in a vase to fill the space between the flower stems.

Accessories are a decided asset for certain types of floral designs. When used directly in the container they are usually small pottery figures which set the scale for the composition. Unless there is proper-scaled proportion between the floral portion and the accessory the mind of the viewer is immediately distracted from the pleasing picture the arranger intended to create. An accessory that becomes part of a composition should be a secondary point of interest and it should only be used where the composition is kept simple by virtue of the small number of flowers used. Often the accessory is used outside of the container in a subtle or dramatic way. Here the color and texture of the accessory are important; and there is a definite size relationship between flowers, container, and accessory that must be maintained to keep the over-all effect pleasing. This type of accessory generally brings out the theme which the composition is designed to suggest. However, it can also be useful in providing width to a tall composition or in accentuating a line which is faintly suggested within the floral portion. Selection of an external accessory is strictly within the sphere of whimsy, although once selected for use in a composition the dominant characteristic of the accessory should influence the selection and placement of the flowers.

COMPANION MATERIALS

Chrysanthemums by themselves are such perfectly formed blooms that they can be matched like jewels in a floral setting. Quite often, though, it is desirable to break up the monotony of perfectly round blooms with spikes of flowers or other natural vegetation, thus giving a line diversity to the arrangement. Fortunately when chrysanthemums are in bloom there are many products of nature which make ideal companions for mums in an arrangement. Cattails, heads of wheat, oak leaves, and even weed pods will blend well with mums in a colorful suggestion of the autumn season. Restraint must be used when adding companion materials, for an equal balance between round and spiked forms will again produce monotony. Since the arrangement is one of chrysanthemums, they should dominate. During a walk in the country sufficient interesting materials can be found for countless chrysanthemum arrangements.

Here a Chinese figure combines with white chrysanthemums in a Chinese vase to create a pleasing combination. Hold a piece of paper over the figure to see how Myra J. Brooks used the accessory to obtain a balanced composition. *(Photography by Roche)*

157

COLOR AND VISUAL WEIGHT

The shape of the container and the position of the components set the over-all design of any arrangement, but only color can bring it to life. The almost complete range of colors available in chrysanthemums makes this phase of arranging so simple that it is often overlooked, although color has a very definite part to play in the effectiveness of a good arrangement. Red, yellow, and orange are bold colors that are stimulating, while purple, violet, and green are soothing colors. Men generally are attracted more toward arrangements that make liberal use of bold colors, but women show a preference for soothing colors and blendings of pastel shades. Harmony is the most important factor in achieving color effectiveness, and for this a knowledge of color blending is necessary. For example, red and yellow are both distinct primary colors which demand equal attention when the eyes are focused on an arrangement. If all yellow mums appeared on one side of an arrangement and all red ones were used on the opposite side there would be two centers of interest and a distracting arrangement. Mixing both colored mums in the arrangement makes it even more disquieting to the viewer's color sensibility. If orange, a harmonizing secondary color, is added, the gap between red and yellow is bridged and the arrangement is brought into clear color focus. The blending of colors, like the blending of chrysanthemums and companion materials, should not be one of equality. One color should be the star of the show with a supporting cast of harmonizing colors.

Harmony is much more than just a blending of colors, for it has had its development in the civilized mind through centuries of conditioning by the impulses registered through the eyes and ears. The music of primitive tribes sounds jarring to civilized ears and the mind rejects it as being unharmonious. The skillful blending of notes by a great composer, on the other hand, evokes thoughts of soothing harmony. Our eyes also have reported to the brain that an ascending balloon seems smaller as it drifts further away. Colors too, which are brilliant close by, fade as they recede. These are a few of the conditions the human mind has accepted as normal; therefore anything which seems to contradict these impressions is unharmonious.

An informal arrangement by Mrs. Ackerson in which the roundness of the white mums has been offset by their incorporation in an asymmetric triangular design. *(Photography by the author)*

Here is flower arrangement at its best in this beautiful composition by Myra J. Brooks. Note how the knee of the driftwood piece is repeated in the stance of the Japanese swordsman. *(Photography by Roche)*

This arrangement by Myra J. Brooks combines chrysanthemums, accessories, and a background to create a beautiful composition with an oriental theme. *(Photography by Roche)*

The bold-colored vase was selected by Mrs. Ackerson to display the large blooms of Indianapolis White and William Turner. Note the informality of the arrangement to avoid the too-perfect symmetry of the large round blooms. *(Photography by author)*

Applied to flower arranging these accepted conditions might be called visual weight. Thus, the clever arranger instinctively keeps the largest blooms and the boldest colors low in the arrangement. Also, to prevent an arrangement from appearing too heavy to the eyes, the larger blooms and darker colors should not be placed too close to the outside of the arrangement.

The color of the container should also be selected with an eye to harmony. Many good arrangers develop the color of the container by using slightly lighter shades in the flowers above, or, when multicolored containers are used, the colors are often repeated in the materials used in the arrangement.

PROPORTION AND SYMMETRY

Closely allied to harmony are such other words as proportion and symmetry, together with composition, design, and simplicity. These words describe the sense of fitness we feel when viewing a good example of architecture, a great work of art, or a beautiful floral arrangement.

Proportion by definition is the relationship of the parts to the whole. In a floral arrangement there is a relationship of size of flowers to size of container, as well as a dimensional relationship between the height of the arrangement and the width of the container which is harmonious and pleasing to the eye. There is a rather narrow range within which the dimensions may be varied without upsetting the proportional balance.

Symmetry is the relationship of equality between parts on either side of an imaginary line. A tight-wire artist represents a perfect example of symmetry, for an imaginary line projected vertically upward from the wire will pass through the center of gravity of the performer. Then an equal weight will project on either side of the line.

The mind is receptive to examples of symmetry and rejects a picture of imbalance. In floral arrangements this becomes important, for a floral projection upward to the left requires a downward projection to the right to balance it. Similarly, in a geometric mass shape the left side must be in balance with the right side. Various tricks are used in flower arranging which seem to contradict the definition of symmetry. However, in every case the seeming imbalance in flower placement is corrected by a balancing factor in the container, or by use of an accessory. Perfect symmetry can be a fault in many arrangements, for it suggests monotony when each flower on the right is exactly matched by one on the left. The overall picture should be one of symmetry, but the individual flower placement should not be done by measurement. To achieve an interesting symmetry without monotony is the artistry of a good flower arranger.

STYLES IN FLOWER ARRANGING

The above discussion has involved the fundamentals which apply to all flower arrangements, but there are many well-defined types of arrangements that reflect the individuality of the arranger. Basically there are two distinct styles into which type arrangements fit. All arrangements are either informal in style, where the flowers themselves are most important, or formal. In a formal design, theme development assumes a greater importance.

Fortunately preferences do vary, and nowhere is this more evident than in a flower show. Agreement with the judging is seldom unanimous, and in some cases the majority of visitors would select an honorable-mention arrangement as more beautiful than the first-place winner. This merely indicates the conflict between a trained judge's appreciation of an artistically designed arrangement and the average flower lover's admiration for a beautiful bouquet of flowers.

Selection of the container for an informal arrangement is important, since it must complement the floral portion, but it should never draw attention away from the fact that it acts solely as a setting for a pretty picture.

The formal arrangement, on the other hand, is designed to carry out a theme or inspire a thought by combining flowers, foliage, and often accessories in a manner which conforms to a definite geometric pattern. A certain amount of artistic ability and a good sense of

Perfect symmetry is obtained in this arrangement by Myra J. Brooks by a clever combination of chrysanthemum mass and companion material line diversity. *(Photography by Roche)*

proportion and symmetry are required in making an informal arrangement. In addition to the requirements needed to complete a pleasing informal arrangement, the creator of formal arrangements needs considerable imagination. Often the judging between two technically correct arrangements is swayed in favor of the one which has a little better touch of inspiration.

TYPES OF ARRANGEMENTS

Tracing through the history of flower arrangement, we find a development from the early concept of a massive collection of blooms in a large container. Such arrangements were designed to fit the large rooms favored in early architecture. Today the linear theme in arrangement is more suitable to the dictates of modern decoration. Out of the desire to achieve expression through the use of flowers there has come a well-defined pattern of types into which most arrangements fall. The evolvement of types will doubtless continue, along with the changes in modes of living, but at present the following distinct types of arrangements are in vogue:

MASS ARRANGEMENTS

The vase full of flowers is characteristic of this type of arrangement, but the modern concept differs from its earlier counterpart in that the display should never be crowded. The color and beauty of each flower should be apparent, with the impression of mass created by using companion material, or by sprays of much smaller flowers.

The over-all outline of a mass chrysanthemum display would first be made by firmly inserting the individual blooms with regard to symmetry and proportion. A large dark-colored mum or a group of smaller ones should provide a definite point of interest by their location at the top of the vase, with perhaps a few petals falling below the edge of the vase. Smaller and lighter-colored blooms, with varying stem lengths, are then added above to complete the outline. The top bloom should be no higher above the top of the vase than twice the vase height in order to keep a pleasing proportion. The blooms on either side of the center line of the vase should appear to radiate outward from the point of interest and, to obtain the necessary width to match the proportion of the height, the lowest stems must be placed nearly horizontal. To avoid a too perfect symmetry, the blooms should be staggered in groups of 3. There seems to be something magical about the number 3 in connection with flowers, for we also find directions for landscaping with perennials in groups of 3. Three round chrysanthemums with their centers equidistant create a triangle effect which softens the endless repetition of roundness.

The arrangement thus far creates an oval impression which is only slightly lessened by grouping some blooms in 3s. To blend the over-all contour into a pleasing design, a contrasting shape is required. Stalks of goldenrod, evergreen sprays, or complementary colored leaves will complete the arrangement. However, care should be taken to keep the companion material from obscuring the flowers. Variation of this simple mass type can be obtained by shifting the top of the arrangement to the right or left with a counterbalancing portion of the mass on the opposite side below the top of the vase.

Another favorite variation of the mass arrangement is made in a low, oval, metal or pottery container. Here a rounded mass arrangement looks out of place in an oval container. Thus it is necessary to make further use of the triangle's ability to soften the round impression created by the curvature of the container and blooms. This is done by visualizing an isosceles triangle above the container, with the ends of each equal sloping side terminating about 3 or 4 inches from the ends of the container (*see Fig. 10*). The chrysanthemums are selected as before, with the larger, deeper-toned blooms placed at the front rim of the bowl. Smaller, lighter-colored mums are then placed first on one side, and then on the other, of a line running from the center of the bowl to the apex of the imaginary triangle. Still lighter shades of bloom on progressively longer stems are added until the sides of the triangle become a reality. The stems of the smaller and lighter-colored sprays are progressively longer as they are placed further toward the back of the container. The basic design now portrays a curved face terminated by two sloping lines. The design is given grace and proportion by adding spikes of goldenrod or similar-shaped material.

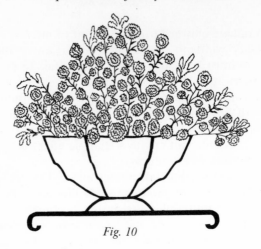

Fig. 10

These are added almost horizontally at the ends of the container. A formal mass arrangement such as this is designed primarily for display in a niche where only the front is visible. However, it is advisable to fill in the back of the arrangement with flowers so that it is pleasing from both sides. Also if the arrangement schedule requires a draped cloth over the top of the niche, the line of the arrangement may be captured by allowing the folds of the drape to follow the arrangement line. Attention to such seemingly unimportant details is often the winning margin in shows where the competition is tough.

LINE ARRANGEMENTS

As a general rule the spirit of a line arrangement is caught by fewer flowers, often in a shallow container, where a linear theme is dominant. The line may be straight or curved, although for years many arrangers did not feel free to deviate from either the crescent design or Hogarth's "line of beauty." All of the fundamentals of color and size of blooms apply even more forcibly to line designs, for here a new illusion, that of motion, is created by a skillful arranger. This effect of motion is obtained by providing a gradual decrease in size of closely spaced flowers along the line, or by having diminishing color tones along the line.

The very nature of a line arrangement seems to be more adaptable to the formal style of arranging. Here the container, the companion materials, and the accessories should all be more formal and should either accentuate the linear theme, or at least not detract from the desired affect. Often the shape of the companion material suggests the type of line to be followed by the flowers. In *Fig. 11* the graceful curves of the branch serve as a perfect background for a straight line of simple daisy-type mums which seem to move out into space.

The container used for such an arrangement should be simple and should have the holder securely fastened to the bottom. The additional material required to hide the mechanics involved in supporting the arrangement should be kept simple and should not pull the attention away from the simple lines of the design.

While line arrangements are usually seen in low containers, a less formal line arrangement can be made with a relatively tall vase (*see Fig. 12*). Here the line effect may be a reversed curve suggestive of an airplane propeller. The junction of the two curves should be located at the top of the vase, where the greatest mass

Fig. 11

and darkest colors will provide a center of interest. A carefully selected spray of mums, rather than individual blooms, should suggest the upper line.

Long-leaf pine or other green material which adds the effect of
a sweeping curve should be used as a background behind the
flowers. The upper ends of this material fix the proportional height

Fig. 12

of the arrangement. A few long twigs of yew, with their short horizontal needles, add the contrast required to neutralize the effect of
the long pine needles. Larger sprays or individual pompons should
be placed below the top spray of mums in a widening pattern to
the top of the vase.

The lower curvature should be recessive in comparison to the
upper. This is obtained by use of the green companion material
only. Since this material must hang down below the top of the
vase, the ends cannot be immersed in water. They must be hidden
behind the point-of-interest blooms. As a final check for symmetry,
hold a piece of cardboard edgewise at the vertical center line of the
vase and optically weigh each side of the arrangement.

Myra J. Brooks has created here an excellent example of a line composition. The container seems made for the type of arrangement, and the accessory arrangement adds the necessary visual weight to balance the composition. *(Photography by Roche)*

In yesteryear this style of line arrangement often had a spray of flowers laid, as if by accident, at the base of the vase. Fortunately, such a waste of good flowers is not in vogue today.

LINE MASS

Flower arrangements need not adhere to a strict set of designs, for it is possible to make combinations of the mass and line designs. This is done by use of a strong diagonal line through a mass design. A standard mass arrangement is made in a medium-tall vase, with the line formed by a cattail or other heavy-line material projected from each side of the mass.

JAPANESE ARRANGEMENTS

Of the various types of arrangements the Japanese is the most stylized. Here the use of flowers is secondary to the interpretation of the theme. The classic form of *Ikebana,* which is Japanese for the art of flower arranging, depicts heaven, man, and earth by use of flowers or other plant material. These must appear to be growing from within the container. For this reason, a Japanese arrangement must be simple and graceful; yet great pains must be taken to preserve the central theme and still achieve the naturalness of living plants.

The two basic styles of Japanese arrangements are the naturalistic informal *Moribana,* or horizontal arrangement, and the more formal *Heika,* or vertical design. In selecting a container for a *Moribana* arrangement the height should be kept below 2 inches, but the length should be 12 to 15 inches. White or a soothing color shade is essential, and the design of the container should be simple. A heavy-base pin holder or mound of floral-arrangement clay is placed ⅔ of the distance from one end along the center line of the container. This serves as the point from which the design will appear to grow. The primary or heaven line may be formed by a single spray of spider mums or reflex pompons, with the stem rising directly from the center of the holder. If the placement of blooms along the stem is interesting, with each one distinct, it will be satisfactory. Should any pedicle cross another, or should a bloom appear damaged, it must be cut off, for crossing lines and imperfect flowers are taboo in a Japanese arrangement. The stem may rise almost perpendicular, or it may be curved. However, when curved, the center of the spray must be exactly over the point of origin of the stem to give the proper balance. The top of this stem is always the tallest part of the arrangement and, for proper proportion, its length should be slightly greater than the over-all length of the container.

The function of the stem symbolizing man is to show a wide dispersion at a height below the stem symbolizing heaven. The only satisfactory way to achieve this effect is to use a material having graceful clusters widely spaced. A pine branch is perhaps the most suitable and it should be chosen carefully so it slants along the center line at the longer end of the container. This branch must project in a horizontal direction with a slight upward tendency. The main stem should be slightly irregular with a curve upward at the end. It should protrude beyond the container about 4 or 5 inches and upward at that point to about ⅔ the height of the first stem. The individual clusters of needles will project from the main stem at various angles; however, clusters which do not curve upward should be carefully removed.

The third stem representing earth should be placed so that it is slightly forward of the center line. If pine is used, all of the needle clusters should also point upward. This stem should project slightly upward 3 or 4 inches beyond the short side of the container. Its over-all height should be about ⅓ that of the first stem. A mound of moss, small stems of leaves, or other natural-growing plant material can be used at the base of the holder to cover it and give the proper mass for the arrangement.

The *Heika* style, usually arranged in a tall vase, is perhaps a little more difficult for occidental arrangers, although the same stem placement is followed. The proportions are slightly different, for the stem symbolizing heaven should be 1½ times the height of the container; the stem representing man should be ⅔ as tall as the first stem; and the earth stem should be ½ the length of the heaven stem.

DRIFTWOOD ARRANGEMENTS

A recent outgrowth of the Japanese type of arrangement has been the driftwood arrangement. It lacks the symbolism of the normal Japanese design, but it maintains its simple naturalness.

This unusual driftwood piece serves as both a container and as an inspiration for a well-designed line-mass arrangement by Myra J. Brooks. *(Photography by Roche)*

The driftwood piece may be used directly in the arrangement or as an external accessory. In either case the size and contour of the piece sets the pattern for the over-all design. Not every piece of driftwood is suitable for use in an arrangement, for, unless it has some interesting feature which can be given expression, it remains just a stick of wood.

When looking for driftwood the sandblasted tree roots sold as nature's creations should be avoided, for they have lost their naturalness. It is much better to walk along an ocean beach or lake front with a small saw and an eye peeled for unusual formations. Perhaps a large weathered knothole, a root that has twisted its way through a maze of rocks, or a malformation, such as a burl, will be a feature capable of expression in an arrangement. No fresh cut should show in a driftwood arrangement, although it may be possible to saw the piece in a flat plane to provide a base to rest on a table or container bottom. If it is necessary to make additional saw cuts, they may be made at a very oblique angle. Then the piece may be used against a wall with the new wood to the rear.

There can be no definite rules for making a driftwood arrangement, although the fundamentals of proportion, color, and symmetry will apply. The spirit of each piece of driftwood must be caught by the individual arranger and brought out with a simple forceful design.

CHAPTER 18

Chrysanthemum Shows

Most gardeners take considerable pride in the appearance of their gardens and in the perfection of their flowers; and for most of them the sheer pleasure they obtain from the results of their efforts is an adequate reward. Some gardeners derive their greatest satisfaction from the prize-winning arrangements or the blue ribbons their flowers may provide. All gardeners, however, are striving to enrich their lives with the beauty of flowers, regardless of the direction their hobby leads them. Gardeners who enjoy the thrill of horticultural competition find flower shows an excellent stimulus to their gardening hobby, particularly if their flowers are worthy of trophies or ribbons.

Chrysanthemums, due to the diversity in their bloom classification, have no peer as show flowers. Local and regional shows are staged each fall in most sections of the country by the chapters and affiliates of the National Chrysanthemum Society. The most important show for N.C.S. members, however, is the national show and meeting.

A very complete set of rules and procedures for staging a chrysanthemum show is contained in the N.C.S. *Show Handbook.* For this reason the contents of this chapter will deal primarily with shows from the exhibitor's point of view.

It is not at all unusual for a neophyte chrysanthemum hobbyist, with no previous exhibition experience, to enter a show and win one or more blue ribbons. However, it is much better for the novice to absorb some of the exhibiting techniques and learn some of the judging objectives first. Enough information can be gained from visiting several chrysanthemum shows to enable the conscientious grower to compete successfully against veteran exhibitors.

JUDGING SCALES

Objective scoring of entries in any flower show in accordance with a scale of values is usually very difficult, even for qualified judges. The natural tendency in judging chrysanthemums is to place too much emphasis on size alone, for this is perhaps the uppermost objective in the mind of the grower. However, unless some consideration is given to all of the factors which make up the ideal chrysanthemum bloom the conscientious grower is placed at a disadvantage. English chrysanthemum shows differ from American shows in that the method of exhibiting the large blooms is deliberately designed to place all of the emphasis on the bloom itself. The bloom heads are mounted on flat boards so that only the bloom is visible. Since only crown buds are used, the absence of real leaves below the bloom is not a disadvantage in this case. In American shows 3 blooms are displayed in a container, except where the show schedule calls for a single bloom. Three blooms are usually more representative of a grower's skill than a single bloom. Here foliage and over-all form and substance of the bloom are given more consideration in judging. Of course, where single-bloom entries are scheduled, size assumes more importance.

It is general practice for the usual group of 3 judges to first eliminate those entries in any class which are definitely inferior. Then the appropriate judging scale in the N.C.S. *Show Handbook* is used to select the winners from the few remaining entries. Where emphasis is placed upon size by the show committee (as it would be in single-bloom divisions for chrysanthemums), the judging scale will give up to 25 per cent for size. Where the division specifies 3 blooms of large bloom chrysanthemums, form and fullness, together with over-all appearance of the stem and foliage, will be assigned 45 per cent of the perfect score. Size in this case is worth only 10 per cent. When sprays are being judged the character and form of the stem and foliage are judged separately. Thirty-five per cent of the scale is allotted to this part of the entry. The color, form, equality of bloom size, and freshness of the blooms make up the balance of the judging scale. A knowledge of judging scales and their application is a definite advantage to a grower who exhibits.

HOW TO WIN PRIZES WITH MUMS

The first activity connected with a prize-winning entry starts long before the first spadeful of earth is turned over in the garden. Varieties must be selected that have the basic qualities required of a good show flower. Many chrysanthemum catalogues emphasize the suitability of certain varieties for show purposes, but a list of the winners at any large chrysanthemum show is an even better guide. Chapter 22 will contain a selection of varieties that have been successful over the years. It usually pays, however, to grow a few of the new introductions each year, along with the old stand-bys.

Sufficient plants of each variety should be grown to permit selection of the best blooms at show time. Six of each variety would be a minimum planting, and any number over 20 may create such a feeling of complacency that inadequate care will be given to them.

The actual culture of exhibition mums does not differ materially from the procedure already given, but it does require a little more emphasis on each phase of the program. There is no intent here to enter the organic versus inorganic controversy; however, the organic content of a chrysanthemum bed does play an important part in its ability to produce prize-winning blooms. If the manure layer is incorporated a little more thoroughly in the soil and the summer mulch is a little thicker than it would be in an average chrysanthemum garden, the chances of success are greatly improved. It is virtually impossible to supply too much organic fertilization, but too much inorganic fertilizer on soils that are low in organic matter can do more harm than good. Soils that are rich in organic matter can absorb much higher amounts of chemical stimulants which they release to the growing plants in more uniform doses.

Proper control of the blooms through pinching becomes more important when show mums are grown, for a minimum stem length of 20 inches is required for the single-bloom exhibits. Sprays must have well-formed terminal bud clusters that can only be obtained by a last pinch at the specified time.

Insect and disease control assumes a greater importance when mums are grown for show purposes. Disfiguration of the leaves due to insect attack, or disease-damaged foliage, may eliminate an otherwise excellent bloom from competition.

Careful attention should be given to the supporting, tying, and disbudding operations. The stems of all possible show varieties should be kept as straight as possible during the entire growing period. The plant ties used to attach the stem to the support system should be loose enough to prevent binding of the stem, and yet they must hold the stem securely. It is advisable to check these ties often and move them upward as the new succulent growth elongates. The disbudding operation should be performed carefully to avoid scars. As the axillary growths develop along the stem they should be removed systematically in such a way that the leaves are not damaged. Also, it is better to do this job every few days so there will be no unsightly stubs resulting from removal of growths that developed over a period of several weeks. This is particularly true when the time arrives to remove the buds surrounding the terminal bud. When the petals of this bud begin to unfold it is important to see that they do not become deformed by the support system.

As show time approaches there is often considerable doubt that entries will be ready in time for the show. However, chrysanthemums are very reliable as to their blooming date, whether grown for natural blooming or in accordance with the shading schedule. In general, a bloom which is a few days past its peak of bloom will stand a better chance of winning than one which is not fully opened. Consequently, it is safer to grow varieties that bloom as much as a week before the show than it is to select varieties whose blooming dates coincide with the show date.

The show schedule should be carefully checked to be sure that the maximum number of entries can be made with the minimum number of blooms. For example, divisions for large blooms will specify either 1 or 3 blooms of a variety. In addition, there is usually a division for a collection of 5 blooms, each of a different variety. The exhibitor should do his own judging in the garden several days before the show. Where one bloom of a variety is outstanding it should naturally be entered in a division for single blooms. Where all blooms of a variety are about equal, and their form and foliage is good, the 3 best should be entered in a division for 3 blooms. The least perfect blooms should be combined together with other varieties for entrance in the class for collections.

In order to make selection easier when it becomes time to cut the entries, it is a good policy to tag each possible entry with the information required by the show schedule. If this is done a day or so before the show there will be less confusion when entries are placed on the show tables.

When the exhibitor plans to deliver personally his entries to the show the blooms should be cut late in the afternoon preceding the show. An overnight conditioning in water will put them in good shape for the trip. Blooms that must be shipped will have to be cut in time to meet the schedule of the transportation system used.

TRANSPORTING BLOOMS TO A SHOW

There are several methods used to transport blooms to the show. They may be carried in a container of water, or, to avoid spilling water in a car, they may be plunged into wet sand or vermiculite. A container can be made for transporting large-bloom chrysanthemums from a 24-inch open-head drum of light-gauge metal. Wire clips fastened around the top edge may be used to support each stem individually.

The standard florist's shipping box may also be used to transport chrysanthemums to a show. A roll of crushed newspaper which has a diameter slightly greater than the blooms should first be placed near each end of the box for a neck support. A layer of florist's green wax paper should then be placed over each newspaper roll. This paper prevents bruising of the petals. The necks of the blooms are then placed on the newspaper rolls so that the blooms do not strike any portion of the box. The stems will then point toward the center of the box. As each bloom is placed in the box there should be a layer of waxed tissue between it and the adjacent bloom. One or more layers may be placed in each box, with the rolls of newspaper placed progressively toward the center of the box. When blooms are shipped to a distant show the same method may be used with a little more care in packing.

Air express is the safest method to use when chrysanthemums

are shipped a long distance. Charges for air shipment are based upon both the actual weight and the dimensional weight. The physical weight of the box is usually quite low, but a large box may increase the shipping cost two or three times above the weight charge. The airline rules and limitations should be checked beforehand. Also, sufficient time should be allowed for possible delay in transit.

The entries should be cut short enough to leave only 1 or 2 inches over the minimum stem length allowed by the show schedule. All excess foliage should be removed, but leaves should be left on the stems for a distance of 8 to 10 inches below the blooms. A row of blooms should be placed at each end of the box as described above, with waxed tissue separating each bloom. The stems should be securely tied by strings which pass through the sides of the box. A second and possibly third row of blooms may be securely tied in each end of the box, as long as the stems do not interfere with the blooms already packed. Spray entries, with their shorter stems, may be placed in the center of the box between the 2 groups of larger blooms.

A soaking period before packing may be sufficient to supply enough water for the trip; however, additional moisture can be supplied by orchid tubes. These tubes are actually test tubes with rubber caps. Florists receive their orchids from wholesalers in these tubes and usually the tubes may be obtained from them. The holes in the rubber cap will stretch over the chrysanthemum stems, and the tubes will hold an ounce or so of water.

SHOW PROCEDURE

A great deal of time has been spent by the chrysanthemum hobbyist in the culture of his exhibition blooms. Also, considerable thought has gone into each phase of the program. However, once the blooms reach the exhibition hall there is very little time to stage the entries and attend to last-minute details. Usually all exhibitors must leave the floor an hour or so before judging begins; so there is bound to be some confusion in a large show when several thousand entries must be set up by 10 or 11 o'clock in the morning. Careful tagging of each entry in accordance with the show schedule can help eliminate some confusion.

Most shows have a committee to assist out-of-town exhibitors with the problems of containers and entry cards. These people can be most helpful; however, each exhibitor should set aside sufficient time to check each of his entries after they have been placed on the show tables. Then he can blame no one but himself if an entry is misplaced or improperly labeled. If an exhibitor is unable to attend the show personally, the same committee will stage the entries he has shipped. Needless to say, all of the information required for the entry card should be attached to each entry.

Before the actual judging takes place the classification committee checks each class of entries. The people selected for this committee are experienced chrysanthemum exhibitors whose function it is to see that each entry conforms to the regulations for a particular class. They will reclassify an entry where an obvious error has been made, but in the short time allotted to them it is impossible for them to detect every error which may have been made.

After the judging has been completed there are bound to be some disappointments, for all entries cannot win a blue ribbon. It is always a temptation to find fault with the judging, but it is far better to look for the reasons which prompted the judges to select the prize winners. Prizes should rightfully be considered a reward for excellence in chrysanthemum culture, but the true value of a chrysanthemum hobby may be lost if prizes become the chief goal.

CHAPTER 19

Making a Profit from Mums

THE chrysanthemums grown in bush form for cutting are so prolific that it doesn't take a new grower long to have more than he can use himself, or give to friends and neighbors. Many a grower with sufficient space has developed a profitable part-time business from just such a situation. Paradoxical as it may seem, the sale of chrysanthemums by amateurs helps rather than hurts the florist trade. Generally, the people who stop to buy roadside flowers do not regularly patronize a florist, but the satisfaction they get from arranging and living with these flowers in their homes often leads them to purchase flowers from the florist during the winter months. The use of flowers in the home is much more prevalent in many of the foreign countries, but fortunately America is becoming more a nation of gardeners. This has made appreciation of flowers a contributing factor to gracious modern living and has raised flowers above their usual status as necessary adjuncts for weddings and funerals.

GROWING FLOWERS FOR SALE

It usually takes a few years and thorough appreciation of two important factors to show a profit from a mum garden. First, the quality of the flowers must be equal to those displayed in florists' windows; and, second, they must be sold at a bargain when compared to the prices charged by the florist. It is really not the customer's fault that he expects to buy better flowers than he can raise himself and pay far less than he would to a florist. However, these are factors that affect the sale of flowers from the home garden year after year.

Selling chrysanthemums is not much different than selling any good product, except that it can be done over such a small portion of the year. Advertising thus becomes very important, and by far the best form is a good display of mums along a well-traveled road. If the location of the garden is such that it cannot be constantly seen by new people, word-of-mouth advertising becomes very important. By far the least important form of advertising is newspaper or other printed forms of advertisement.

Every sales display of chrysanthemums should have a "come-in row" located in front, where it is easily seen quite a distance from either direction along the road. Here there should be the most unusual colors, with many of the new, well-advertised introductions. This one row can often lead to a sale by prompting a driver to stop during that moment of indecision when his mind is shifting from driving to thoughts of transferring such a beautiful display to his own home. Invariably the customer will insist on having his flowers cut from the "come-in row," for these are the flowers which caused him to stop. Considerable tact is needed to prevent him from walking off with the bait. For this reason, additional plants of the same varieties should be grown in other parts of the garden to enable the "come-in row" to remain intact.

There is perhaps more sales psychology required in selling flowers from an outdoor garden than there is in selling a manufactured product in a retail store. Here the customer walks right into the workshop where he can see all of the gardening mistakes, as well as the choice blooms that are either not for sale or are reserved for a prior order. This means careful planning of the sales garden. If possible to do so, the sales garden should be separated from a mum garden where flowers are grown for exhibition or personal use. The sales garden can then be laid out in the best sales-promotional manner.

Flowers for sale should be those not normally grown by the average home gardener. This requires greater use of the varieties grown by the commercial growers. There should be a wide choice of colors and types. Also, they should be well mixed so there are not too many plants of a variety together. Customers like to buy whatever flowers seem scarce, and by spreading out the planting often the grower tempts them to buy more than they had originally intended.

One special row or bed should contain many of the new varieties in order to test customers' reactions, and also to draw those customers who return year after year just to see the new varieties. Careful records of sales from this section will help plan future gardens. The success of a mum sales garden depends, as it does in any type of selling, upon flowers that appeal to the customers. It may be possible for the grower to push a certain variety he is particularly fond of, but repeat business is best obtained when the customer makes his own selection and knows he can come back year after year for his favorite varieties.

Customers' tastes do, however, vary quite widely, so there must be enough diversity to interest all types of customers. Male customers generally pick the bold red, bronze, and yellow colors without regard to the color scheme at home. They also are more attracted to the spiders and unusual forms of bloom. Women, on the other hand, are much more careful to select colors which blend well together with the color scheme of the rooms in which the flowers will be used. Garden-club members, and women who practice the art of flower arranging, like to pick out the individual flower stems to be cut so they have some fully open flowers, some partly open, and some buds. They also like curved or crooked stems, contrasting color combinations or blending tones, and the unusual types of smaller blooms. Several years of experience are required to indicate the proportion of colors and types to plant to meet the demand.

The discussion of selling so far has dealt primarily with spray types of bloom, since the greatest demand will be for this type of bloom. These are the flowers the customer usually buys for use in his own home, but for special occasions, and for presents, he often will buy either standards alone or in a mixed bouquet with spray types. Some of the commercial and exhibition types should be grown to supply this demand and to draw the interest of those who like to look now, but who may either buy later or advertise the display to their friends.

The time-pinching date should be followed for all of the pompon types in order to produce good-quality, uniform terminal sprays.

This makes possible maximum production from a given area and keeps the number of flowers for each stem more or less equal. This is rather important, for, early in the game, the decision regarding number of stems to a bouquet and the price per bouquet must be decided upon. The pricing practice should be standard. Without uniformity some customers will complain that their bouquets are smaller than those obtained by their friends. A good practice to follow would be to charge a round figure, such as 50 cents, for so many stems. This figure should be posted and explained to customers while they are selecting flowers so they don't have more flowers cut than they had intended to pay for. The number of stems produced by following the time pinching schedule will permit a good profit from chrysanthemums grown in bush form, even when they are sold considerably below the price charged by a florist. With the standards it is a little more difficult to realize the same profit margin from an equivalent area. These blooms must be sold individually, or in units of a dozen, and this price may seem high to the customer. There is more work involved in raising standards, for the removal of side buds in a large bed takes considerable time. The average customer doesn't appreciate this even when it is explained to him.

The commercial florist usually obtains 2, or at the most 3, flowers per plant from a 12-inch spacing of plants. Thus, he is able to charge as much as 50 cents per bloom. The part-time grower can't approach this figure, so many of them compromise by allowing 5 or 6 flowers to develop on each plant. These flowers will be smaller and have a flat appearance, but customers will accept them at a price which will be profitable to the grower. Although uniformity in prices charged for a given quantity of flowers is important, it is a definite aid to future sales to add a few extra flowers. This stimulates business, but care must be taken to treat each customer equally.

Sales of chrysanthemums usually pick up after frost has killed flowers in home gardens; so the part-time grower should plan his sales garden to have more or less uniform bloom from early in the season until as late as possible. Some method of frost protection is required to do this. In general, the later varieties should occupy the rear portion of the garden where a frost-protection structure will not interfere with the view of the garden during the early part of the season. The "come-in row" can be kept in full bloom constantly by transplanting plants from a reserve plot. However, a carefully constructed frame should be used to protect these plants. Oblong frames, equal in dimensions to the standard 3- by 6-foot hotbed sash, can be made of 1 by 2 shingle lath and covered with clear polyethylene plastic. These frames should be placed on the top and front of the row and held in place with hooks and hinges. The rear wall and ends can be made solid, using wooden boards nailed to posts. The rear wall should be 4 to 4½ feet high to permit run off of water and clearance for the taller plants. With the cover in place the flowers will receive ample protection from frost and, on cold days, the flowers can still be seen through the plastic. During warm sunny days the cover should be folded back to permit air circulation among the plants. This will also prevent overheating within the enclosure.

The rear enclosure should be more permanent and should more nearly approach a greenhouse in construction, for there must be sufficient room for customers to come in and make their selections. Great ingenuity has been displayed by growers in designing this type of protective unit. Some have built permanent side walls and roof-support members. Then hotbed sash are placed on the roof when frost appears imminent.

Others have used frames constructed as outlined for the "come-in row" with, either polyethylene plastic, or the heavier, less clear vinyl plastic covering. The new Fiberglas corrugated panels, now widely used in construction of patios, offer considerable promise for use in either permanent or semipermanent greenhouse-type structures. These panels come in several widths and are 12 feet long. At present the cost is rather high. They should be the clear, or transparent, type to permit maximum light penetration. This material may be sawed and nailed with the ease of wood.

Any of these grower-constructed structures may be supplied with heat from portable oil or electric heaters. Thus it is possible to grow December-blooming varieties in them. A well-constructed unit of this type may be left up all winter to provide protection for the stock plants, and in the spring it will be very useful in getting an early start for the garden. Fortunately the price customers will pay for later-blooming varieties will help offset the increased cost of such a structure plus its heating. However, it probably will not be profitable to try to extend the season much beyond the first week of December in the area around New York City.

The amount of time which can be devoted to a chrysanthemum sales garden will determine the extent of the undertaking, but if it can be run as a retirement activity, or on a partnership basis, it is possible to extend the scope of activities considerably. Sales of cut flowers only should be made from a well-planned sales garden. However, if additional space is available for a reserve plot to supply not only the grower's needs but extra plants as well, a landscaping service can provide added income. The ability of the chrysanthemum to withstand careful transplanting without suffering ill effects makes it possible to transfer plants to customers' gardens just before blooming. The hardy varieties are best for this purpose. A good price can be obtained for this service from customers who are willing to pay for a well-laid-out display without any work attached to it. This phase of chrysanthemum selling can all be completed in late summer before the sale of cut flowers begins. Any plants unsold by early October can be balled in burlap and sold in full bloom to roadside stands or disposed of at the auction markets now becoming quite popular in some sections of the country.

The demand for pot plants is usually not sufficient to warrant much attention by the part-time grower, for such plants have their greatest sales appeal during the spring holidays. Commercial florists grow many of these plants in 3-inch pots for sale at this season. Many florists are now capitalizing on the sale of flowers and potted plants in grocery stores and 5-and-10-cent stores by supplying them with plants packaged in cellophane bags. These bags are made of 450 MSAT 87 cellophane. They will keep plants fresh on a store shelf for a week without watering. The part-time grower might use such bags to package cut chrysanthemums for sale in local stores.

Existing conditions in a given locality will determine the potential for sale of chrysanthemums; however, the grower who wants to realize a profit from his hobby will find the chrysanthemum a very adaptable flower for this purpose.

SELLING PLANTS

The ease of propagation of chrysanthemums makes it possible to realize quite a profit from the extra plants raised by the amateur who wishes to capitalize on his hobby. This phase of chrysanthemum selling makes an additional selling period and it has several very important advantages to the grower. First, the customers who buy plants are not nearly as selective as those who buy cut flowers. They usually will permit the grower to select plants having the desired characteristics for their gardens. Thus it is possible to dispose of plants that make a lot of suitable cuttings in the spring. For the grower this is often easier than it is to sell the flowers from the same plants, even though they may be superior in every way to varieties which do not winter over as readily. Second, if the part-time grower sells excess plants, it permits him to buy wholesale plants where the minimum order of 50 plants of a variety gives him more than are required for his own use.

Plants from the wholesale growers are bare root cuttings packaged 25 to a section of carton. The unit price is about 8 cents apiece. To make a profit from these plants requires a fast turnover at a price below the retail catalogue price for the same varieties. To do this properly the grower should plan his own garden and order sufficient extra cuttings to meet his expected demand for plants. The order should specify the first delivery as early as possible, with subsequent orders to follow at intervals of 1 to 2 weeks, depending upon the demand for plants. Many wholesalers have a minimum shipping order of 500 cuttings, so this will have a bearing on the number of deliveries to be made. Spreading delivery permits both a more uniform work load and a longer period of plant sales. There is one word of caution necessary concerning early delivery. Some varieties, notably the hardy ones, have the same day-length conditions to permit flowering in April as they have at their normal blooming time. If terminal buds are to be avoided on these plants they must have an additional lighting period.

When the cuttings arrive they should be potted in plant bands and set on damp sand in a cold frame. Within a few days they will be making active growth. Then they will remain in good condition to sell for a period of 2 to 3 weeks. Plants unsold at the end of this period should be topped to make new cuttings, and the bottom portion can be planted in the reserve garden. Plants in bands can be sold below the retail price a customer would have to pay if he ordered from a catalogue. The seller may realize a 100 per cent profit and provide plants in a better condition to set out immediately in the customer's garden.

Local conditions will again determine the potential sale of plants. If there are not sufficient individual purchasers of plants, a good turnover of plants can often be made through garden centers and stores that cater to the gardening public. An effective way to sell such plants is to place each variety in a flat, with a colored catalogue picture pasted on a sign attached to the flat. In addition to the picture, the flowering date, height of plant, and brief cultural directions should appear on the sign. A fair price for these plants would be 15 cents, which still permits the store or garden center to make a good profit selling the plants at approximately the retail catalogue price.

There are other ways of making a profit from a chrysanthemum hobby, such as selling well-designed arrangements, supplying flowers to churches, or selling plants for municipal gardens. In each case the success of the project will depend upon the inclination and ability of the individual grower.

CHAPTER 20

Historical Background and Modern Development

THERE is considerable romance, adventure, and painstaking development involved in the introduction of plants from all parts of the world to modern gardens. In the case of the chrysanthemum there has also been an element of mystery, for, through its long history of cultivation, the relationship to an original wild species is somewhat obscure. Plant explorers who travel to the remote corners of the earth seeking new species of plants; taxonomists who compare and classify plants into a recognizable pattern of nomenclature; and plant hybridizers who develop the best characteristics of these plants have all had a hand in making our modern chrysanthemum the superior flower it is today. An account of this work is interesting in itself, but it has a special significance for those who grow and love chrysanthemums.

Since chrysanthemums were grown before the advent of the printing press there is no written record of their origin. However, Chinese pottery depicts the chrysanthemum in much the same form as we know it today; so it can be safely assumed that China was the point of origin. From there it was undoubtedly imported to Japan, where it became a symbol of royalty and was called Ki-Ku, or "Queen of the East."

INTRODUCTION TO EUROPE

It was not until the eighteenth century that any attempt was made to import the chrysanthemum for commercial development.

The first recorded variety which was imported was a ball-shaped purple flower which was rather small when compared to the large blooms seen in florists' windows every fall. This variety became the dominant parent in the breeding of the large double types which we refer to as Chinese incurves. Although many growers in Europe should be credited with a hand in the development of the chrysanthemum, the name of John Salter of England stands out as the foremost breeder of the regular incurved type of chrysanthemum.

In 1862 Robert Fortune brought back with him to England several varieties of chrysanthemums which he had obtained in Japan. These varieties in all probability had been derived from the species imported much earlier from China. However, due to the Japanese concept of artistic beauty as exemplified by the graceful curve and irregularity of petal deployment, the development in Japanese hands over the centuries had produced a fully double flower with a tendency to incurve irregularly. Evidently the English growers felt more akin to the Chinese concept of beauty evidenced in the regular marshaling of the petals into an incurved ball-shaped bloom, for the Japanese imports met with disfavor in England. However, in later years, after considerable success in France, they became as popular in the English shows as the Chinese incurves.

Also among Fortune's plants were several that produced small blooms which varied in color and degree of doubleness. These also seemed inferior to the English growers, but French growers recognized in them a new form of chrysanthemum. Much of the credit for the development of the small multiflowered bush-type plants should be given to the French gardeners. They gave the appropriate name "pompon" to these blooms which we now list in Class 5.

TAXONOMIC HISTORY

The preceeding factual account has traced the actual chrysanthemum plant introduction to Europe, but the nomenclature was still an enigma. This was a job for the taxonomists, and many years were required before this phase was completed.

In 1753, Linnaeus, the founder of that branch of taxonomy dealing with plants and embracing the science of classification and identification, made a Greek composite word from *chrysos,* meaning gold, and *anthemon,* meaning flower. He applied this to the small yellow species we now know as *C. indicum.* In accordance with the rules of taxonomy followed since the time of Linnaeus, the name "Chrysanthemum" became the valid generic name for a group of species which closely resembled each other. This collection of species, called a genus, together with others bearing a family resemblance, are joined together by taxonomists in the Compositae or daisy family. Thus, a flower which had been in cultivation for over 2000 years before Linnaeus was born became known as "gold flower"; even though the Chinese as early as the fourth century A.D. grew ball-shaped progenitors of our present chrysanthemums in a variety of colors.

Without discussing the minute plant characteristics involved in a taxonomic classification, it is possible to trace the botanical history which led to the adoption of *C. morifolium* as the valid name.

In 1792 Ramatielle described a fully double incurved flower recently imported to France from China as *Anthemis grandiflora.* The specimens he sent to the Botanical Garden at Paris as a new species were identified as being botanically consistent with *C. indicum.* Linnaeus had published a complete description of *C. indicum* in his *Species Plantarum.* Ramatielle agreed that his specimens were generically compatible with *C. indicum.* Theoretically he should then have used the designation *C. grandiflora* for this species to indicate a much more showy type of bloom. However, since there was already a valid description for a plant named *C. grandiflora,* it was impossible under the rules of nomenclature approved by the International Botanical Congress to use that name. As an added complication, another botanist named Lamarck had published his findings that radiate flowers having yellow florets do not produce varieties with red, white, or purple florets. Ramatielle then concluded that his multicolored varieties should be included in another genus, leaving *C. indicum* as a single-species genus. He therefore proposed the name *Matricaria morifolium,* using the valid generic name Matricaria that had been used by Lamarck for several other species of Compositae. This seemed to close the issue as far as Ramatielle was concerned, but this solution was not universally acceptable. Most botanists continued to classify the newly imported chrysanthemum varieties under *C. indicum.*

In 1823 Joseph Sabine reasoned that Ramatielle had been correct in his assumption that the Chinese chrysanthemums were a species apart from *C. indicum,* but he did not agree to their classification under Matricaria. He tried to reconcile matters by proposing the name *C. sinense,* but this violated the rules of nomenclature which state that an older name supersedes any younger name until all differences are resolved.

Hemsley, in the British gardener's chronicle of 1889, attempted to correct the nomenclature picture by proposing the name *C. morifolium.* This name used the older species designation of Ramatielle in the generic classification acceptable to most botanists. The only problem left open was the inability of botanists to trace the Chinese chrysanthemum back to a wild species.

Botanists generally concluded that the Chinese chrysanthemum was a cultigen, or plant which occurred in cultivation as a sport of some hybrid that was derived from *C. indicum.* This would seem to settle the problem, except that the previously published names, *C. sinense* and *M. morifolium,* were still in use in some references and catalogues.

America's eminent botanist Bailey tried to reconcile the cultigen theory with the obvious *C. indicum* characteristics of the Chinese chrysanthemum by proposing the new name *C. hortorum* in 1914. This name indicated that the Chinese chrysanthemum was of horticultural origin rather than a native species, but Bailey did not continue use of this name. The newest edition of Bailey's *Manual of Cultivated Plants,* as well as the *Dictionary of Gardening,* published by the Royal Horticultural Society in England, list *C. morifolium* as the valid name for the varieties of chrysanthemums we grow today.

INTRODUCTION TO AMERICA

During the middle nineteenth century period, development of the chrysanthemum was carried on in the United States through use of varieties imported from England. During the Civil War and the period of westward expansion the general public had scant time for gardening; so little progress was made in American chrysanthemum culture, except at a few private estates. As a result it remained, as it did in England, a pampered conservatory beauty raised for the sole purpose of winning prizes in the various shows. Size was the primary consideration, and each estate vied for the services of the most experienced chrysanthemum growers from abroad. The first American show devoted exclusively to chrysanthemums was held in 1868 under the auspices of the Massachusetts Horticultural Society, and from that time on fall chrysanthemum shows have been very popular.

The early European and American development of the chrysanthemum followed along two broad lines. One aim was the breeding of the large incurves to produce still larger and more beautifully colored blooms, while the other goal was carried on, largely on the continent, by breeders who sought finer strains of pompons for the cut-flower trade. Both types of flowers were considered greenhouse or half-hardy perennials and no attempt was made to popularize them as garden flowers, until a French grower named Lebois produced two pompon seedlings that flowered as early as August. From these two plants have come many of the early-flowering garden chrysanthemums we enjoy today. This was purely an accident of nature because our recent horticultural research has revealed that the chrysanthemum is a short-day plant. In other words, the time of the blooming of the plant is controlled only by the length of day. It is possible that some early-flowering species used in the many crosses involved in the complex history of the chrysanthemum had its tendency towards early blooming submerged for centuries before reasserting itself in accordance with Mendelian law.

MODERN DEVELOPMENT

The impact of changing world conditions had its effect on the development of the chrysanthemum, as it did on almost every phase of human endeavor. In order to chart the course of autumn's favorite flower it might be well to see just what present trends are evidenced in the principle chrysanthemum-growing countries.

AUSTRALIA

Throughout the course of history there are instances where the efforts of one man have had a profound influence on the horticultural development of a country. Such is the case in Australia. Thomas Pockett began hybridizing irregular incurve types of chrysanthemums from stock plants imported from England. His introductions bearing the famous Pockett name have been consistent prize winners in shows held throughout the world. These large exhibition-type flowers have set a trend in the development of exhibition-type chrysanthemums that has made Australian introductions eagerly sought after the world over. Since the southern part of Australia, where most of the chrysanthemum development has been done, lies in the 30- to 40-degree south latitude range, the day length that determines blooming time in their fall season coincides with the day length which occurs in November in the United States.

ENGLAND

The effect of two world wars, high taxation, and the trend towards socialism have closed many of the estate conservatories that formerly housed the stately blooms for which England was famous. The English, however, are a very adaptable race and they have an inborn love of flowers. It is not surprising, therefore, that the trend of chrysanthemum development in England for the past few years has been toward earlier flowering varieties suitable for use in an English cottage garden. These new English chrysanthemums are larger than the French-developed pompons, and they have an informal grace that makes them a welcome addition to our American gardens. It must be remembered, however, that England lies in the same latitude as Labrador and is north of any point in the United States; consequently, the shorter fall days make these plants bloom earlier in England than they do in more southern latitudes.

HOLLAND

The Dutch have been the foremost growers of cut flowers for the European market for many years. Flowers are so much a part of Dutch life that the Dutch housewife shops for flowers in the same manner women of other lands do in their daily marketing. Since

Dutch chrysanthemums are destined for use as cut flowers in the home, their development has been along lines which would produce a graceful spray of double flowers. These flowers must remain fresh and salable after a trip to the market on the flower barges which ply the canals. The flowers of the Dutch hybrids, while not so large as the early English varieties, have the same open appearance with the slightly incurved petals radiating outward from the center in increasing lengths to the outside petals.

JAPAN

The chrysanthemum, since its introduction from China, has been the national flower of Japan, and each fall, in October, the feast of chrysanthemums, called *Kiku-No-Sekku,* is observed. With such a long background of culture it is not surprising that the form of the flower and the shape of its petals have undergone many changes. Japanese development has stressed the artistic interpretation of the petals in addition to the horticultural goal of larger and finer flowers. Some of the names give a clue to this trend. For example, *Yado-no-hitomoto* means "solitary tree in retreat," and the flower bearing this name can be described as mobile-petaled with a few downward hanging petals on one side and a full complement of interlaced petals protruding at right angles on the opposite side. This gives the flower the appearance of a dish mop in a hurricane. "The Steed under Cherry Blossoms" and "The Crane on the Sacred Peak" are other apt descriptions of Japanese chrysanthemums that convey a meaning but would be regarded as freaks by Western standards. These flowers are fully double and the petals, although flat, are twisted and often bear two colors, one on each petal surface. One of the wide-petaled varieties, called "Powdery Hair," has small hairlike projections on the outer surface of the irregular incurved petals.

Another Japanese trend is toward development of tubular petals that are quill-shaped throughout, or are spatula-shaped at the end. Here again there are endless variations, ranging from a variety called "Radiance of Gems," which has as few as 21 quilled petals radiating outward from a naked core or eye similar to that found in the familiar daisy, to *Mie* (name of a prefecture) which resembles a badly tangled mass of string. Generally speaking, the fewer the petals on the Japanese quill, spider, and thread forms of flowers, the straighter and more horizontal they are. The fully double spiders become hopelessly hooked and coiled. Still another variation of this tubular petaled type is the thistle type in which the petals surround the core vertically, so that the flowers have the appearance of our common wild thistle.

The core, or eye, of the chrysanthemum, which is hidden in fully double types and apparent in the single varieties, is actually composed of tiny petals that surround the seed-bearing part of the flowers. The clever Japanese hybridizers found a way to develop these core petals into a far greater size, so that the entire core measures several inches across and is mound-shaped like a pincushion. These varieties have a few rows of stubby wide petals radiating from the enlarged cushion, and, due to the likeness of the core to the shape of the anemone flower, these varieties are known as anemone chrysanthemums.

The pompon and single types of chrysanthemums have also been subjects for Japanese cultivation, although they seem to be far too regular in shape to fit the Japanese concept of beauty. It is during the growth of the plant, however, that the Japanese grower can give vent to his artistic urge, for the plants are trained to achieve the same appearance that is evidenced in the cultivation of the Bonsai miniature trees. The shell pompons they have developed are like little round buttons and combine very effectively with other types of chrysanthemums, as well as with other flowers, in arrangements and bouquets.

While Japan lies on the opposite side of the world from the United States, the same north-latitude relationship exists, so the Japanese varieties, most of which bloom in November, will have the same blooming date in most of the northern chrysanthemum-growing countries. In the southern countries having the same relative degree of latitude, the date of blooming will differ by 6 months. The Japanese seem to have been able to reverse the chrysanthemum's response to nature's short-day blooming schedule in at least one case, for one Japanese variety called, *Haru-Giku,* blooms in May. This is a pretty pompon having the same general shape as the early-flowering English varieties, but apparently it is a novelty, for it does not appear in available catalogue listings.

Not content with developing the physical structure of the chrys-anthemum bloom to endless conformations, the Japanese have de-veloped an edible chrysanthemum called *Ryori-Giku.* To the oriental taste the petals of this chrysanthemum are probably de-licious, but in the Western mind they probably would be classed with bird's nest soup and ancient egg omelet as things to be be-lieved without tasting.

In the matter of color, too, the Japanese have run the gamut, for their chrysanthemums appear in almost every color and combina-tion, except for blue. However, early Japanese pottery depicted a blue chrysanthemum. Probably the ceramics used in these early pieces were incapable of capturing the purple color evidenced in the later chrysanthemum imports to England, or else a little artistic license was employed. At any rate, the search for a true blue chrys-anthemum by the chrysanthemum breeders of the world assumes the same intriguing importance as the search for a blue rose and a yellow African violet. In addition to the solid colors, Japanese chrysanthemums come in regular bicolors with each side of the petal a contrasting color, and mosaic-colored flowers having a few adjacent petals a different color than the majority of the petals. There is even a green chrysanthemum whose translated name is "Verdant Hill."

UNITED STATES

When the chrysanthemum reached America, the United States was not noted as a nation of gardeners, so the development of the flower was directed toward production of good commercial vari-eties. There was a good market for the large incurved varieties so familiar in florists' windows every fall, and breeders sought to cap-italize on this by developing what florists call a "hard" bloom. Such a flower has stiff petals that resist crushing during shipment in the standard florist's shipping box.

Elmer Smith, by virtue of the long list of commercial hybrids he developed, is recognized as the man most responsible for the com-mercial success of the large-flowered chrysanthemum in the United States. He started his breeding in 1887 and over the years he in-troduced over 400 varieties. His life gave credence to the legend of longevity associated with the chrysanthemum, for he died at the age of eighty-five. As if it were a fitting climax to a lifetime devoted to the chrysanthemum, his death occurred while he was attending the annual meeting of the Chrysanthemum Society of America. Two of his introductions, Mrs. H. E. Kidder (1930) and Silver Sheen (1924), are still the largest-selling commercial varieties. Of all the chrysanthemums grown by amateurs, these two varieties have been at, or near, the top in the "100 favorite varieties" poll conducted by the National Chrysanthemum Society.

As American inventiveness has made possible shorter working hours, more and more people have turned to gardening as a healthful and relaxing hobby. This trend has focused attention on the chrysanthemum as the logical flower with which to close the outdoor gardening season, but unfortunately in many sections of the country early frosts made it too much of a gamble to grow the available types of chrysanthemums outdoors without protection. There was a definite need for earlier-blooming chrysanthemums that had the necessary hardiness to withstand the rigors of a New England winter. As many an American soldier can attest, Korean winters can match anything New England can produce; so it was only natural that plant exploration for suitable hardy species of chrysanthemums should center in Korea and the colder parts of China.

Much of the credit for the development of the modern hardy chrysanthemums, called Korean hybrids, should be given to Alex Cumming. He began in 1925 the tedious job of crossing and re-crossing to incorporate the hardiness of the recently discovered single Korean variety *C. coreanum* into the breeding work then in progress toward the development of hardier chrysanthemums. *C. coreanum* was introduced in the second crossing of the two hardiest double pompons then known. In subsequent crosses *C. yezoense* and *C. nipponicum* were added. The problem became one of developing hardiness without sacrificing quality. A successful solution to this problem is evidenced in the wide acceptance of these varieties by the American gardening public. The Bristol Nurseries of Bristol, Connecticut, has been largely responsible for popularizing this important development in American chrysanthemum breeding.

Many other chrysanthemum breeders, working as individuals, or in conjunction with commercial nurseries, have engaged in the development of chrysanthemums to produce new varieties for special applications. All of the chrysanthemums developed prior to 1932 were either large-flowered types growing to a height of about 6 feet or small multiflowered bush-type plants that produced their flowers at a distance of 2 to 3 feet from the ground. Thus in mass plantings the front edge of the bed presented a wide area of bare stems and leafy branches. To complete the chrysanthemum picture there was a definite need for dwarf types of chrysanthemums that had the full range of bold colors evidenced in the taller types. In 1932 the R. M. Kellogg Co. of Three Rivers, Michigan, introduced a hardy low type of chrysanthemum that produced a mound of flowers from ground level up to a height of approximately 15 inches. The Kellogg trademark for this type of chrysanthemum is "Azaleamum," although, due to their appearance, they are often referred to as cushion chrysanthemums. These plants start to bloom in August and are in full bloom by the latter part of September. Of course, the short stem length precludes their use as cut flowers, but they keep blooming until November. As the flowers become older they tend to fade, but the delicate color shadings of the month-old flowers have a softening effect on the bright colors of the taller and later blooming varieties. This makes them a definite asset in the over-all picture of a mass planting.

America has a world-wide reputation as the land of opportunity and the melting pot of the world. That is true with regard to our acceptance of people from other lands, as well as the products of their factories and research. We do not shun a development because it is not our own, nor do we cease our efforts toward perfection because of it. Thus, in the field of chrysanthemum culture, we have continued to seek better plants for American gardeners from our own chrysanthemum breeders as well as from the experts in other countries. The catalogues of American chrysanthemum growers list the best introductions from Australia, England, Holland, Japan, and the United States, along with the old stand-bys that have been successful over the years.

There has been a definite trend in the past few years that has tended to lessen the gap between the hardy garden-chrysanthemum enthusiast and the greenhouse specialist. The amateur grower, seeking larger flowers with better colors and firmer petals, has discovered that many of the earlier-blooming greenhouse varieties can be grown outdoors with no protection. Other enterprising amateurs have contrived various forms of protection that permit the flowering of even later-blooming greenhouse types in the garden. The chrysanthemum in all its varied forms has now reached a point of development in the United States where it can be grown and enjoyed by anyone who loves to grow flowers.

CHAPTER 21

Classification of Bloom Types and Species of Chrysanthemums

In Chapter 2 a brief description of chrysanthemum bloom types was given. Here the more detailed discussion of the difference between bloom types is further explained and illustrated. While this National Chrysanthemum Society classification is designed primarily to provide standards for chrysanthemum shows, it provides a universal terminology that can be used by all who grow and love chrysanthemums.

DIVISION A

Ray florets with straplike or ligulate corolla. Disk floret vase-shaped and relatively short.

SECTION 1 — Disk conspicuous, made up of unmodified disk florets surrounded by one or more rows of ray florets.

Class 1 — Single. Straplike ray florets in not more than 5 rows. Disk flat with florets short.

Courtesy J. Horace McFarland Co.

JOAN HELEN

Subclass — Broad-Petaled Single. Ray florets fewer and much broader in proportion to their length than in the typical single.

(a) *Small,* blooms not over 2 inches in diameter.

(b) *Intermediate,* blooms over 2 inches but not over 4 inches in diameter.

(c) *Large,* blooms over 4 inches in diameter.

The open central disk of the singles is an invitation to cross-fertilization by many insects; so it is not surprising that the so-called "volunteer" seedlings that occasionally spring up in mum gardens turn out to be single varieties. Some of these are worth keeping, but generally it is better to buy named single varieties whose color, height, and growth habit fit into the planned garden picture. There are many varieties of singles whose brightly-colored ray petals combine with the usually brilliant yellow central disk to provide contrast to the more formal double varieties. Some of the single varieties provide early patches of color in a massed display, while others bloom later and are more suitable for growing where frost protection can be given. In the late-blooming group there is a wide variation in growth habit. Some varieties have been developed to produce one large flower on a 5- or 6-foot stem for exhibition purposes; and, as a rule, these varieties will not make good multi-flowered bushes, nor will any of the bush types produce a comparable large flower if grown as a single-stem plant.

One of the most interesting of the singles is the cascade chrysanthemum, which the Japanese call mountain chrysanthemum. These actually are not a type of mum, but are rather a method of training the stems. Cascade mums produce long pliable stems having many short flowering stems evenly distributed along their length. Without training, the long stems will topple over in utter confusion, but a planned program of tying and pinching can produce a mass of bloom in a predetermined shape. Formerly, at many estates where chrysanthemums were raised for exhibitions, the cascade varieties were grown in large pots or tubs and trained into various forms (see Chapter 13).

Class 2 — Semidouble. Ray florets in more than 5 rows; disk apparent in fully opened blooms, flat, with short florets. Classification for bloom size as in Class 1.

RONALD

The semidouble lacks the simple appeal of the daisylike single and the more formal grace of the fully double, so it is apt to be ignored in the plans of many mum gardeners. The semidouble flowers, however, provide that slightly different flower form that can make the winning margin in a chrysanthemum arrangement contest. The red and copper-colored varieties are particularly good in metal containers.

Class 3 — Regular Anemone. Ligulate ray petals in not more than 5 rows, broad, evenly spaced, and equal in length. Disk florets longer than in the singles. Disk prominent, approximating a hemisphere in form.

CRIMSON GLOW

The central disk in this class is so much larger in every way than it is in the single varieties that to a novice these varieties might appear to be entirely different flower species. Unfortunately, these are the least familiar types of mums and, since they do not stand shipment as well as other varieties, they are not often seen in florists' windows. Anemones, in the past, have been grown primarily as single-stem exhibition flowers, but many of them will also make excellent multiflowered bush plants. Generally, the earlier blooming a variety is, the better it will be if desired as a bush. This, of course, makes possible the use of anemone-type chrysanthemums in outdoor plantings. Actually, when grown this way, the sprays of flowers have a much more pleasing proportion between size of ray petals and central disk than is the case where only one flower per plant is permitted to develop.

Class 4 — Irregular Anemone. Like Class 3 except that the ray petals are irregular in length, may be flat or quilled, and, when flat, may be twisted. Are apt to be large, but are subdivided for size as in Class 1.

Courtesy R. M. Kellog Company

QUEEN ELIZABETH

The applications of irregular anemone chrysanthemums are the same as for the regular anemone varieties.

SECTION 2

Group A: Ligulate corollas incurved. Disk may be present and concealed, or the disk florets may be scattered singly or in small groups among the ligulate florets, or absent. In any case, if present, the disk florets are concealed by the numerous ligulate florets that give character to the bloom.

Class 5 — Pompon. The ray florets are short, broad, and typically incurved to form a globular bloom, although smaller blooms are often flattened and buttonlike.

   (a) *Small,* less than 1½ inches in diameter.

   (b) *Intermediate,* blooms at least 1½ but not over 2½ inches.

   (c) *Large,* blooms over 2½ but not over 4 inches. Blooms of this type larger than 4 inches are placed in Class 6, Regular Incurves.

Courtesy J. Horace McFarland Co.

MASQUERADE

Pompons are the bread-and-butter crop of the commercial florist, for the techniques worked out by the large wholesale growers make this class of chrysanthemums a dependable cut-flower crop with a steady demand at relatively good prices. The florist uses the varieties developed for greenhouse growing, but more and more of these have proven hardy with amateurs who wish to grow professional-quality flowers. An amateur can successfully flower all of the early-blooming varieties in the open ground; and, with frost protection, some of the November-blooming varieties can be grown outdoors. Since these formal pompons were designed primarily for cutting, it is for this use that the amateur should grow them. The range in size from tiny buttons to perfect 3-inch ball-shaped blooms makes this class of chrysanthemums most useful in arrangements. The fortunate greenhouse owner can work many types of flower magic with potted pompons by using the techniques developed by experiment stations and commercial growers which are discussed in the section covering advanced chrysanthemum culture.

Class 6 — Regular or Chinese Incurve. Disk florets hidden as in Class 5. Ligulate petals longer than in Class 5, but broader in proportion to their length, incurved and overlapping smoothly and regularly. Petals not twisted and bloom globular when fully developed.

(a) *Small,* blooms over 4 but not over 6 inches.

(b) *Large,* blooms over 6 inches.

INDIANAPOLIS WHITE

Subclass — Skirted Incurve. Lower tiers of petals not incurved, standing out at right angles to the stem or hanging vertically to hide the upper portion of the stem. Otherwise like the regular incurves of Class 6.

These are some of the stately blooms that dominate the florist's windows each fall; and there is a special thrill waiting for any chrysanthemum hobbyist who has never raised them in his own garden, for they are not so difficult to grow as they might appear.

The firm petalage of the Chinese incurves makes them good shipping flowers, and they have long been favorite show flowers, particularly where the blooms had to be sent long distances. The regular petal formation and large size of these flowers make them very effective cut flowers for use both in churches and other public buildings, as well as in private homes. As corsage flowers they have no equal for ruggedness and lasting ability.

Class 7 — Irregular or Japanese Incurve. Much as the regular incurves except that the petals are even wider in proportion to the greater length. The twisted ligulate petals are the distinguishing characteristic which gives the bloom an open, airy appearance and makes for irregular overlapping of the petals. The blooms are globular when fully opened.

   (a) *Small,* over 5 but not over 7 inches.
   (b) *Large,* over 7 inches in diameter.

WHITE TURNER

These flowers are often referred to as exhibition blooms because that is their primary application; however, they can be used separately or in combination with regular incurves anywhere that a tall container of these large cut flowers would be appropriate. The size of these blooms is tremendous when grown one bloom to a plant, and this is the only satisfactory way to grow them, for they quickly lose their distinctive individuality when grown as multiflowered sprays.

SECTION 3 — Ligulate Corollas Reflexed.

Class 8 — Reflexed or Decorative Pompon. All the characteristics of the pompons in Class 5 except that the ligulate petals are reflexed instead of being incurved. Subdivisions for size are the same as for Class 5. Specimens of this type larger than 4 inches are classed with the regular reflexes, Class 10.

Courtesy J. Horace McFarland Co.

CARNIVAL

Subclass — Carnation-Flowered. Ligulate petals laciniated as in a carnation. Otherwise as in Class 8.

The flower formation of the Class 8 pompons lacks the formal appearance of the regular incurved pompon, but it achieves an effectiveness all its own, whether the blooms are used in a cut-flower arrangement or left on the plant for a colorful display. Many of the hardy chrysanthemums, ranging from the low cushion varieties to the tall cutting varieties, fall in this class and Class 9, although petal formation has no bearing on hardiness. These two classes form the backbone of any amateur display or cutting garden, and a wide choice of varieties is available from the many chrysanthemum specialists. Since reflexed pompons are not usually as pure colored nor as professional appearing as the Class 5 incurved pompons, many amateurs feel that the florist uses some trick growing method. Actually, the varieties used in each case are different; however, any amateur can get professional results by using the same early-blooming pompons the florist grows. For the grower who is not interested in exhibiting but who wishes a good landscape picture from a chrysanthemum display, as well as good quality cut flowers, it will pay to grow many of the hardy varieties of classes 1, 2, 8, and 9 in the display garden and plan a separate garden for the most hardy Class 5 pompons. With the formal pompons together in a cutting garden it will be much easier to provide that little extra winter protection which may mean the difference between losing a favorite variety and having it perform well year after year.

Class 9 — Decorative or Aster-Flowered Reflexes. The ligulate petals are longer and narrower in proportion to their length than in the pompons of Class 8. They are apt to be pointed. The inner petals

Courtesy J. Horace McFarland Co.

APACHE

may be incurved for a time, but are reflexed in the fully open bloom. The bloom is flatter than those in Class 8. The width may be two or three times the depth, but the disk should not be apparent.

There is considerable confusion between Class 8 and Class 9 in classifying the many varieties of chrysanthemums because the variations between them are so slight, and there is no clear line of demarcation between the 2 classes. For this reason, many chrysanthemum shows combine the 2 classes and, for the average grower, the differences are not important.

Class 10 — Regular or Chinese Reflex. All the characteristics of the regular incurves of Class 6 except that the ligulate petals are reflexed. Subdivisions for bloom size are the same as in Class 6.

GARNET KING

These blooms generally do not approach in size those of the regular incurves, and there are not so many varieties available. They are grown as exhibition flowers, although the number of entries in this class is usually small, for hybridization efforts in recent years have been directed more toward the larger reflexes of Class 11. There are several deep red varieties in this class, one of them shown in the accompanying photograph, that contrast well in arrangements and bloom late enough in November to provide a good centerpiece for Thanksgiving Day.

Class 11 — Irregular or Japanese Reflex. This class has all the characteristics of the irregular incurves of Class 7, except that the ligulate petals are reflexed. Subdivisions for bloom size are the same as in Class 7.

Courtesy the Kruckeberg Press

MUTO'S CRIMSON

Many of the recent introductions of exhibition chrysanthemums from England and Australia are in this class, although until a few years ago the emphasis seemed to center on the Class 7 varieties. These large reflexes are suitable both for exhibiting and as striking accents in a large container of chrysanthemums.

DIVISION B (*Tubular Flowered*)

Class 12 — Spoon — Single. Ray florets regular and tubular, opening at the end to form spoonlike or spatulalike tips. No more than 5 rows of petals. Disk conspicuous and flat.
Subdivisions for bloom size as in Class 1.

Courtesy J. Horace McFarland Co.

CHARM SPOON

Class 12A — Semidouble and Double Spoon. This class has the same characteristics as Class 12, except that the ray florets occur in more than 5 rows and the disk may or may not be apparent.
Subdivisions for bloom size as in Class 1.
The spoons enjoy all of the hardy qualities of the singles, but provide a contrasting flower formation. For this reason, in a large display, spoons can be very effective when planted in groups of 3 among larger groups of singles or doubles.

Class 13 — Quill. Ray florets elongated and tubular with tips usually spoonlike, but may be closed to the tip and curved or rarely hooked. The bloom is fully double with no disk apparent.

Subdivision for bloom size as in Class 1.

Quills are usually grown one bloom to a stem for exhibition or for use in a large arrangement. Of all the chrysanthemums grown in

Courtesy The Kruckeberg Press

MISS GENA HARWOOD

this manner the quill varieties have the weakest stems; so at shows it is not uncommon to see a beautiful quill-shaped bloom with its head held erect by a splint tied to its neck.

Class 14 — Thread. Ray florets long, slender, tubular, may be straight or gently curved. Tips are closed and straight or slightly curved, but not significantly coiled or hooked. The disk may or may not be apparent.

(a) *Small,* blooms not over 6 inches in diameter.

(b) *Large,* blooms over 6 inches in diameter.

There is some disagreement, even among professional growers, as to the classification of certain varieties that have tubular petals closed to the tip. This is due to the lack of arbitrary limitation to the number of ligulate petals that exists in the division between single and semidouble blooms. Generally, the thread varieties are, as their name implies, more delicate, with fewer and more slender petals than the quill varieties. The method of growing and the uses are the same for both classes.

Class 15 — Spider. Ray florets long and tubular, usually more or less curved and twisted. The tips may be open and spoonlike or

Courtesy The Kruckeberg Press

CHERIE

closed, but in either case they should be definitely coiled or hooked. The disk may or may not be apparent.

Subdivision for size as in Class 14.

The coiled and hooked petals are the distinguishing characteristic of this class of chrysanthemum and one that creates quite a problem for the grower. There is always trouble when two spider mums get together, for their petals are as engaging as fishhooks. On the other hand, when spider mums are used in one of the exotic oriental arrangements they are sure to draw many a complimentary glance.

Any classification of chrysanthemums is bound to be somewhat arbitrary because the potential for variation is so great. However, the efforts of specialists to create novelties tend to be toward improvements within the well-defined classes mentioned above; so it does not appear that any changes in classification need be made for some time to come.

SPECIES OF CHRYSANTHEMUMS

The word "chrysanthemum," to those who grow and love flowers, may bring to mind a beautiful autumn display. Or perhaps thoughts of a football stadium, where the large colorful blooms of chrysanthemums have become a traditional part of the pageantry of the game. However, these typical blooms represent but one segment within one generic branch of the Compositae family of plants.

Within the genus Chrysanthemum there are many other annuals and perennials which are not too well known by the average gardener. However, many of these species are worthy of a place in the garden or greenhouse. To describe them all would require a separate book, but those that are particularly useful in combination with, or as supplements to, our more familiar chrysanthemums are included.

C. ARCTICUM (sny. *C. sibiricum*)

This hardy little plant from the cold regions of Alaska and Japan is a perennial which grows to a height of 12 inches. The white daisy-type blooms often become tinged with pink as they age on the plant. This characteristic has had an effect on the development of our modern chrysanthemums, for *C. arcticum* has been widely used in hybridization to impart the qualities of low growth and hardiness. However, this does not detract from the value of this species as a rock-garden plant.

C. arcticum may be divided as easily as most low-growing perennials by cutting through the roots with a spade near the plant center. Since the natural growth is prostrate rather than bushy, sections of the divided plant can be transplanted intact without the necessity of making a Dutch cutting.

C. CARINATUM

In its native Morocco this is a summer-blooming half hardy annual that grows about 2 feet high. Its 2-inch daisylike flowers are carried on the ends of the many short branches. These branches are covered with dark green leaves cut into many narrow segments. In the wild state the species has white flowers with a yellow area at the base of the petals, but, by hybridization, double forms have been produced. The named variety, *annulatum*, has flowers in white or yellow that have a circular band of red, maroon, or purple at the base of the petals. The fact that these flowers must be grown from seeds started very early has perhaps made them less popular than the earlier-blooming hardy garden chrysanthemums. They do, however, have a place in the greenhouse as spring-blooming cut flowers.

C. COCCINEUM

The term "painted lady" has often been used to describe these plants that are listed in perennial catalogues as Pyrethrums. While the flowers look like daisies that have been painted all the rosy shades between purest white and deepest red, the vivid green fernlike leaves combine to produce a plant worthy of a place in any respectable perennial border. The long stems of this 2-foot-high plant make the species ideal for the cutting garden. However, it is not always hardy in northern climates. The insecticide, pyrethrum, is obtained from this flower, which is extensively cultivated in its native Iran for this purpose.

C. CORONARIUM

This quite hardy annual, called the crown daisy, is similar to *C. carinatum* but grows almost twice as tall. The Chinese and Japanese cultivate a variety of this species for its edible shoots, but for American gardeners it is more suitable as a rear border plant for August and September blooming. It may also be forced for spring bloom in the greenhouse. Hybridizing has produced varieties which vary both in shades of yellow and in extent of doubleness. Usually seeds are sold as a mixture of varieties including some of *C. carinatum.*

C. FRUTESCENS

The Paris daisy, or Marguerite, is an almost continuous blooming perennial if it is alternated between the greenhouse and the garden border. Its continuous growth habit made it ideal as a tub specimen in an estate greenhouse. Often the species is exhibited in flower shows as a globe-shaped plant grown to a 4-foot height, with hundreds of white or yellow daisies in simultaneous bloom. The variety called "Boston Yellow" makes the best plant for the greenhouse. The poorest blooming period occurs during the summer and early fall; so, if plants are grown for indoor blooming during the winter, they should spend their summer vacation in some out-of-the-way spot in the garden.

C. LEUCANTHEMUM

The old-fashioned ox-eye daisy has been much improved in recent years. The new double-flowering types are larger than the Pyrethrums and come into bloom by Memorial Day. This makes a good early-cutting perennial that should be handled like *C. arcticum.*

C. MAXIMUM

This is the old favorite Shasta daisy that has been modernized by plant breeders so that it is more double and more pleasing as a garden perennial. However, it still is best treated as a biennial, for it lacks the persistence of other members of the genus. Like the Pyrethrums it grows to a height of 2 feet and its 4-inch-wide white flowers combine well with them in arrangements.

C. PARTHENIUM

Medical lore is full of references to the actual or supposed efficacy of certain plants in the treatment of mankind's ills. This member of the chrysanthemum genus, which bears the common name of feverfew, was an important plant in grandmother's medical herb garden. Even though it, too, has been improved by hybridization, it is not commonly grown today. The characteristic spicy odor of the chrysanthemum foliage is more pronounced in this species. Also, the leaves are more finely cut and divided. The feverfew, like many other plants whose taxonomic classification remained long in doubt, was classified as *Matricaria capensis* long enough to make that name more familiar. As a minor florist's crop for the spring greenhouse, the terminal sprays of dainty white ¾-inch flowers, borne on 3-foot bushy plants, are a welcome variation to the flower types then in season. In the outdoor garden the small button chrysanthemums are more suitable.

An entirely different variety of feverfew classified as *aureum,* and commonly known as golden feather, is widely used as an edging plant in English border gardens. This is a dwarf form with yellow crisped or curled leaves. The insignificant flowers, like those of the coleus, should be removed before they open. This variety should be treated as an annual grown from seeds sown in March.

C. SEGETUM

The 2-inch golden-yellow flowers of this European species have oval ray petals that broaden out and are notched at the tip. Thus, it received the common name of corn marigold. The plant is a compact little annual which grows to a height of 18 inches and blooms in July and August. It is more popular in Europe than it is in the United States as a garden flower, although it is sometimes used as a spring blooming plant in American greenhouses.

C. ULIGINOSUM

This 4- to 6-foot leafy perennial carries its 3-inch white flowers on long stems. It is a native of Hungary where it grows in rich moist soil. It is useful as a tall cutting flower in the rear perennial border.

CHAPTER 22

Varieties for Every Purpose

MANY facets of the interesting hobby of chrysanthemum culture have been discussed in preceding chapters, but mention of specific varieties has been purposely avoided. In this chapter are listed the varieties which have been favorites over the years, mingled with the best of the new introductions. An alphabetical sequence is used, since no individual's personal preference can meet with universal approval. However, each listed variety is well suited to the purpose described in the following brief preface to the tables.

HARDY GARDEN CHRYSANTHEMUMS

The varieties contained in Table 4 were bred primarily for their hardiness. In this case the word "hardy" refers to winter survival of the plants. However, all varieties of chrysanthemums have this trait to some extent, for the genes of hardiness were inherent in the original species from which our modern chrysanthemums are derived. Ability to withstand autumn storms and cold weather is also characteristic of the hardy mums. Many of these varieties lack the form and clearness of color found in the bush-type mums listed in Table 6; however, great improvements along these lines have been made in the past few years.

The cushion mums are included in a separate section of Table 4, since they are both early blooming and hardy. They have a definite place in landscape planning and so are classified separately.

The small button mums are likewise listed in an individual section, for they will provide bloom diversification for landscape effects and special floral arrangements.

Spoon varieties as a class are generally hardy; so they, too, are included in Table 4, for they are primarily a landscape type of bloom.

EXHIBITION CHRYSANTHEMUMS

Technically it is possible to groom almost any chrysanthemum for exhibition, but the varieties contained in Table 5 are limited to those which are grown to produce one large bloom on each stem permitted to develop. The table includes the so-called standards of the florists, since they are often entered in chrysanthemum shows, as well as the Japanese incurves, reflexes, spiders, anemones, and large singles. Many of the early-blooming varieties will do well in the outdoor garden with no protection, and many more can be grown outdoors under various types of protecting covers.

The major winners of the various N.C.S. shows held in the past few years are included in this table. The chrysanthemum exhibitor, however, will find the table of winners contained in each December issue of the N.C.S. *Bulletin* a practical way to keep abreast of the variety trends in exhibition chrysanthemum popularity.

A separate division of Table 5 has been reserved for the top winners of the English shows. These varieties bloom later in the United States, but the quality of the blooms is equal to that of our own varieties. There are a few varieties from Australia, France, and Japan which are included in the main portion of the table. They, too, represent the best of the foreign imports, but their number is insufficient to warrant placing them in a separate section.

The cascades are normally grown for exhibition usage; so they have been included in Table 5. However, many of the early-blooming varieties may be used for special landscaping effects.

POMPON CHRYSANTHEMUMS

There is no definite line of demarcation between hardy mums and those contained in Table 6. Actually, many of them will bloom satisfactorily, and winter over under a good mulch, in the normally colder chrysanthemum-growing areas. Most of these varieties are the pompons displayed in florists' windows, and, since they are grown in large quantities in commercial greenhouses, they are customarily called greenhouse varieties in many catalogues. Only by actual test can the amateur grower determine their ability to bloom and survive the winter. The blooming date and the coincidence of freezing weather in any given locality will determine whether a variety will bloom outdoors without protection.

DUAL-PURPOSE CHRYSANTHEMUMS

The ability of some chrysanthemum varieties to produce well-proportioned blooms, whether grown as single-bloom plants or bush-type plants, was discussed in Chapter 2. The most satisfactory of these varieties are included in Table 7. Most of them are pompons or the so-called large English decorative varieties, with a few spider and anemone varieties. All of the other bush-type varieties would produce a very small single bloom if grown in the same manner as the large-bloom type. On the other hand, large-bloom-type varieties will produce poorly proportioned sprays of flat flowers if grown in the bush form.

OUT-OF-SEASON CHRYSANTHEMUMS

It is possible to make any chrysanthemums bloom at any season, provided the following requirements are met:

(1) Day length — Once the day length required to initiate buds is reached, a mature plant will bloom at the end of its response period of short days.

(2) Stem maturity — There must be sufficient time for a plant to develop from the cutting stage until the time short days occur.

(3) Temperatures — Varieties vary in the degree of temperature variation they will withstand. Thus, only those varieties which are thermozero or thermopositive (see Chapter 15) will be most satisfactory.

To bloom satisfactorily in the heat of summer a chrysanthemum bloom must resist bleaching. During the short sunless days of winter the ability of chrysanthemum varieties to develop true colors is equally important. Degree of doubleness is also a factor which affects the quality of an out-of-season bloom. Generally, the varieties which bloom well in summer will also do equally well in winter. The varieties in Table 8 are recommendations of the leading commercial propagators, combined with the results of blooming tests in the author's greenhouse and garden.

Code letters are used in the tables to identify the dealers who catalogue the listed varieties. The names, addresses, and special sales conditions of these chrysanthemum suppliers will be found in Appendix A.

TABLE 4

HARDY GARDEN CHRYSANTHEMUMS

Variety	Color	Height and N.C.S. Class	Blooming Date	Code List of Suppliers
Alex Cumming	Rose cerise	Tall — 8	Oct. 5	ABILMNPTWYZ
Apache	Bright red — gold overcast	Med. — 9	Sept. 15	ACEFHIOTVWZ
Autumn Beauty	Reddish chestnut	Med. — 8	Sept. 15	DIN
Autumn Song	Wine red	Med. — 8	Sept. 10	IN
Avalanche	White	Tall — 8	Oct. 1	BCEFHILMNPS TWY
Baltimore Oriole	Golden yellow	Med. — 8	Sept. 20	FJ
Betty	Rosy pink	Tall — 8	Oct. 10	ABCDEIMNOS TXYZ
Bokhara	Rosy crimson	Med. — 8	Oct. 15	HIN
Brigadier	Carmine red	Med. — 8	Oct. 1	IW
Burma	Copper bronze and pink	Med. — 8	Oct. 15	I
Canary	Clear deep yellow	Med. — 8	Oct. 1	J
Carnival	Burnt orange	Med. — 5	Oct. 10	ABCEFHILMNO PRTWXYZ
Cecil Beed	Deep lavender	Med. — 8	Sept. 1	ACDFHMNOPRS VWZ
Cedar Waxwing	Cherry red	Med. — 8	Sept. 5	J
Charles Nye	Yellow	Tall — 5	Oct. 5	ABEFHILMNP RSTWXYZ
Chickadee	Orchid lavender	Med. — 8	Sept. 15	J
Chippa Red	Reddish maroon	Med. — 8	Sept. 20	BLNT
Chippewa	Aster purple	Med. — 8	Sept. 20	ABEDINPW
Chris Columbus	Ivory white	Tall — 8	Oct. 1	ADFLNWXY
Cockatoo	Cream white	Tall — 8	Sept. 10	J
Coppersmith	Copper bronze	Med. — 8	Sept. 25	BT
Cuckoo	Clear yellow	Med. — 8	Sept. 20	J
Delight	Butter yellow	Med. — 5	Sept. 20	BNPTV
Desert Quail	Soft lavender pink	Med. — 8	Sept. 15	J
Early Crimson	Crimson maroon	Med. — 8	Sept. 15	BLMNOPT
Elizabeth Hood	Light lavender rose	Med. — 8	Oct. 15	AHLNOWXYZ
Fascination	Silvery lavender	Med. — 8	Oct. 1	ABCILMNRTZ
Flamboyant	Scarlet orange and bronze	Med. — 8	Sept. 15	BEFMNPTW

Variety	Color	Height and N.C.S. Class	Blooming Date	Code List of Suppliers
Flicker	Reddish tan	Tall — 8	Sept. 20	J
Giant Kingbird	Rose-pink, buff-tan center	Tall — 8	Sept. 25	J
Ginny Lee	White	Med. — 1s	Oct. 10	CI
Granite Bronze	Bronze	Tall — 8	Sept. 25	D
Granite Buttercup	Deep yellow	Med. — 5	Sept. 25	D
Granite Harvest	Light orange	Med. — 2	Sept. 25	D
Granite Promise	Red	Tall — 1	Sept. 25	D
Granite Radiance	Red	Med. — 5	Sept. 25	D
Gretchen Piper	Brilliant yellow	Tall — 1	Oct. 20	HI
Horizon	Pure white	Med. — 5	Oct. 5	FIMNPXY
Huntsman	Scarlet orange	Tall — 8	Oct. 5	ABCFHILMNOP TWXYZ
Jean Treadway	Pink — red-tipped center	Med. — 8	Sept. 25	ABHZ
Joan Helen	Garnet red	Med. — 1	Sept. 15	BEFMPTW
Jubilee	Deep red	Med. — 5	Oct. 1	CEIMNPZ
Kathleen Lehman	Orange bronze	Med. — 8	Oct. 1	AHIN
Kristina	Rose	Med. — 1	Oct. 1	AMRW
Lady's Choice	Ivory pink	Med. — 2	Sept. 25	BEFNRT
Lavender Lady	Lavender	Tall — 8	Oct. 10	ABEFINPSWY
Lee Powell	Rich yellow	Tall — 8	Oct. 10	BCEFHILMNOP RTVWY
Macaw	Reddish orange	Med. — 8	Sept. 15	J
Malinda Brown	Lavender rose	Med. — 5	Oct. 1	ACFHINOPRTVZ
Masquerade	Silvery rose	Med. — 5	Oct. 10	ABCFHILMNOP TWXYZ
Mrs. P. S. Du Pont III	Peach pink	Tall — 8	Oct. 10	AEFHINPWXYZ
Myrtle Walgren	Amaranth purple	Med. — 5	Oct. 1	AFINPT
North Platte	Orange yellow	Med. — 8	Sept. 25	EFRT
Old Lavender	Silvery lavender pink	Med. — 8	Oct. 1	BFLNORTV
Olive Longland	Apricot and peach	Med. — 8	Sept. 25	ABFMNSTZ
Orchard Oriole	Orange bronze	Tall — 8	Sept. 25	J
Patricia Lehman	Pink and peach	Tall — 8	Oct. 1	AFHILMNTZ
Phoebe	Golden tan	Tall — 8	Sept. 15	J
Queen Anne	White — yellow cushion	Med. — 4	Oct. 1	K
Queen Elizabeth	Pink — golden cushion	Med. — 4	Oct. 1	KS
Queen Mary	Yellow — yellow cushion	Med. — 4	Oct. 1	K
Queen Victoria	Red — yellow red cushion	Med. — 4	Oct. 1	K
Red Velvet	Deep red	Med. — 8	Oct. 10	ABFNOPWXYZ

Variety	Color	Height and N.C.S. Class	Blooming Date	Code List of Suppliers
Ronald	Plum	Med. — 2	Oct. 10	HO
Ruffed Grouse	Rose salmon	Med. — 8	Oct. 5	J
Silver Thrush	Silvery peach	Tall — 8	Sept. 25	J
Swallow	Light tan	Tall — 8	Sept. 10	J
Thrush	Soft peach	Tall — 8	Sept. 15	J
Tiffany Rose	Deep rose	Med. — 1	Oct. 5	HIN
Titmouse	Lavender pink	Med. — 8	Oct. 5	J
Towhee	Deep red — gold reverse	Med. — 8	Sept. 15	J
White Wonder	White	Med. — 5	Oct. 5	HINPTXY
Yellow Avalanche	Light yellow	Tall — 8	Oct. 1	BCFILMNT

CARNATION-FLOWERED MUMS

Pathfinder	Golden yellow	Med. — 8s	Sept. 25	DEFNORTVWZ
Plainsman	Orange bronze	Med. — 8s	Sept. 25	DFNTVWZ

CUSHION MUMS and AZALEAMUMS

Amelia	Lavender pink	Short — 1	Sept. 30	BHINP
Amethyst Cushion	Purple	Short — 8	Sept. 10	B
Autumn Star	White — white cushion	Short — 3	Oct. 20	C
Blazing Red	Bronze changing to red	Short — 8	Sept. 25	K
Bowl o' Gold	Canary yellow	Short — 8	Sept. 10	ABEILW
Commander Cushion	Red	Short — 8	Sept. 25	NZ
Coquette	Rose pink	Short — 8	Sept. 25	BENT
Crimson Cushion	Wine red	Short — 8	Sept. 10	HI
Early Gold	Yellow	Short — 5	Sept. 5	BT
Hallowe'en Moon	Pink	Short — 5	Sept. 1	KS
Honey Chile	Reddish purple	Short — 8	Sept. 15	K
Lipstick	Brick red	Short — 8	Sept. 28	BCEILNT
Major Cushion	Pink and salmon	Short — 8	Sept. 10	AFHMRXZ
Mischief	Red	Short — 2	Sept. 30	BEFHLMNPRTWZ
Nugget	Clear lemon yellow	Short — 8	Sept. 15	IKS
Pink Dream	Silvery pink	Short — 8	Sept. 15	K
Powder Puff	White	Short — 8	Sept. 15	BHNW
Rouge Cushion	Red	Short — 1	Sept. 25	ABCFHILNPRT
Snow Fairy	White	Short — 8	Sept. 1	S
Summer Sunset	Orange apricot	Short — 8	Sept. 1	S
Tam-o-Shanter	Reddish orange	Short — 2	Sept. 1	K

BUTTON MUMS

Annette	Pink	Med. — 5	Nov. 5	HI
Baby	Clear yellow	Med. — 5	Nov. 5	AHI
Chiquita	Deep yellow	Med. — 5	Oct. 1	ABCEFHLNOPTXZ
Irene	White	Med. — 5	Oct. 20	ACEHINWY
Pepita	White	Med. — 5	Sept. 25	BFHINOPTWXZ

Variety	Color	Height and N.C.S. Class	Blooming Date	Code List of Suppliers
Pinocchio	White	Tall — 5	Oct. 25	AHMNWXYZ
Rosita	Persian rose	Med. — 5	Oct. 1	ABCFHINOPWZ
Yellow Irene	Yellow	Med. — 5	Oct. 20	ACIN

SPOON MUMS

Variety	Color	Height and N.C.S. Class	Blooming Date	Code List of Suppliers
Cardinal Spoon	Yellow — red spoons	Med. — 12	Oct. 1	CNPRW
Charm Spoon	Ivory — red spoons	Med. — 12	Oct. 3	ABHNPTV
Davy Crockett	Orange yellow	Med. — 12A	Oct. 15	CM
Garnet Spoon	Garnet — purple spoons	Med. — 12	Oct. 1	BCFLMV
Grand Canyon	Purple	Med. — 12	Oct. 8	CMRV
Hazel	Yellow	Tall — 12	Oct. 10	C
Loveliness	Carmine pink	Med. — 12A	Oct. 5	ACRTW
Paula	Buff yellow — crimson spoons	Med. — 12	Oct. 25	HIW
Remember Me	Bright red	Med. — 12	Oct. 5	CFWVZ
Scintillation	Orchid pink	Med. — 12A	Oct. 25	HI
White Spoon	White	Med. — 12A	Oct. 10	HINPSTWZ
Wilma Lee	Silver white — red spoons	Tall — 12	Oct. 20	C

TABLE 5

EXHIBITION CHRYSANTHEMUMS

Variety	Color	N.C.S. Class	Blooming Date	Code List of Suppliers
Albatross	White	6	Nov. 1	AHINWXY
Ambassador	White	7	Oct. 25	INMPSYZ
Ambassador Yellow	Yellow	7	Oct. 25	AINY
Appert	Bronze	6	Nov. 5	AI
Apricot Queen	Yellow bronze	6	Nov. 1	AINY
Autumn Blaze	Oxblood red	6	Oct. 15	AI
Ben Leighton	Wine red	6	Nov. 10	CEI
Blazing Gold	Deep yellow	6	Oct. 25	ACHILMNPXY
Chattanooga	White	6	Nov. 20	ANXY
Dark Pink Orchid Queen	Lavender	6	Nov. 10	ANXYZ
Detroit News	Light bronze	6	Nov. 1	AEINXYZ
Friendly Rival	Deep yellow	6	Nov. 20	AHINY
Garnet King	Deep red	10	Nov. 15	ACINVY
Giant Betsy Ross	White	7	Nov. 5	AINWXYZ
Good News	Golden yellow	6	Nov. 1	AINXY
Harvester	Deep yellow	6	Nov. 23	CNXY
Harvest Moon	Bright yellow	6	Nov. 10	A
Hilda Bergen	Reddish bronze	6	Oct. 20	AFHIMNPSWYZ
Honeydew	Light yellow	6	Nov. 5	ANY
Indianapolis:				
Bronze	Bronze	6	Nov. 5	ACINXY
Golden Bronze	Golden bronze	6	Nov. 5	INXY
Pink	Lavender pink	6	Nov. 5	ACINWXYZ
White	White	6	Nov. 5	ACINWXYZ
Yellow	Yellow	6	Nov. 5	ACINXYZ
Major Bowes	Lavender	6	Oct. 20	ABCEFILMNPSWYZ
Mary Palmour	Rosy purple	6	Oct. 20	CILM
Miss Frances Lowe	Raspberry bronze	6	Nov. 8	HI
Miss Osaka	Light pink	7	Oct. 25	IL
Mrs. David Roy	Red — bronze reverse	6	Nov. 10	AINXY
Mrs. H. E. Kidder	Medium yellow	6	Oct. 25	ABCEFHILMNPSWYZ
Muto's Crimson	Deep crimson — gold reverse	7	Nov. 15	AIXY
Oriole	Golden yellow	7	Nov. 5	HI

Variety	Color	N.C.S. Class	Blooming Date	Code List of Suppliers
Philip Kay	Lavender pink	6	Nov. 10	AIN
Pockett, John	Rose crimson	7	Nov. 10	IL
Pockett, Louisa	White	7	Nov. 10	AHINY
Pockett, Thomas	Deep pink —silver reverse	7	Nov. 8	INY
Pockett, Yellow	Light yellow	7	Nov. 10	AINY
Pockett's Maroon	Oxblood red — buff reverse	7	Nov. 8	CHI
Say Edgar	Wine red — silver reverse	6	Nov. 1	HI
Silver Sheen	White	6	Oct. 20	ACFHLMNORWYZ
Smith's Late White	White	6	Nov. 28	AXY
Tobin's Yellow	Deep yellow	6	Dec. 5	ANXY
Turner, William	White	7	Nov. 10	AHIOW
Turner Pink	Pink	7	Nov. 10	HI
Turner Yellow	Yellow	7	Nov. 10	AHI
Watanabee	Light yellow	6	Oct. 25	CFI
Yellow Mefo	Yellow	6	Nov. 20	ANXY

ENGLISH EXHIBITION CHRYSANTHEMUMS

Variety	Color	N.C.S. Class	Blooming Date	Code List of Suppliers
Dennis Wroe	White	7	Nov. 1	IO
Doreen Monte	Rose pink	6	Oct. 20	FILT
Enid Woolman	Yellow	6	Nov. 10	H
Fred Yule	Orange bronze	6	Oct. 20	CFHIO
Hilda Birch	White	6	Oct. 20	CHIM
Jaffa	Orange and terra cotta	7	Nov. 15	HIO
Jessie Habgood	Pure white	7	Nov. 10	HI
Pamela James	Salmon pink	6	Oct. 25	FHIOV
Shirley Perfection	Bright pink— silver reverse	7	Nov. 10	HIO
Sylvia Riley	Deep pink	7	Oct. 30	FHIO

SPIDER and QUILL CHRYSANTHEMUMS

Variety	Color	N.C.S. Class	Blooming Date	Code List of Suppliers
Albert Witt	Yellow	15	Oct. 15	CFHIL
Ami Charles Souchet	Rose and gold	odd French import — 13	Oct. 20	AFHILO
Bess Witt	Bronze	15	Oct. 15	ACFHILMW
Bunbu	Lavender pink	15	Nov. 1	ACFILMOPWZ
Cathay	Copper red	15	Nov. 1	FHIW
Cherie	Orchid pink	15	Nov. 5	I
Dalwin	Light bronze	15	Oct. 25	MNY
Georgina Hedinger	Pink	15	Oct. 25	ACFHIOWZ
Heros Jean Guizonnier	Deep rose purple	odd French import — 13	Oct. 20	AFHT

Variety	Color	N.C.S. Class	Blooming Date	Code List of Suppliers
Lorraine	Clear yellow	15	Nov. 5	AHILNY
Luyona	Yellow	15	Oct. 25	NYZ
Mamoru	Light bronze	15	Oct. 28	ACFHINOPWYZ
Mary Garden	Lavender pink	15	Oct. 28	AEFLNPXYZ
Miss Gena Harwood	Straw bronze	13	Oct. 30	ACINORY
Oriental Knight	Deep red — silver overcast	15	Nov. 20	HI
Patricia Grace	Rose pink	13	Oct. 25	FHW
Paul Miller	Bronze — red hooked tips	15	Oct. 28	CFHLMW
Peggy Ann Hoover	Light pink	15	Oct. 28	AFIMNRWY
Queen's Lace	White	15	Oct. 25	AFHINPXYZ
Rayonante	Pink	13	Oct. 28	AFILNRVY
Rayonante, White	White	13	Oct. 28	AFHILNRVY
Rayonante, Yellow	Yellow	13	Oct. 28	AFHILNRVYZ
Sarah Morasch	Rose pink	15	Nov. 5	I
Sondra Gail	Bronze and red	15	Nov. 1	IM
Sunnyslope Splendor	White — greenish petal base	15	Oct. 25	HIMOR
Yellow Frill	Clear yellow	15	Oct. 20	I
Yellow Lace	Yellow	15	Oct. 25	AEFINPY

ANEMONE

Variety	Color	N.C.S. Class	Blooming Date	Code List of Suppliers
Bronze Frieda	Bronze — yellow cushion	3	Nov. 5	AI
Dark Pink Frieda	Deep pink — yellow cushion	3	Nov. 5	AN
Elizabeth	Light pink — yellow cushion	3	Nov. 5	HI
Francis Schoen Park	Pure white — white cushion	3	Nov. 20	ACHI
Long Island Beauty	White — yellow cushion	4	Nov. 20	ANXY
Norma	Lavender — yellow cushion	3	Nov. 10	ANWY
Rolinda	Yellowish bronze	3	Nov. 15	A
Rose Madder	Lavender — darker cushion	3	Nov. 15	AH
Sincerity	White — white cushion	3	Oct. 25	CHI
The Titan	Red — red cushion	3	Nov. 10	WY
Tuxedo	Rose — yellow cushion	4	Nov. 5	AHIWYZ
Yellow Estrelita	Yellow — yellow cushion	3	Nov. 17	HI
Yellow Sincerity	Yellow — yellow cushion	3	Oct. 25	CHL

Variety	Color	N.C.S. Class	Blooming Date	Code List of Suppliers

CASCADE and SPECIMEN CHRYSANTHEMUMS

Variety	Color	N.C.S. Class	Blooming Date	Code List of Suppliers
Anna	White	1	Nov. 5	CHIW
Jane Harte	Yellow	1	Nov. 5	HIV
Lavender Mist	Pink — yellow cushion	3	Nov. 5	HI
Mount Hood	White	8	Nov. 1	W
Opal	Pink — yellow cushion	3	Oct. 20	I
Pink Sweetheart	Pink	1	Oct. 25	I
The Real Mackay	Pink	1	Nov. 1	HW
White Castle	White — yellow cushion	3	Nov. 1	I

SINGLE MUMS

Variety	Color	N.C.S. Class	Blooming Date	Code List of Suppliers
Crimson Valencia	Red	1	Nov. 15	INY
Mensa	Pure white	1	Nov. 10	ANY
White Valencia	White	1	Nov. 15	AINXY

TABLE 6

POMPON CHRYSANTHEMUMS

Variety	Color	Height and N.C.S. Class	Blooming Date	Code List of Suppliers
Beauregard	Orange bronze	Tall — 5	Nov. 10	AINXY
Blue Chip	Lavender pink	Tall — 5	Nov. 1	NXY
Bronze Thyra	Salmon bronze	Tall — 5	Nov. 5	IY
Cassandra	Orange bronze	Tall — 5	Nov. 5	ANYZ
Christmas Red Improved	Deep red	Med. — 8	Dec. 20	HI
Coral Frost	Bronze coral and pink	Med. — 8	Oct. 25	HI
Daybreak	Soft pink	Med. — 8	Oct. 20	I
Deanna Lee	Bright red	Med. — 8	Oct. 25	ACI
Gold Coast	Deep yellow	Tall — 5	Oct. 25	ACHNWXY
Golden Herald	Rich yellow	Tall — 8	Oct. 25	AHINXY
Highlander	Deep yellow	Tall — 8	Nov. 25	INXY
Kramer Bronze	Light bronze	Med. — 8	Dec. 20	AIN
Kramer Peach	Peach pink	Med. — 8	Dec. 20	IN
Kramer Pink	Deep pink	Med. — 8	Dec. 20	AIN
Kramer White	White	Med. — 8	Dec. 20	IN
Kramer Yellow	Yellow	Med. — 5	Dec. 20	AIN
Legal Tender	Gold and red	Tall — 5	Nov. 20	AHNY
Maid of Orleans	White	Med. — 8	Oct. 25	HI
Mary MacArthur	Raspberry rose	Tall — 5	Oct. 25	ACNXY
Pristine	White	Med. — 5	Oct. 25	ACINXY
Queen of Pinks	Deep pink	Med. — 5	Nov. 1	AHINXYZ
Revelation	White	Med. — 5	Dec. 20	NY
Silverplate	White	Med. — 8	Oct. 20	AIMNWXY
Silversmith	White	Tall — 8	Dec. 15	ANXY
Thyra	Lavender	Tall — 5	Nov. 5	AHINY
White Doty	White	Tall — 5	Nov. 1	ACMNWYZ
Yellow Dot	Yellow — pink center	Med. — 5	Oct. 25	AHINWYZ
Yellow Seagull	Soft yellow	Med. — 5	Nov. 1	AINWXY

TABLE 7

DUAL-PURPOSE CHRYSANTHEMUMS

Variety	Color	Height and N.C.S. Class	Blooming Date	Code List of Suppliers
Bronze Doty	Bronze	Tall — 5	Oct. 25	H
Bronze Frieda	Bronze — yellow cushion	Med. — 3	Nov. 5	AI
Coral Frost	Bronze coral and pink	Med. — 8	Oct. 25	HI
Davy Crockett	Orange yellow	Med. — 12A	Oct. 15	CM
Doreen Monte	Rose pink	Med. — 6	Oct. 20	FILT
Fred Yule	Orange bronze	Med. — 6	Oct. 20	CFHIO
Frieda	Pink — yellow cushion	Med. — 3	Nov. 5	AIN
Granite State	White	Med. — 6	Oct. 20	HNXYZ
Lillian Doty	Shell pink	Med. — 5	Oct. 25	AHNWYZ
Masterpiece	Lilac pink	Med. — 5	Nov. 10	AHINY
Pamela James	Salmon pink	Med. — 6	Oct. 25	FHIO
Queen of Pinks	Deep pink	Med. — 5	Nov. 1	AHINXYZ
Red Doty	Red	Med. — 5	Nov. 1	HZ
Richard Mandel	White	Med. — 6	Nov. 1	NXY
Rolinda	Yellow bronze	Med. — 3	Nov. 15	A
Rose Madder	Lavender — darker cushion	Med. — 3	Nov. 15	AH
Silver Ball	White	Med. — 5	Oct. 10	HNW
Snowy	White	Med. — 15	Nov. 5	W
Sylvia Riley	Deep pink	Med. — 7	Oct. 30	FHIO
Thyra	Lavender	Tall — 5	Nov. 5	AHINY
White Doty	White	Tall — 5	Nov. 1	ACMNWYZ
Yellow Doty	Yellow	Tall — 5	Nov. 1	AHYZ

TABLE 8

OUT-OF-SEASON CHRYSANTHEMUMS

Variety	Color	N.C.S. Class	Response Group	Code List of Suppliers
Beauregard	Orange bronze	5	10-week	N*
Bluechip	Lavender pink	5	9-week	N
Chattanooga	White	6	12-week	N
Dark Pink Orchid Queen	Lavender	6	10-week	N
Detroit News	Light bronze	6	9-week	N
Giant Betsy Ross	White	7	10-week	N
Gold Coast	Deep yellow	5	9-week	N
Golden Herald	Rich yellow	8	9-week	N
Good News	Golden yellow	6	9-week	N
Harvester	Deep yellow	6	11-week	N
Indianapolis:				
Bronze	Bronze	6	10-week	N
Golden Bronze	Golden bronze	6	10-week	N
Pink	Lavender pink	6	10-week	N
White	White	6	10-week	N
Yellow	Yellow	6	10-week	N
Kramer Bronze	Light bronze	8	14-week	N
Kramer Peach	Peach pink	8	14-week	N
Kramer Pink	Deep pink	8	14-week	N
Kramer White	White	8	14-week	N
Kramer Yellow	Yellow	8	14-week	N
Mary Garden	Lavender pink	15	9-week	N
Masterpiece	Pink	5	10-week	N
Mrs. David Roy	Red — bronze reverse	6	10-week	N
Pinocchio	White	5	9-week	N
Queen's Lace	White	15	9-week	N
Silversmith	White	8	14-week	N

* This nursery will supply cuttings out of season, either retail or wholesale.

TABLE 9

CHRYSANTHEMUM SPECIES

Variety	Form and Color	Species	Height	Code List of Suppliers
	SHASTA DAISY			
Aglaya	Semi-double — white	C. maximum	Med.	RV
Cobham Gold	Double — yellow overcast	C. maximum	Med.	HJV
Esther Reed Improved	Double — white	C. maximum	Med.	JSV
G. Marconi Improved	Large double — white	C. maximum	Tall	SV
Horace Reed	Double thick petaled — white	C. maximum	Med.	HSV
Phyllis Elliott	Semi-double frilled — white	C. maximum	Med.	V
Snow Princess	Double feathery — white	C. maximum	Tall	H
Snow Queen	Large single — white	C. maximum	Tall	V
	PYRETHRUM			
Brilliant	Double — rose red	C. coccineum	Med.	V
Crimson Giant	Single — red	C. coccineum	Med.	V
Lady Dawn	Double — pink	C. coccineum	Med.	V
Lady Garnet	Double — deep pink	C. coccineum	Med.	V
Pasadena	Double — Silvery pink	C. coccineum	Med.	V
Poinsetta	Double — bright red	C. coccineum	Tall	V
Robinson's Hybrids	Pink red and white	C. coccineum	Med.	ER
Senator	Double — deep rose	C. coccineum	Tall	V
The Pearl	Full double — white	C. coccineum	Med.	V
	MISCELLANEOUS			
Giant Daisy Seed	White daisy	C. uliginosum	Tall	*
Ox-eye Daisy	Double white daisy	C. Leficanthemum	Med.	V
Paris Daisy Seed	Single — white and yellow	C. frutescens	Variable	*
Shasta Daisy Seed	Single and double — white	C. maximum	Med.	*
Turfing Daisy	Prostrate white daisy	C. Tchihatchewii	Short	V
Annual Seed	Single — shades of yellow	(C. coronarium) (C. carinatum)	Med.	*
Feverfew Seed	Double white buttons	C. Parthenium	Med.	*
Perennial Seed	Korean hybrids	C. morifolium	Med.	*
Pyrethrum Seed	Single — pastel shades and red, single white	C. Coccineum	Tall	*

* Rex D. Pearce, Moorestown, N.J.

CHAPTER 23

Calendar for a Chrysanthemum Hobby

THE ebb and flow of activities connected with most horticultural hobbies in the temperate zones can be made a smooth progression of interesting work when chrysanthemums become the chief interest. Mums are so adaptable to a hobbyist's schedule. Few growers will undertake every phase of chrysanthemum culture which has been discussed, but the possibility exists for variation of the hobby from year to year. For this reason the activities discussed have been summarized on the basis of a monthly schedule.

JANUARY

Sketches and plans for landscape improvements should be made in this season most fitted for indoor activity. Catalogues should be checked for promising new varieties, and orders should be sent as soon as possible. All of the planning type of work which may be done at this season will help make the program operate smoothly as the year unfolds.

Winter mums in the greenhouse will benefit from additional plant food applied as a foliar spray. The foliar food may be placed in one of the proportioning devices which attaches to a standard faucet connection. A fog nozzle on the other end of the hose will provide good coverage of the leaf surfaces with a fine mist of fertilizer-enriched water.

If chrysanthemum stock plants in pots are now taking up too much bench space in the greenhouse, cuttings may be taken for future stock plants.

Seeds of perennial chrysanthemum crosses, and seeds of annual chrysanthemums for summer bloom, should be started in the greenhouse this month.

FEBRUARY

The winter mulch on the outdoor garden should be checked during periods when no snow is on the ground. If it has packed too tightly it should be loosened.

Mums from the greenhouse will brighten up the dreary atmosphere which is characteristic of this in-between season. The novelty of chrysanthemums at this season, together with their lasting quality, makes them ideal for winter arrangements.

Cuttings for small specimen plants or basket cascades should be started in the greenhouse.

If a hotbed is used in place of a greenhouse to provide an early start for the gardening year, the seed-sowing activities listed for the January greenhouse program may be undertaken during late February.

MARCH

Spring makes its appearance in many chrysanthemum-growing areas during March. As temperatures moderate, the mulch should be gradually removed. The glass on cold frames should also be slightly raised on sunny days. In this season of weather contrasts snow will do no harm. Temperatures below 20 degrees, however, will damage new growth. For this reason, it is better to leave the mulch near the plants so that it may be put on the plants if cold weather threatens.

March is a good month to incorporate organic matter in a new mum garden, or one from which the stock plants have been removed. In fact, any preparatory work which can be done now will make for smoother operation in the normally busier spring months.

APRIL

Plants ordered for delivery in April should be placed in the cold frame to make growth for additional cuttings.

Cuttings for plunge-pit culture, or for the exhibition garden, should be started in the greenhouse or in a hotbed. These early cuttings will produce tall plants of the large-bloom mums; so if height is a limiting factor, postpone this phase for a month.

April is a good outdoor working month and perhaps the best one for preparation of the soil mixture required for greenhouse benches and plunge-pit mums.

MAY

This is the month of greatest propagation activity. Cuttings of all hardy mums, as well as greenhouse pompons, will root readily at this season.

If soil sterilization with chloropicrin is necessary, May is the best month, for the ground must be warm for best results. With the cuttings in the rooting medium and the planting date a few weeks away, there will be ample time to do this job.

JUNE

June is planting month for all outdoor mums; and the plunge-pit mums also receive their final shift to flowering pots at this time.

JULY

The greatest number of operations connected with a chrysanthemum hobby occurs at this season. The work, however, is varied, and careful attention to each phase determines, to a large extent, the success of the chrysanthemum year. The operations of mulching, pinching, supporting, spraying, fertilizing, and watering which are discussed in Chapters 8 and 11 should be completed or started this month.

AUGUST

Axillary shoots begin to develop along the stems of the large mums during August, and a systematic process of removal must be started now. It must continue until blooming time.

The final steps which determine the success of a specimen plant or cascade display take place during August and continue into September and October (see Chapter 13).

The shading program must be started for the normally late-blooming exhibition chrysanthemums that are grown for entry in October and early November shows (see Chapter 15).

Cuttings for winter-blooming chrysanthemums should be started this month. Be sure to take extra cuttings to allow for poor rooting at this season.

SEPTEMBER

Warm humid nights that begin in September and continue into October are conducive to development of fungus diseases. During this period when petals begin to unfold a careful check should be made for evidence of brown or white fungus spores. If necessary, the specific fungicide recommended in Chapter 7 should be used.

If the landscape plans are based upon succession of bloom, now is the time to move chrysanthemum plants from the reserve plot. They may replace annuals which have passed their peak of bloom. If they are kept well watered after transplanting they will be ready to bloom with asters and other late perennials, without any indication that they have been moved.

Brush support or unobtrusive staking may be provided for both transplanted mums and those grown all season in the display garden.

OCTOBER

October is a month of comparisons after a long period of preparation. It is important to make notes of the blooming characteristics of each variety as it reaches its peak of bloom, for impressions written down at blooming time are much more reliable than recollections when planning time rolls around.

The frost cover should be assembled early in October in preparation for an unexpected frost (see Chapter 12).

The sunpit gardeners should also get ready for winter.

The blooms which will be entered in chrysanthemum shows should receive their last-minute grooming. Insect and disease control assumes considerable importance with these entries, and no spray should be used which might damage the petals. Proper un-hurried preparation for chrysanthemum shows will make this phase of the hobby more enjoyable and will improve the chances of win-ning awards (see Chapter 18).

NOVEMBER

For the hardy chrysanthemum grower, November is the month to put the garden to bed for the winter. All plant stems should be cut down after blooming and preferably burned to minimize the spread of nematodes or disease. If the plants are to remain in the garden over the winter they should be covered with a winter mulch.

When stock plants are lifted for storage over the winter in a cold frame, it is possible to sterilize the soil with a fumigant which is effective in cool weather.

Gardeners who grow late-blooming chrysanthemums under a frost cover will be able to enjoy outdoor mum gardening until Thanksgiving in favorable areas. However, it is advisable to take down and store a plastic frost cover on a sunny day before the end of the month. Any blooms not completely open at that time may be brought indoors where they will develop normally. Cleaning up and winter mulching may then be completed before the weather makes this an unpleasant task.

DECEMBER

While December is a month of no activity for the hardy chrysan-themum hobbyist, the greenhouse or sunpit gardener will find many interesting things to do.

The winter-blooming chrysanthemums will be making good growth at this season and, to insure bloom by February, the lights should be turned off early in December (see Table 3). Most of the outdoor cultural requirements are repeated for the same varieties grown as winter-blooming chrysanthemums.

The cuttings for large specimen and cascade chrysanthemums should be started in December. Be sure to use November-blooming varieties, or else light the cuttings and young plants of early bloom-ing varieties to prevent premature budding. This trouble may also be avoided by waiting until January or February to take cuttings, but of course the blooming-sized plants will be smaller.

Although much has been learned about the effect of short days, temperatures, and stem maturity in the production of chrysanthemum bloom, there are still many avenues for horticultural research. The amateur with a greenhouse, sunpit, or even a homemade enclosure may enrich his life, and possibly add to the fund of horticultural knowledge about that interesting perennial, the chrysanthemum.

Code List of Chrysanthemum Suppliers

ALL of the varieties of chrysanthemums listed in Chapter 22 may be obtained from one or more of the chrysanthemum specialists listed in this Appendix. On the basis of floral returns to the gardener, chrysanthemum plants are one of the least expensive investments connected with a gardening hobby. These concerns will supply quality chrysanthemum cuttings or plants at reasonable prices.

Company name and address	Sales conditions
A — F. A. Spivey, Box 574, Montgomery, Ala.	Retail sales. Quantity prices on request.
B — Bristol Nurseries Inc., Bristol, Conn.	Retail sales. Wholesale upon request.
C — Echo Valley Floral Gardens, Magnolia, New Jersey	Retail sales. Blooming plants sold from fields in fall.
D — Pine-Croft Nurseries, Hampton Rd., Exeter, N.H.	Retail sales, collections and quantity discounts.
E — Spring Hill Nursery, Tipp City, Ohio	Retail sales.
F — J. C. Smith Co., 107 Highland St., Brockton 19, Mass.	Retail sales including collections.
H — Cascade Gardens, 4511 Pasadena Ave., Sacramento 21, Calif.	Retail sales, quantity discounts.
I — Sunnyslope Gardens, 8638 Huntington Drive, San Gabriel, Calif.	Retail sales plus collections.
J — Jackson & Perkins Co., Newark, N.Y.	Retail sales only.
K — R. M. Kellogg Nurserymen, Three Rivers, Mich.	Retail sales.
L — A. Ladygo Nursery, 4800 Van Epps Rd., Cleveland 9, Ohio	Retail sales, quantity discounts.
M — Daliahdel, Vineland, N.J.	Retail sales and quantity discounts.

N — Neal Brothers, Toledo, Ohio — Wholesale suppliers on an all year basis.

O — Garland Nursery, Route 1, Box 403, Corvallis, Ore. — Retail, wholesale and garden club group orders.

P — Glass City Floral Gardens, 5950 Stickney Ave., Box 56, Station H, Toledo 13, Ohio — Retail sales and group offers.

R — Rocknoll Nursery, Morrow, Ohio — Retail sales and group specials.

S — The Conard Pyle Co., West Grove, Pa. — Retail sales and group offers.

T — Terrace View Gardens, Greencastle, Ind. — Retail sales, quantity discounts.

V — Lamb Nurseries, E. 101 Sharp Ave., Spokane 2, Wash. — Retail sales, quantity discounts.

W — Wonderland Nurseries, Ellerson, Va. — Retail sales, wholesale to florists, group orders a specialty.

X — Mikkelson & Sons Greenhouses, Samuel Ave. & Nickel Plate R.R., Ashtabula, Ohio — Wholesale suppliers. Will handle group orders.

Y — Yoder Brothers, Inc., Barberton, Ohio — Wholesale suppliers. Minimum order 50 of a variety.

Z — Athalia Gardens, Athalia, Ohio — Retail and wholesale.

Good equipment is required to get the best results in any hobby. The following items which are useful in the culture of chrysanthemums represent a partial list of such equipment, and a source of supply.

TRADE NAME	SUPPLIER
Fertilizers, Bulk	
Mum Food — 4–8–4 high organic content	Doggett-Pfeil Co., Springfield, N.J.
Vigoro — balanced dry plant food	Swift & Co. — sold at garden supply stores
Fertilizers, Soluble	
Atlas Fertilizer Emulsion — organic	Atlas Fish Fertilizer Co., No. 1 Drum St., San Francisco 11, Calif.
Dyna-Gro — inorganic fertilizer for use with sphagnum moss	Mosser Lee, Millston, Wisconsin
Heller-Gro — inorganic paste or powder	Heller Greenhouse Labs., 218 E. Pikes Peak Ave., Colorado Springs, Col.
Instant Vigoro	Swift & Co. — sold at garden supply stores
Kapco 20–20–20 — inorganic mum fertilizer	The Summers Fertilizer Co., Inc., McKeesport, Pa., Wholesale supplier
Miracle-Gro — inorganic	Sterns Nurseries, Inc., Geneva, N.Y.
Ra-Pid-Gro — the original foliar feeding fertilizer 23–21–17 plus trace elements	Sold by nurseries and garden supply stores
XL-36, 12–12–12 XL-60, 15–30–15 — inorganic	Doggett-Pfeil Co., Springfield, N.J.

Fertilizer Applicators

Hozon — hose suction proportioning applicator from pail of soluble fertilizer	The Hozon Co., Box 703 Cleveland 22, Ohio
Mix Mizer — attaches at faucet, sealed container holds one cup of dry soluble fertilizer	Breck's, Boston 10, Mass.

Greenhouses

Everlite Aluminum Greenhouses	Aluminum Greenhouses, Inc., Cleveland, Ohio
Glass O Plastic — vinyl plastic with glass wool reinforcing mesh	American Associated Cos., Box 272, Red Bank, N.J.
Orlyte — complete line of aluminum home greenhouses	Lord & Burnham, Irvington, N.Y. or Des Plaines, Ill.
Waldor Greenhouses	Horto Corp., Pequot Center, P.O. Box 188, Salem, Mass.

Greenhouse Suppliers

Bench fittings, glass, vents, putty, paint, hotbed sash, etc.	Lord & Burnham, Irvington, N.Y. or Des Plaines, Ill.

Growth Stimulant

Gibberellic acid	Doggett-Pfeil Co. Springfield, N. J.

INSECTICIDES AND FUNGICIDES

The amateur gardener may purchase the separate ingredients required to make the basic compounds discussed in Chapter 7 at garden supply stores, or he may buy prepared mixtures which approximate these compounds.

TRADE NAME	SUPPLIER
Agri Spray — 50% DDT	Doggett-Pfeil Co., Springfield, N.J.
Apomite — Rotenone plus associated resins	Liberty Chemical Laboratories, Box 98, Franklin Park, Ill.
D & P Lindane Aramite Emulsion — insecticide portion of Basic Compound #2	Doggett-Pfeil Co., Springfield, N.J.
Dapspray — 30% DDT, 1% Rotenone	Doggett-Pfeil Co., Springfield, N.J.
Detex — a complete agricultural insecticide	Liberty Chemical Labs., Box 98, Franklin Park, Ill.

Dithane Z 78 — (Rohm & Haas tradename for zineb) — Doggett-Pfeil Co., Springfield, N.J.

End-O-Pest Garden Dust — Swift & Co. — sold at garden supply stores

End-O-Pest Garden Spray — contains malathion — Swift & Co. — sold at garden supply stores

Fermate (DuPont trade name for Ferbam) — Doggett-Pfeil Co., Springfield, N.J.

Isotox Garden Spray M — basic Compound #4 when combined with Orthocide Garden Fungicide — California Spray Products Co. — sold at garden supply stores

Multi Purpose Dust — Basic Compound #3 — sold in wholesale quantity only — Plant Products Corp., Blue Point, Long Island, N.Y.

Mist Propagating Equipment

Mistic Bubble — complete mist propagating unit — Mist Methods Co., 600 South High St., Winchester, Tenn.

Nozzles, Fog, and Mist

Fogg-It Nozzle — used on hose end for mist spray — Ray Sanders & Co., 133 North Santa Anita Ave., Pasadena 8, Calif.

Mist Nozzles — brass — used on copper tubing for mist propagating — William Steinen Mfg. Co., 43 Bruen St., Newark, N.J.

Mist Nozzles — stainless steel — Mist Methods Co., 600 South High St., Winchester, Tenn.

Plant Bands

Wood Veneer Plant Bands — sold in units of 2000 — Geo. J. Ball, Inc., W. Chicago, Ill.

Plant Ties

Life Ties — plastic-covered wire for twist-type plant ties — The Garden Spot, 170 Washington St., Marblehead, Mass.

Plastic Covers

Vinyl Plastic — 4 and 8 mil. — American Associated Cos., Box 272, Red Bank, N.J.

Pots, Composition

Cloverset Pots — asphalt composition pots for easy moving of blooming plants — Cloverset Flower Farm, 105th and Wornall Rd., Kansas City 5, Mo.

Jiffy Pots — composition pots for rooted cuttings — wholesale

Geo. J. Ball, Inc.,
W. Chicago, Ill.

Shading Cloth

Black cloth of various weights

American Associated Cos.,
Box 272, Red Bank, N.J.
Brand & Oppenheimer,
229 Fourth Ave., N.Y. 3,
N.Y.

Soil Sterilization

Larvacide — chloropicrin

Larvacide Products Inc.,
Ringwood, Ill. or
1515 Third St.,
San Francisco, Calif.

Soilene — contains chlordane

Liberty Chemical Labs.,
Box 98, Franklin Park, Ill.

Soil Testing

Soil Testing Kits

Sudbury Laboratory,
South Sudbury, Mass.

Sphagnum Moss

Milled Sphagnum Moss

Mosser Lee
Millston, Wis.

Sprayers and Dusters

Champion portable sprayers and dusters

Champion Sprayer Co.,
657 Heintz Ave.,
Detroit 11, Mich.

Hudson sprayers and dusters

H. D. Hudson Mfg. Co.,
589 E. Illinois St.,
Chicago 11, Ill.

Plastic tank sprayer

b & g Co.,
4725 Rising Sun Ave.,
Philadelphia 20, Pa.

Supports

Bench wire, stake fasteners and steel stakes — all sizes of stakes in bundles of 100

Schupp Florist Supply Co.,
P.O. Box 114,
1143 Greenleaf Ave.,
Wilmette, Ill.

Glossary

THE following glossary combines definitions adopted by the National Chrysanthemum Society for use in chrysanthemum shows, as well as horticultural terms used by growers:

Accessory — Anything other than freshly cut plant material, whether in the container, on the lip, or placed apart from the container. This includes such items as background fabrics, lids, and figurines.

Accessory container — A figurine or added adornment, regardless of its attachment to the container, which creates a secondary focal point. Any floral arrangement in such a container must be entered in the composition class.

Amateur — A person who grows chrysanthemums because he loves them. He does not derive a significant portion of his income from his hobby.

Axillary — From the axis or stem. In chrysanthemum culture any vegetative growth developing from the leaf axils is called axillary growth.

Bicolor — A bloom with one color for the inner surface and a different color for the outer surface (See Reverse). For show purposes, a bicolor bloom should be entered in the color class indicated by the color of the inside petal surface.

Bloom — The chrysanthemum inflorescence is made up of both ray and disk florets, hence the word "bloom" is more comprehensive than the word "flower."

Bract — A leaf which is modified to a much smaller straplike form. Found on the stems of crown buds only.

Breadth — The diameter of a bloom taken at right angles to the stem.

Commercial bloom — A term used by florists for Chinese incurve chrysanthemums to indicate good shipping qualities.

Compositae — The largest family of plants in the world, comprising shrubs, trees, vines, and thousands of herbs. There are over 800 genera embracing more than 12,000 species in a world-wide distribution. With the exception of several taxonomically correct deviations, the inflorescence of all genera contains both ray and disk florets in the same flower head.

Composition — An arrangement with one or more accessories. It may include dried, treated, or weathered materials.

Corolla — The inner tube portion of distinct or united petals.

Crown bud — Any chrysanthemum blooming bud which is surrounded by leaf buds. Removal of the leaf buds will force this bud to bloom at the normal time. Without bud removal the crown bud may not bloom.

Cushion — A term which denotes the low growth habit of some varieties of chrysanthemums. This term embraces the trademarked names, Azaleamum and Ameliamum. (Also applied to disk of Classes 3 and 4.)

Cutting — A portion of a chrysanthemum stem consisting of terminal growth and several pairs of leaves. When no roots are included on the stem portion it is a softwood cutting.

Depth — The height of a bloom measured along an extension of the stem.

Disbud — Term used by commercial growers to indicate bud removal required to improve the quality of the remaining blooms.

Disk — The central portion of the chrysanthemum inflorescence. In the singles it is apparent and is often referred to as the button. The disk in anemone blooms is greatly enlarged and is often called the cushion.

Disk florets — The complete flowers which, combined, make up the disk.

Disqualify — To remove an entry from judging because it does not conform to the show schedule (See Eliminate).

Disseminate — To offer a new chrysanthemum variety, either a seedling or a sport, for sale to the public.

Double — Any bloom in which the disk is not apparent. Any bloom in classes 5 to 11, inclusive, should be disqualified if the disk is evident.

Eliminate — Rejection of an entry from judging because it is unworthy.

Exhibition — A popular term used mainly for the Japanese incurves and more broadly for any chrysanthemum bloom entered in a class where size is of greatest importance. In an N.C.S. show, the class number is used in place of this broad term.

Floret — The individual flowers that are combined into the inflorescence of members of the Compositae.

Form — This refers to the shape of the bloom, and in judging it refers to the approved shape for the type and variety.

Fullness — This refers to the number of ligulate petals when used in connection with double blooms, and the number of disk florets when anemones are being judged.

Gene — The smallest unit of plant cell structure that determines hereditary characteristics. It is analogous to the chemical atom.

Inflorescence — A single flower or a flower cluster which fulfills its mission by flowering.

Inorganic — Applied to fertilizers which are derived from mineral sources.

Laciniated — Applied to petals that are cut or notched like those of a carnation.

Ligulate — Straplike. This term describes the flattened corollas of the ray petals.

Obverse — The opposite of reverse (See Reverse). Applied to the upper surface of the ligulate corolla of any reflex bloom; the inside corolla surface of any incurved bloom; or the exposed inner corolla surface of a spoon or spider bloom.

Organic — Applied to fertilizers derived from vegetable or animal matter.

Pedicel — The stalk portion connecting each bloom of a spray with the main stem.

Peduncle — The main stem of a single bloom and the stem to which the pedicels are attached.

Petal — The colored segment of a flower which may be distinct, as in a ray floret, or united, as in a disk floret. This portion of a bloom is the attraction for pollination by insects but it has no connection with the sexual parts of the flower.

Pinch — Removal of terminal growth to induce branching.

Ray florets — The imperfect flowers which surround the disk portion of the chrysanthemum inflorescence.

Receptacle — The cuplike portion of the stem which contains the flower head of disk and ray florets.

Reverse — The outer or lower surface of the ligulate corolla.

Seedling — A hybrid chrysanthemum plant which has not received a varietal name nor been disseminated.

Size — The size of a bloom for all classes except 15 and 16 is the largest diameter measured at right angles to the stem. This measurement is taken without disturbing the petals, however, since the threads and spiders of class 15 and 16 have drooping petals, it is customary to extend the petals on a flat surface at right angles to the stem before measurement.

When 2 blooms have an equal diameter the value of depth is considered in determining size by measuring over the top of the bloom with a tape measure.

Specimen — A plant grown for the purpose of exhibiting a large number of blooms in a prearranged geometric pattern.

Spray — The term "spray" is used by a florist to denote any multibloom branch of a bush type chrysanthemum. The N.C.S. recognizes two types of sprays:

(a) *Terminal Spray* — Any multibloom branch which meets the following requirements:

1. The bloom at the end of the main stem is the highest bloom on the spray.

2. This bloom is developed from the central bud of a terminal bud cluster.

3. Each pedicel which developed below the top bloom supports a single bloom.

(b) *Crown Spray* — Any multibloom branch where the bloom at the end of the main stem is below any other blooms.

The time-pinching procedure required to produce terminal sprays has been discussed in Chapter 11. However, this is not an exact science and such things as high temperature or cloudy weather may prevent a perfectly proportioned terminal spray. For this reason, it is customary for judges to consider as a terminal spray any entry where the bloom at the end of the main stem is not more than ½ its diameter below the highest bloom of the spray.

Sport — A plant which has been asexually reproduced from a mutation or hereditary change not due to hybridization. Usually a sport is produced by a change in a single gene, such as a color gene.

Stomata — Porelike openings in leaf surfaces through which gases and water vapor pass.

Stool — A chrysanthemum clump consisting of the stub of the previous year's stem, plus all of the stolons which radiate from it.

Stopping — This is a term widely used by English growers to denote a time pinch, since it stops the upward growth.

Substance — When applied to a chrysanthemum bloom this refers to the over-all qualities of thickness, texture, and firmness of petals which are necessary for a prize-winning entry.

Standard — This term is applied by florists to any large bloom chrysanthemum which has but one bloom per stem. However, in horticulture it refers to any chrysanthemum which is grown in tree form. To accomplish this the cutting must be started a year ahead of the normal blooming time. Terminal growth must be pinched many times; and the leaves on the lower portion of the thick woody stem will dry up and fall off. A standard, if trained to a specific shape, becomes a specimen.

Taxonomy — Classification of plants and animals according to their natural relationships.

Terminal Bud — In chrysanthemum usage only this is the last bud produced in the growth cycle. Unlike the crown bud it is surrounded by identical, but smaller, flowering buds.

Transpiration — The process by which a plant gives up water in the complex exchange of gaseous chemical compounds required to produce growth.

Two-toned — A bicolor having the same basic hue for obverse and reverse petal surfaces, but with a darker tone for the reverse surface. Jean Treadway and Pink Dot are varieties which have this characteristic.

Variety — A seedling which has been disseminated and/or registered with a varietal name applied.

Acknowledgments

Often after years during which he has specialized in a horticultural hobby, the gardener will hear the statement, "You ought to write a book." This may provide the initial impetus, but the end product cannot be arrived at as casually.

The book you hold is a fine example of the publishing art. It represents not only the mechanical perfection of modern printing and illustration, but also the efforts of a great many people. While it is true that the text is supplied by the author, the publisher's editorial staff, consultants, photographers, typesetters, and printers all play an important part in the production of any book.

As I look back on the months of preparation before the final page-proof correction, I realize how much credit is deserved by so many people. My fellow chrysanthemum growers and my many friends in the National Chrysanthemum Society are certainly deserving of my sincere thanks for the stimulus they have provided. There are, however, specific contributions which deserve individual mention.

Most of the line illustrations were done by Miss Allianora Rosse, whose artistry faithfully portrays nature in *Flower Grower* magazine. Her faithful reproduction from nature is most helpful in depicting characteristics which may be hidden in the clearest of photographs. The three drawings showing flower arrangements were done by Miss Consuelo Joerns.

Where photography seemed to offer the best method of illustration, the photographic team of Jack and Mary Roche was most co-operative. They have made a partnership career of flower photography which has gained them an international reputation.

Chapter 17 became a necessary part of this book, since the book includes not only complete cultural directions, but directions for the enjoyment of chrysanthemum blooms. The floral-arrangement field has always been considered the special province of the female of the species. Hence, it took considerable courage on the part of the author, a mere male gardener, to presume to discuss it. The author, however, is deeply grateful to Mrs. William Mulheron, General Zone Chairman of the Garden Club of New Jersey, for her criticism of and contribution to Chapter 17. Also, the author was very fortunate to be able to use arrangements by Myra J. Brooks for illustration. Her artistry with flowers is unsurpassed.

The author is also indebted to Mrs. Elmer Bahrenburg of Hazlet, New Jersey. Her successful chrysanthemum sales garden techniques furnished much of the material included in Chapter 19.

Last, but by far the most important contribution has been the understanding and co-operation of my wife. She has worried with me when storms threatened and shared my enthusiasm over prize-winning blooms. Her appreciation for and clever arrangements of the chrysanthemums I have raised have been a constant spur to my efforts.

Index

The following Index has been prepared in an effort to provide ready reference to specific points in connection with the culture and use of chrysanthemums. Specific varieties of chrysanthemums will be found in Chapter 22; terms and definitions will be found in the Glossary; and suppliers of plants and equipment will be found in the Appendices. Where possible, all other references have been grouped under the key word which would identify a particular subject:

Acid soil, 31
Aerosols, 49
Alkaline soil, 31
Aluminum sulphate, 32
Ameliamum, 150
Ammonium sulphate, 32, 75
Anemone, 7, Table 5, 227
  irregular, 202
  regular, 201
Anthemis grandiflora, 189
Aphids, 112
  black, 53
  green, 53
  root, 53
Aramite, 52, 57
  spray, 58
Arrangements:
  accessories, 155
  color, 158
  companion materials, 156
  containers, 154
  driftwood, 169

  harmony, 159
  Heika, 168
  holders, 155
  Ikebana, 168
  Japanese, 168
  line, 164
  mass, 162
  Moribana, 168
  proportion, 159
  styles, 160
  symmetry, 159
  types, 162
  visual weight, 158
Ascochyta, 60
Asobenzine, 112
Aster-flowered chrysanthemum, 207
Aster wilt, 60
Automatic cutting bench, 40
Auxin, 38
Axillary growths, 94
  stems, 16
Azaleamum, 67, 71, 150, 197, Table 4, 223

Bacterial diseases, 60
  collar rot or stem rot, 62
  fasciation, 62
  wilt, 62
Bacterial wilt, 62
Bailey, L. H., 190
Bench culture of chrysanthemums, 110
Blindness, 64
Bloom classification:
  anemone, 7
    irregular, 202
    regular, 201
  decorative, 8
  incurve, 8
    irregular, 205
    regular, 204
  pompon, 7, 203
  quill, 10, 211
  reflex, 8, 206
    irregular, 209
    regular, 208
  single, 6, 199
    semidouble, 6, 200
  spider, 11, 211
  spoon, 10
    double, 210
    semidouble, 210
    single, 210
  thread, 11, 211
Boron, 33
Boston yellow daisy, 215
Botrytis, 60
Bracts, 20
Break bud, 14
Bristol Nurseries, 196
Bromex, 85
Bush-type chrysanthemum, 12
Button mums, Table 4, 223

Calcium, 33
Captan, 53, 113
Carnation-flowered chrysanthemums,
  206, Table 4, 223
Cascade chrysanthemums, Table 5, 228
Cellophane bags for chrysanthemum
  packaging, 184

Chlordane, 54
Chloropicrin, 62, 85
Chrysanthemum
  anemone, 7, 201, 202, Table 5, 227
  aster-flowered, 207
  beds, 146
  borders, 145
  button, Table 4, 223
  calendar of operations, 233
  carnation-flowered, Table 4, 223
  cascade, Table 5, 228
  cushion mum, Table 4, 223
  decorative, 8, 207
  definitions, Appendix C, 245
  diseases, 59
  dual purpose, 219, Table 7, 230
  edging, 147
  English exhibition, Table 5, 226
  equipment, Appendix B, 241
  exhibition, Table 5, 225
  first show, 191
  from seed, 127
  growing for profit, 179
  hardy garden, 217, Table 4, 221
  in Australia, 191
  in Holland, 192
  in United States, 195
  incurve, 8, 204–5
  judging scales, 173
  landscape borders, 150
  miscellaneous, Table 9, 232
  name, origin, 21
  out-of-season, 219, Table 8, 231
  pompon, 7, 203, Table 6, 229
  quill, 10, 211, Table 5, 226
  records, 80
  reflex, 8, 206
  seed production, 122
  single, Table 5, 228
  species, 213, 232:
    C. articum (syn. C. sibiricum), 213
    C. carinatum, 214
    C. coccineum, 214
    C. coreanum, 196
    C. coronarium, 215
    C. frutescens, 215

Chrysanthemum, species (*cont.*)
    C. grandiflora, 189
    C. hortorum, 190
    C. indicum, 189
    C. leucanthemum, 215
    C. maximum, 215
    C. morifolium, 189
    C. nipponicum, 196
    C. segetum, 216
    C. sibiricum, 213
    C. sinense, 190
    C. uliginosum, 216
    C. yezoense, 196
  spider, 11, 211
  spoon, 10, 210
  thread, 11, 211
Classification committee, 178
Cold frame construction, 42
  storage of stock plants, 87
Collar rot, 63
Combination dusts and sprays, 51
Commercial, 5
Compositae family, 4
Copper naphthenate, 42
Corn-ear worms, 54
Corn marigold, 216
Crown bud, 94
Cultigen, 190
Cushion mum, 14, 150
Cuttings for out-of-season mums, 139
Cutworms, 54

Damp-off fungus, 127
  organisms, 63
Day length for bud formation, 130
DDT, 52, 54, 56, 59
Decorative, 8, 9, 207
Disbud, 5, 12
Disk petals, 6
Display gardens, 79
Dithio fumigation, 58
Dodder, 64
Dual-purpose chrysanthemums, Table 7, 230
Dusts, 48
Dutch cutting, 36

Early delivery advantages, 27
  care, 27
Electric soil-heating cable, 43
Emulsified sprays, 48
Equipment for rooting cuttings, 40
Ethylene dibromide, 85
Exhibition chrysanthemums, Table 5, 225
English, Table 5, 226

Fasciation, 63
Feeding, greenhouse mums, 112
Ferban, 51, 62, 113
Fertilizer analysis, 33
  deficiency symptoms, 75
  high analysis, 33
  trace elements, 33
Fertilizing, 74
  schedule, 74
Feverfew, 216
Fiberglas, 183
First crown bud, 12
Flower spot, 60
Fluorescent-lighted cabinet, 140
Foliar feeding, 33
  nematodes, 57
Formaldehyde, 85
Formalin, 85
Fortune, Robert, 188
Frost-protection cover, hotbed sash, 102
  temporary, 101
Fumigants, 49
Fumigation in a greenhouse, 112
Fungicides, 49
  dusts, 49
  wettable powders, 49
Fungus diseases, 60
Fusarium, 60

Genera, 4
Gibberellic acid, 34. *See* Appendix, 242
Glossary, Appendix C, 245
Greenhouse ground beds, 110
  soil preparation, 109
Greenhouses for chrysanthemums, 108
Guano, 33

Hard pinch, 71
Hardy, 5, Table 4, 221
Hemsley, 190   ,
Hotbed construction, 42
Humus, 31
Hybridizing, 122
Hydrogen ion concentration, 32

Incurve, 8
    Chinese, 204
    Japanese, 205
Indolebutyric acid, 38
Inorganic fertilizer, 74
Insecticides, 48
    aerosols, 48
    basic compounds, 51
    dusts, 48
    fumigants, 48
    and fungicides, Appendix B, 242
    sprays, 48
Insects and pests, 53
Intergeneric crossing, 5
Iron, 33

Judging scales, 173

Keeping chrysanthemums fresh, 82
Ki-Ku, 187
Kiku-No-Sekku, feast of chrysanthe-
    mums, 193
Korean hybrids, 67, 196

Lamarck, 189
Landscape planning, 144
Large-bloom types, 12
Larvabrome, 85
Leaf miners, 54
Leaf-spot disease, 62
Leaf tiers, 56
Lebois, 191
Lighting procedure, 138
    schedule, 142
Lime and limestone, 32
Lindane, 52, 54, 57, 58
Linnaeus, 188

Magnesium, 33
Malathion, 51, 54, 56
Manure water, 74
Marguerite, 215
Matricaria capensis, 216
    morifolium, 189
Mealy bugs, 56
Mendel's law of heredity, 122
Methyl bromide, 85
Midges, 56
Mildew, 60, 113
Mist propagation, 44
Mist-spray cutting bench, 140
Mites, 57, 112
Morifolium, 4
Mosaic, 63
Mrs. H. E. Kidder, 196
Mulch:
    buckwheat hulls, 69
    ground corn cobs, 69
    peat moss, 69
    pine needles, 69
    sawdust, 69
    straw, 69
    tobacco stems, 69
Mulching, 67

National Chrysanthemum Society, 3
    bloom classification, 6–11, 119
    Bulletin, 218
    100 favorite varieties, 147
    Show Handbook, 172
    shows, 80
Nematodes, 57
    root knot, 57
    foliar, 57
Nemex, 85
Nicotine-smoke generator, 121
Nitrate of soda, 32, 75
Nitrogen, 33, 74, 75
    loss (when mulch is used), 69

Ompa, 50
Organic fertilizer, 74
    matter, 29
    phosphate, 50

Out-of-season chrysanthemums, Table 8, 231
Ox-eye daisy, 215

Painted lady, 214
Parasites, 60
Parasitic bacteria, 62
Parathion, 51
Paris daisy, 215
Pathogenic agents, 49
    bacteria, 59
    fungi, 59
    viruses, 59
Peat moss, 69
P40, 50, 58, 99
pH, 32
Phosphorus, 33, 74, 75
Photographing chrysanthemums, 81
Photosynthesis, 31
Pinching, 14, 16, 70
Planning chrysanthemum gardens, 144
Plant band, 28
Planting, 66
    and spacing of large-bloom
        chrysanthemums, 89
Plant lice, 53
Plant support systems, 90
Plunge-pit mums, 95
Pockett, Thomas, 192
Polyacrylonitrile soil conditioners, 35
Polyethylene plastic, 183
Pompon, 5, 7, 71, 203, Table 6, 229
    greenhouse spacing, 110
Potash, 75
Potassium, 33, 74
Preventive spraying, 72
Protection of chrysanthemum blooms, 83
Pyrethrum, 232, Table 9, 232

Quill, 10, 211, Table 5, 226

Ramatielle, 189
Ray blight, 60
Ray petals, 6
Red spider, 58, 112

Reflex, 8, 9, 206
    Chinese, 208
    Japanese, 209
Response groups, 131
Rhizoctonia, 63
R. M. Kellogg Co., 197
Root knot nematodes, 57
Root-promoting substances, 38
Rooting mediums, 38
    procedure, 44
Rosette, 63
Rust, 62
Rust pistules, 62

Sabine, Joseph, 190
Salter, John, 188
Saprophytes, 60
Saprophytic bacteria, 62
Schrader systemic poison developer, 50
Second crown bud, 12, 16
Seed sowing, 128
Seidewitz disease (verticillium), 62
Septoria, 62
Shading material, 131
    procedure, 131
    schedule, Table 1, 135; Table 2, 136
Shasta daisy, 215, Table 9, 232
Sheet composting, 69
Short-day plants, 17
Silver Sheen, 196
Single, 6, 199, Table 5, 228
Smith, Elmer, 195
Smoke generators, 112
Sodium selenate, 50, 54, 99
Soft pinch, 71
Softwood cutting, 37
Soil chemistry, 31
    conditioners, 34
    for chrysanthemums, 29
    preparation, greenhouse, 109
    sterilization, 84, 128
    structure, 30
    testing, 32
    kit, 33
Soot water, 96
Sow bugs, 54

Spacing, 67
Species, 4
Species Plantarum, 189
Specimen chrysanthemums, Table 5, 228
   plants, 113
Sphagnum moss, 129
Spider, 11, 212, Table 5, 226
Spoon, 10, Table 4, 224
   double, 210
   semidouble, 210
   single, 210
Spores, fungus, 60
Sports, 126
Sprayer operation, 74
Spraying, 72
Sprays, 48
Spreader for insecticides and
   fungicides, 51
Stakes, 90
Standard, 5, 12
Standards, greenhouse spacing, 110
Stem rot, 63
Sterilization of soil in an oven, 128
Sterilizing greenhouse soil, 113
Sting fly, 59
Stolon, 36
Stool, 36
Stunt, 64
Sulfur, 51
Sunpit, 117
Superphosphate, 29, 74
Supporting and tying, 90
Supports, 75
Support systems, greenhouse mums, 111
Symmetry in chrysanthemum beds, 71
Symphylids, 58
Systemic poison, 49
Systox, 50, 54, 58

Tarnished plant bugs, 59
Taxonomists, 4
Temperature classifications:
   thermonegative chrysanthemums, 141
   thermopositive chrysanthemums, 141
   thermozero chrysanthemums, 141

Temperature for rooting cuttings, 39
Terminal bud, 94
   cluster, 16, 17
Test gardens, 79
Tetraethyl-ditho-pyrophosphate, 58, 112
Thermonegative chrysanthemums, 141
Thermopositive chrysanthemums, 141
Thermozero chrysanthemums, 141
Third crown bud, 12
Thread, 11, 211
Time pinch, 70
   greenhouse mums, 111
Time pinching and disbudding, 93
Time switch for lighted mums, 138
Tips on buying plants, 26
Trace elements, 33
Transporting show entries, 176

Varieties, names of: Tables 4–9, 221–32
Vermiculite, 128
Verticillium, 62
Vinyl plastic, 104, 183
Virus diseases, 60
   mosaic, 63
   rosette, 63
   stunt, 63
   yellows, 63

Watering, 71
   greenhouse mums, 111
Wettable powders, 48
White fly, 112
Wilt, 62
   See Verticillium and Aster wilt
Winter-blooming chrysanthemums, 139
Winter care of chrysanthemum plants, 85
Winter mulch:
   field hay, 86
   salt hay, 86
   straw, 86

Yellows, 64

Zineb, 52